I0762492

A COMBAT PILOT'S JOURNEY FROM VIETNAM TO BEYOND EARTH

SPACE ACE

A COMBAT PILOT'S JOURNEY FROM VIETNAM TO BEYOND EARTH

SPACE ACE

ROBERT "HOOT" GIBSON

WITH ANTHONY PAUSTIAN, PHD

Published in Des Moines, Iowa, by:

Bookpress Publishing
P.O. Box 71532
Des Moines, IA 50325

www.BookpressPublishing.com

Publisher's Cataloging-in-Publication Data

Names: Gibson, Robert, author. | Paustain, Anthony, author.
Title: Space ace : a combat pilot's journey from Vietnam to beyond Earth / Robert "Hoot" Gibson; with Anthony Paustian, PhD.
Description: Des Moines, IA: BookPress Publishing, 2026.
Identifiers: LCCN: 2025926206 | ISBN: 978-1-960259-45-5
Subjects: LCSH Gibson, Robert. | Astronauts--Biography. | Air pilots--Biography. | Space Shuttle Program (U.S.) | Vietnam War, 1961-1975--Biography. | BISAC BIOGRAPHY & AUTOBIOGRAPHY / Aviation & Nautical | BIOGRAPHY & AUTOBIOGRAPHY / Adventurers & Explorers | BIOGRAPHY & AUTOBIOGRAPHY / Military | BUSINESS & ECONOMICS / Leadership
Classification: LCC TL789.85.A1 .G53 2026 | DDC 629.450092--dc23

First Edition

Printed in the United States of America

10 9 8 7 6 5 4 3 2 1

To my Father, Paul Alexander Gibson,
my hero, mentor, and flight instructor.

Who taught me not just how to fly,
but all the reasons behind how we fly.

The aerodynamics, the structural
considerations, the flying techniques.

If I have been successful as an aviator,
it's because of you.

Thank you, Dad.

1

My life began in Cooperstown. Even if you haven't heard about this little hamlet situated on Lake Otsego in upstate New York, nicknamed "America's Hometown," you already know it. It's the proud home of the Baseball Hall of Fame, that place where every great player hopes their legacy will live on in the end. But this isn't a story about baseball, and it doesn't start with me.

I never knew the small village where I was born, but rather learned about it through my parents' stories and photos. As with many kids, my father was my hero. Paul Gibson was born in 1907 in Pittsburgh, the second child of John Henry Gibson and Edith Bradley Lowe. His father was a piano tuner and music teacher, and Dad apparently inherited a talent for music. He learned to play the piano, keyboard, and guitar by ear. His family wasn't wealthy by any means, there was no money for college, and he dropped out of high school in 1922 after only two years. He worked odd jobs and in 1925 started working as an assistant and a mechanic for a motor sales company, then he enlisted in the Army Air Corps in September of 1927. His experience as a mechanic gave him a foot in the door working on aircraft, but he wanted to fly. He studied hard for his flight school exams, but in the end, the effort proved unnecessary after he walked out on the wing of a B-6A bomber mid-flight to patch an oil leak that would have seized the engine and dropped the plane. Pilot training was his reward, and he learned to fly in the Curtis JN-4 biplane. Later, he would fly jets.

My father rose to second lieutenant in the Army Reserve with the 20th Bomb Squadron, now flying the B-6A, the same plane he'd maintained with such daring and heroism. He also flew the airmail in the notorious winter of 1934 after the Army took over all routes in February. It was a dangerous job with an abysmal fatal accident rate, and therefore the airlines resumed carrying the mail June of that same year. He remained a pilot in the Army Air Corps until 1936, when he returned to work as an aircraft mechanic in a supervisor's role.

Lt. Paul A. Gibson, Army Air Corps 1929. Credit: Paul Gibson Collection / Color by Jay Miller

While he was managing the US Navy propellor shop at Naval Air Station Quonset Point, Pearl Harbor was attacked. He tried to reenter the Army Air Corps to fly in the war, but his request was denied. Because he was serving in a defense-critical position, my father wasn't allowed to leave that job until 1945, when World War II was ending.

My parents met through flight. My mother, Margaret Rita Perrault, a former schoolteacher in Providence, Rhode Island, was also

B-6A "Keystone" Bomber. Credit: Paul Gibson Collection 1934

working for the Navy as an inspector at Quonset Point when World War II began. She and two of her college friends decided they wanted to learn how to fly, and the three of them bought a J-2 Taylor Cub in November 1943 and sought lessons from my father. They married soon after, and my older brother Jon was born in 1945 in Reno, Nevada, where Dad was earning his rating of Certified Flight Instructor. My parents moved to Cooperstown, New York, on October 23, 1946, and I was born one week later.

Dad managed an airport in Fly Creek near Cooperstown. It was a small airport with two grass runways and a single, minimalist hangar. The plan was for Dad to work as a flight instructor, aircraft mechanic, and airport manager. In exchange for basically working three jobs, the airport owner had promised to provide a heated hangar, but the idea never materialized. After enduring two upstate New York winters, we left Cooperstown in April 1948 and moved to a far warmer climate in Santa Monica, California. The postwar economy resulted in many downturns, and our family moved seven times toward various aviation careers that sprung up and faded in the boom-and-bust aftermath of WWII, the Korean War, and my father's pursuit of his degree in aeronautical engineering, which he finally earned in 1956. To this day, I can vividly remember my father's pride as he walked across the stage to receive that diploma. From that point on, Dad worked the rest of his career for the Federal Aviation Administration as an engineer, test pilot, and manager. We grew into a rather large family consisting of myself, Mom and Dad, my maternal grandfather who lived with us, and my five siblings. Several of us inherited our parents' love for aviation, but perhaps none more than I.

I grew up wanting to follow in my father's footsteps. By the time I was ten, I knew I was going to become an aeronautical engineer and a test pilot just like him. In my younger years, I had already begun building model airplanes, first starting with plastic models and then moving to rubber band-powered flying models made from balsa wood covered with tissue. My inherent, early talent for engineering was on display when I designed and built my own model of the Mach One, a Bell X-1—the first plane known to have flown at supersonic speed. I also learned a lot of my basic mechanical ability by constructing three Soap Box Derby racers with Dad. The rules stated that each contestant must do all the construction of the car himself. With Dad being a strict follower of the rules, I constructed all three cars and learned a lot while building them—with Dad's guidance of course. We raced against some stiff competition. All of the participants were from Los Angeles and Orange County, and the winner of that local competition usually went on to win the championship at the national finals in Akron, Ohio. While I didn't make it too far in the competition, what I learned in the process served me well during my development as an engineer.

Dad taught me how to fly, and I've always been exceptionally proud of that. Because of his instruction, I became the aviator I am today. I remember flying as a passenger with both of my parents as early as five years old. Dad first began instructing me when I was fourteen in an Aeronca TC-65 that we rebuilt, completing the project in 1960. It was a fabric-covered trainer known as a "taildragger," with a high wing and conventional landing gear—meaning a wheel under the tail instead of under the nose—and it was powered by a small 65-horsepower engine. I only flew it seven times in 1961 and had logged only four hours and fifty minutes before we sold it and moved from Long Beach to Vienna, Virginia, in September 1961. Dad was rapidly moving up in the FAA and took an engineering position in Washington, D.C., at its headquarters. I had gone through my freshman year of high school in California and then attended James Madison High School in Vienna for the next two years.

By June 1962, my flight training continued in several different planes over the next year, including a Cessna, a Beechcraft, and several Piper models. I learned a great deal from Dad's flight instruction, likely because any time I asked a question, he wouldn't only answer it, but would also tell me all the reasons why as well as the science and the aeronautical engineering principles behind the answer. This tactic prepared me not only to be a pilot, but it also paid off immensely when I started work on my aeronautical engineering degree in college. My first solo flight that year was on my sixteenth birthday in a Piper Colt at the airport in Manassas Virginia. Dad was determined that I be able to fly that first solo on that day because that was the earliest a person could fly alone in a powered airplane. He had to get my Student Pilot License ahead of time because I needed to have that certificate to legally fly, and still, the flight almost didn't happen because of weather. The day was windy, rainy, and overcast. However, after flying several practice patterns with Dad on board, there was a short break in the rain, and I was able to complete my

Dad and Mom with Mom's J-2 Taylor Cub. Credit: Rita Gibson Collection 1943

first solo flight. I was also able to do something very unusual that same day, and that was to fly my first "passenger" with only a Student Pilot Certificate. While not normally legal, this particular passenger happened to be my mother who also held a Private Pilot Certificate, which technically made her the Pilot in Command, though I was doing all the flying.

At the time of my first solo flight, I had only logged about eighteen hours of total flying time and would need at least forty to qualify for my next rating of Private Pilot. We had been renting planes to get me through flight school, but continuing to do so would have been way too expensive, so in July 1963, my parents bought a Luscombe 8A. This was a high-wing airplane with an aluminum fuselage and a fabric-covered wing. It had a small, 65-horsepower Continental engine, but it was able to cruise at 97 miles per hour because of its very efficient design.

The Luscombe was also a taildragger and had the reputation of being somewhat challenging during takeoff and landing. The spacing between the main gear (the two wheels up front) was narrow and as a result required constant attention on the runway to keep the airplane moving straight. Dad was such a good instructor, it only took two flights and less than two hours of flight time for him to sign off on my competency for conventional gear airplanes. I really enjoyed being able to fly the Luscombe solo, and after a few flights staying within the airport traffic pattern, he gave me permission to leave the airport and fly further away, and that's when I got myself into trouble.

I immediately left Manassas and flew to Vienna where I was part of the Vienna Woods Swim Team. I buzzed our outdoor swimming pool, flying just overhead to show off to my teammates. I did this several times before Dad sat me down and asked how I planned to pay the $1,000 fine for low-flying over the town of Vienna. He showed me the letter that the FAA had sent him detailing how a Luscombe, tail number N23038, had been spotted making the objectionable maneuver. I was fortunate Dad was a part of the FAA because they had basically told him to take care of the matter himself, which he did. I received a well-deserved chewing-out, and he told me I'd better never do anything like that again, or my flying days would be over!

My final flight in Virginia was in September 1963, and then we moved again after our two years in Vienna. Dad continued to move up within the FAA and was named Director of Engineering for the entire Eastern Region of the country. He was to be based out of offices at John F. Kennedy Airport, so we moved to Long Island, where I began attending my third high school in four years. By October, I started flying from Deer Park Airport, which had no control tower, just like the uncontrolled field I'd grown accustomed to back in Manassas.

I had to be trained for cross-country flights before I could do them solo. Many of my great memories of flying with Dad in the Luscombe were during practice cross-country flights from Deer Park across Long Island Sound to Groton, Connecticut, from there to Stormville, New York, and finally, from Stormville back to Deer Park on Long Island. After this training, I flew three short solos to airports on Long Island the following week and finally completed my first solo on the same three-leg cross-country I had trained on with my father.

The Luscombe was a minimal airplane—no radio and no navigation avionics—which meant that cross-country flights were made by "dead reckoning." I carried detailed aviation sectional charts which depicted terrain, roads, and cities. The key to navigating successfully was always knowing where I was by viewing ground references against the charts. I flew compass headings and timed how long I had been on a set course to know when to expect the next landmark. I also needed to account for the winds aloft because those could cause a drift angle and move me off my desired ground track.

This was how Charles Lindberg had flown the Spirit of St. Louis across the Atlantic Ocean from New York to Paris in 1927. Over the course of more than thirty-three hours in the air, he flew on heading after heading, each for a calculated and pre-set amount of time. He flew over the Atlantic Ocean for most of the route with no landmarks to help verify where he was.

Lindberg's accomplishment was an incredible milestone in aviation, and I was able to fully appreciate his challenge firsthand many years later when I flew a replica of the Spirit of St. Louis. The Spirit had no forward view other than through a periscope. All the fuel tanks needed to be in front of the pilot on the airplane's center of gravity, which blocked any view. The replica I flew didn't have a periscope, so I had to lean considerably to the left, hanging my head out the side window to see, which made takeoff and landing quite challenging. Yet it was a real thrill to fly such an historic airplane, and it confirmed how well my father had trained me.

Most of my flight time from July 1963 onward had been in the Luscombe, but for my Private Pilot Certification check ride, I needed to be in an airplane with the items the Luscombe didn't have, a radio and navigation aids. I would need to demonstrate my ability to use those for the FAA examiner, so I rented a Piper Colt and made two practice flights just prior to my check ride. It had been fifteen months since I had flown a Piper Colt, so my check ride in 1964 was less than perfect. I had very little experience talking to a control tower since the Luscombe had no radio, but I needed to show that I could do it. I was barely able to manage it, but I think my examiner gave me the benefit of the doubt, possibly because Dad also worked in the FAA. Nonetheless, I passed my check ride for the Private Pilot Rating.

At seventeen, I could take my friends flying, but they had to drive us to the airport because I still didn't have a driver's license. I could fly a plane but not drive a car. It had been a financial burden for the family to have the Luscombe, and after I earned my pilot rating, my parents sold it in May 1964. I was very sad to see that airplane go. I graduated from Huntington High School that next month and only flew a few times in 1965. It was time for me to start college and begin working toward one of the next major goals my ten-year-old self had set—a college degree in aeronautical engineering.

2

Growing up, I had spent my time flying with my parents and building aircraft models. My head was literally in the clouds, and it's an understatement to say I hadn't been a star student in elementary school. Add to that that my mother was Catholic, so I attended Catholic school, and that I had suffered from Attention Deficit/Hyperactivity Disorder, which went undiagnosed until much later in my life.

Following high school, my parents and family of nine couldn't afford the tuition of expensive universities, so I had to look at other options. We lived in Suffolk County, so I began attending Suffolk County Community College (SCCC). Honestly, it was exactly what I needed. The college was part of the New York University system and offered the identical curriculum as the schools with higher tuitions such as the State University of New York at Stony Brook. I pursued a two-year degree in engineering science and planned to transfer into a four-year program in aeronautical engineering. Attending SCCC allowed me to live at home and make the one-hour drive to the college alongside my older brother, Jon, who was a year ahead of me. Driving back and forth to SCCC together provided a lot of time to help us grow much closer.

In high school, I didn't have to work very hard to earn above-average grades, but during my first semester of college, I received a rude awakening. It was the Vietnam War era, so I had a college draft deferment of only four years, meaning I was required to graduate in that amount of time or be drafted before earning my degree, and I didn't have the option to fail any courses during those four years. But I struggled in some of my classes, physics in particular. After our two mid-terms, I held a mere 60 percent average in the course, which meant I was failing.

My physics professor, Dr. Jacobson, announced to the class after the second mid-term that our final grade would reflect the average of those two tests and the final exam. I immediately knew I was in trouble because I had to get at least a 90 on the final to pass. I had no choice but to really buckle down and work hard at learning physics. When the term ended and the grades were posted in the hall outside Dr. Jacobson's door, I had distinguished myself by earning the highest grade on the final. I had learned what it took to succeed—a heavy dose of study and effort. From that point forward, I did well in college.

I earned my Associate of Applied Science (AAS) in June 1966, but our family's financial reality hadn't changed much, so I chose to move on to California State Polytechnic College in San Luis Obispo, better known as "Cal Poly." I was attracted to the school's aeronautical engineering program, the same degree my father had earned, but what sold me was the program's grass runway and several large hangars where some of the classes would be held. In addition, out-of-state tuition at Cal Poly was significantly less expensive than in-state resident tuition in the New York University system. We'd also endured a particularly miserable winter on Long Island, so sunny central California sounded pretty good to me. As an added bonus, I was eager to get back to surfing as I had in my childhood. The Pacific Ocean waves were much larger than those in the Atlantic.

Three of my classmates at SCCC also transferred to California—one joining me at Cal Poly and the other two enrolling at the Northrop Institute of Technology in Los Angeles. One of them was Ed Mygland, who would become a close friend of mine for more than sixty years. In September 1966, the four of us drove together from Long Island to California, an adventure in itself. In Denver, Jimmy, who was going to attend Cal Poly with me, wrecked the car, stranding us for about a week while the car was being repaired. I made it to Cal Poly about an hour before introductions into the new school year.

California Coast looking toward Morro Bay and the Rock. Credit: Hoot Gibson

From the moment I arrived, I was mesmerized by the beauty of San Luis Obispo and the Central Coast area. I recall walking between buildings at Cal Poly and simply stopping in my tracks to marvel at how picturesque it was. I was living on my own for the first time, but I missed my family. The cost of traveling back was just too high, so I had to spend my first Christmas and most of the entire school year away from them, but it felt outstanding to be finally studying aeronautical engineering.

Cal Poly held sacred the mantra, "learn by doing." One of the ways the mantra manifested in the curriculum was in how determined the school was to produce engineers who knew how to design not only aircraft, but all of the components that went into them. This philosophy, and one of the most enjoyable parts of it, required us to take classes in welding, foundry or metal-casting, machining to include lathe and milling machines, and sheet metal fabrication. These skills ensured that as engineers, we wouldn't design something that couldn't be built. I have continued to use these foundational skills my entire life.

While I had enjoyed my studies at SCCC, I really hit my stride with aeronautical engineering. My experience as a pilot and flying model airplanes gave me extra insight into the field. I finished my third year of college in June 1967, and then my family joined me back in California. The FAA had transferred my father again, this time to Los Angeles to serve as a test pilot. However, I only got to spend about a week with them before I had to fly back to Long Island for my annual summer job as a lifeguard on several of the Huntington Township beaches for the summer of 1967. I had certainly enjoyed my time working as a lifeguard for the prior three years, but that year would be my last as a beach guard.

I returned to California for my fourth year of college and immediately faced a situation that would seriously alter the direction of my life. It was the 1960s, the Vietnam War was raging, and all young men, including myself, were affected by it. Early in my fourth year of college, my draft board mailed me a questionnaire to verify that I would graduate the following June.

When I graduated from SCCC, they had waived my completion of one course, called "Strength of Materials." There had not been enough students who had passed the prerequisites to take it, so I was granted my AAS without having completed the course. Since I didn't have the course on my transcript before starting my third year of engineering at Cal Poly, I couldn't begin the Stress Analysis sequence of instruction, meaning I couldn't graduate within the four years of my draft deferment.

I sent that news to the draft board and was immediately reclassified "1A," available to be drafted into the Army right away. As expected, about a week later, I received notice to appear for my Army induction physical in New York City. They told me if I wanted to finish college, I needed to immediately enlist into a military branch.

Initially, I hurried to downtown San Luis Obispo and walked right into the Air Force recruiting office and said, "I want to enlist in an Aviation Officer Program." The officer asked me when I was going to graduate, and I told him, "That's the problem. I'm about to be drafted, and I can't graduate 'til June of 1969."

"You do have a problem," he said, "because we don't talk to any candidates until they're within six months of graduation. If you somehow get to that point, come back and talk to us then."

I walked out of that office terrified that even after all my studies and valuable experience as a pilot, I still was about to be shipped to the rice paddies of Vietnam with an M-14 in my hands. I wasn't about to let that be my future if I could help it.

I found my way to the Navy recruiting office and told the chief petty officer in charge that I wanted to fly in the Navy, and he immediately asked me, "What's your draft status?" When I told him "1A," he pulled out a form letter to the draft board that basically said, "Keep your paws off this guy! We're considering him for an officer program." The chief signed it at the top and handed it to me. I happily added my signature. He slipped it into an envelope and the envelope into his out basket and then told me, "This gives us three months to process you into the Navy, and you will receive a '1Y' deferment in the meantime."

I was impressed. The Navy seemed like my kind of organization.

I still needed to travel south to Naval Air Station Los Alamitos in Seal Beach, California, which was great because it was near where my family was currently living. There, I took two tests—the Aviation Aptitude Test and a Personality Survey. I passed both of those along with an aviation medical exam. I was interviewed by two naval aviators who told me they had never seen an applicant that scored "nines" on both exams. I'm guessing they probably told everyone that, but as a result, I was sworn into the Navy and was given orders to return to Cal Poly, finish college, and notify the Navy when I was about to graduate. This allowed me to finish the fourth and fifth years of instruction I needed to graduate.

My hard work was already beginning to pay off. During my final year of college, I became one the officers of the Tau Sigma Honorary Engineering Fraternity, of which I had been a proud member since my third year of college (only the top 25 percent of engineering students were eligible). I also served as chairman of the Cal Poly student chapter of the American Institute of Aeronautics and Astronautics, the world's largest aerospace technical society. This role helped me overcome my fear of speaking to large groups and also helped me understand the importance of delegation since I couldn't singlehandedly accomplish all the tasks that needed to be done in a single school year. I was forced to share the workload with my friends who also wanted to be part of the AIAA. Whatever free time I could find, I spent dirt biking through the nearly inexhaustible trails of the California desert or surfing. In the winter, the waves would swell to fifteen feet, giants compared to those I'd caught on the east coast.

In 1968, during my last summer of college, I landed a young aeronautical engineer's dream job—engineering assistant at NASA's Dryden Flight Research Center at Edwards Air Force Base. I was surrounded by fascinating, cutting-edge aircraft: the XB-70 Valkyrie, the X-15 Rocket Plane, and several of the NASA and Air Force lifting bodies (fuselages that generate their own lift without wings), such as the HL-10, the M2F3, and the X-24A. My engineering role that summer was to compare wind tunnel test data for the HL-10 Lifting Body against flight test results. I believe it was this interesting work that helped me get selected to become an astronaut many years later.

Test pilot Bill Dana after an HL-10 lifting body flight test. Credit: NASA

The second quarter of my final year, I met a girl who would become a major part of my life at that time. Cathy Von Epps lived in the rental house next door to me. She had already graduated from the school with a bachelor's degree in education and was working on a master's degree. I asked her to marry me at the end of school year, before I left to start Navy Officer Candidate School and Navy Flight Training. But she needed another quarter to finish her master's degree, so we put the marriage on hold, and she stayed in San Luis Obispo while I went on to Pensacola on the other side of the continent to start my Navy journey.

I graduated from Cal Poly June 7, 1969, and had achieved the first life goal I had set for myself at ten years old. I was the second oldest of my parents' six kids, but I was the first one to graduate from college. Dad was so proud, which meant more to me than the degree itself. He had lived a very challenging life for want of a college degree and was determined that all his kids receive one. Ultimately, two of my siblings would also become engineers.

3

I had planned to spend my summer of '69 surfing in southern California prior to the start of my Navy training, but that post-graduation period of rest and relaxation was all fantasy. The minute I graduated, I received orders to report on June 24th to Aviation Officer Candidate School in Pensacola, Florida.

I had a feeling that physical fitness would be an important part of AOCS, so I prepared by taking a weightlifting class during my final quarter at Cal Poly. After moving home following graduation, I also started running every evening, and prior to leaving California, was able to run a full seven miles. I had been told to arrive in Pensacola as late as possible because the minute you showed, you were endlessly harassed by drill instructors and class officers.

I waited until June 23 to fly to Pensacola and checked into the San Carlos Hotel where candidates stayed prior to reporting. I had only brought a very small bag and the clothes on my back. A Navy bus picked us up the following day to drive us to the indoctrination battalion by our noon reporting time. Even before we stepped off, candidate officers began screaming and accusing us of "hanging out" at that San Carlos Hotel rather than taking initiative by showing up early. The candidate officers were those AOCS members who were in their final week of school prior to graduation and commissioning as officers in the rank of ensign. They managed the four battalions—indoctrination and battalions one through three—in partnership with the drill instructors (DIs) and a class officer who was a Navy lieutenant or Marine Corps captain. Our heads were shaved, and my small bag and civilian clothes were confiscated for the next seventeen weeks. I was issued a set of coveralls, affectionately known as "poopy bags," to wear until our uniforms were ready.

We were issued uniforms along with government-issued underwear and toiletries. We spent the first week doing paperwork and learning how to march with our class, Class 26-69. We spent days at the Naval Aerospace Medical Institute for intense physical exams to ensure we were physically qualified to train as either a Student Naval Aviator or Student Naval Flight Officer. Our time at NAMI was a nice break from the constant shouting by our DIs and candidate officers. As pilot candidates, we shed the poopy bags after a week, donned our uniforms, and were sent to NAS Saufley Field to start primary flight training in the Beechcraft T-34B in Training Squadron One (VT-1).

We were required to start primary flight training so early because the Navy needed to ensure that all pilot candidates were truly motivated to fly. Apparently, there had been issues with candidates dropping out of flight training immediately after AOCS. Flying was voluntary, and candidates could "Disenroll on Request" (DOR) at any time. The demands of the Vietnam War and men wanting to avoid being drafted to the Army were to blame. Many men had signed on with the Navy, but OCS for shipboard officers at Newport, Rhode Island, was full. As a workaround, candidates had signed on for AOCS, and once commissioned as officers, went the DOR route instead. They were still in the Navy, but they were no longer flying.

Saufley Field was heaven on Earth for pilot candidates. There were no DIs or candidate officers at Saufley, and we were given rooms in the Bachelor Officers' Quarters. We promptly began ground school on the T-34B and were taught the course rules for flying from Saufley Field. The T-34B was very similar to the Beechcraft Bonanza, an airplane I had previously flown. Its design used the same wings and landing gear but had a narrower fuselage. I had flown Dad's Bonanza, had a Private Pilot License, and had a good head start in flight training with 104 hours in my logbook in twelve different types of planes and helicopters. After spending a while in ground school, we started flying the T-34B. I made my first flight on July 11, 1969, alongside a great instructor, Lt. Junior Grade Weber. He had flown the C-121 with the Navy, the military version of the Lockheed Constellation. He taught us the "Navy way" of flying, meaning we didn't do smooth landings but rather firm touchdowns to prepare for no-flare carrier landings. While I had made one previously "unadvised" loop in the Luscombe on a solo flight back in 1964, LTJG Weber's training in the T-34B provided my first real experience doing aerobatics—that is, loops and barrel rolls.

Captain's List award ceremony.
Credit: M.R. Powell, US Navy

I did well in ground school at Saufley Field and made the Captain's List thanks to my aeronautical engineering degree and previous flight experience. I also did well in the flying portion of Primary Flight Training and flew the T-34B a total of nineteen flights for 26.3 flight hours. It was a nice-flying airplane with no bad habits, but it was a little underpowered with only a 225-horsepower engine. I soloed in the airplane on my thirteenth flight. While the Navy gave us a nice certificate to commemorate our first solo flights, I had already made my first solo many years before on my sixteenth birthday. The citation was amusing, in that it stated, "...AOC Robert L. Gibson did, alone and unassisted, take off and return to NAS Saufley, thereby successfully completing his first solo flight," which was essentially untrue.

I did my final flight at Saufley on August 11, 1969. I returned to NAS Pensacola and AOCS later that week, joining Class 33-69, moving into Battalion III, and spending the remainder of my time in AOCS there. My class had 62 candidates, and our drill instructor was Staff Sergeant Sanders, a decorated Vietnam veteran. He was extremely tough on us but very unforgiving of even the most minor of errors. It wasn't until after we had all been commissioned as officers when I learned that the actual theme of the training was "attention to detail," a skill crucial to aviators, hence the rigorous focus on every minor detail.

I must have done something right during our training because after several weeks in the battalion, SSGT Sanders called four of us into his office and presented us with a "Military" name tag to be worn above my "Gibson" name tag on my shirt. At the time, he said he expected we would become battalion commanders and high-ranking members in our class. I really didn't take it all that much to heart because I knew we still had weeks to go before finishing AOCS. We had plenty of physical fitness training to complete along with academics, including an "opportunity" to run the cross-country course as well as the obstacle course every week. All the running I did my last couple weeks in California really paid off, and I did very well in both of those courses, well enough that I earned my next badge, the red "Military & PT" badge that replaced my simple "Military" badge.

A week before our class's graduation and my commissioning as an officer, I was presented with my final achievement badge. I had earned the rank of candidate lieutenant commander posting as battalion commander of Battalion III, the Honor Battalion, and I would be graduating second in my class of 62 candidates. Suddenly, all my classmates were calling me "Sir," and it kind of made me uncomfortable. I remember saying to my staff in Battalion III, "Hey, guys. Just call me Bob." I hadn't become "Hoot" just yet. As one of the top two graduates in the class, I was then presented with the highly coveted white badge with ACAD MIL & PT emblazoned across it, one that everyone referred to as a "snowflake," because we had received honors in academics, military, and physical training during AOCS.

As commander of the Honor Battalion, I led the parade of the entire regiment, including regimental staff and all four battalions, on and off the parade grounds on graduation day, October 17, 1969. Next came the swearing-in ceremony, where candidates first took the rank of O-1, Navy ensign. We were presented with a certificate naming us as officers and had our moment with the captain. My parents made the trip from California for the event, and I remember Dad, who had served most of his time in the Army Air Corps as an enlisted sergeant, beaming brightly.

The day concluded with a grand tradition—a very proud moment and the most memorable of my training career. For the first time, our drill instructor saluted us as officers. After nine weeks of being abused and yelled at by SSGT Sanders, he proudly stood at attention as we squared off one at a time in front of him and received our first salute. It was a moment I will remember forever, and I will always cherish SSGT Sanders as a defining presence in my Navy career and beyond. After each salute, SSGT Sanders gave us a firm handshake, and when he shook mine, I slipped him a five-dollar bill folded into the shape

Commissioning ceremony as ensign U. S. Navy. Credit: U.S. Navy

of an American flag, which he took and placed into his pocket.

As commissioned officers, we went from being at the "top of the pyramid" in OCS to "bottom of the barrel" in the officer corps. Following graduation, I spent an additional month in Pensacola for an Aviation Systems course to study systems, engines, propulsion, and aviation safety. At the completion of the course, we each learned which aviation "pipeline" we would be assigned to. We had all filled out a preference card for our aircraft preferences—jets, propellors, or helicopters. Obviously, I wanted to fly jets. Our standing had been determined by our combined grades in Primary Flight Training in the T-34B, in AOCS, and in the Aviation Systems course.

I eagerly awaited the news and was relieved to learn I'd been selected for my first choice, the jet pipeline. I packed my things from the Pensacola BOQ, loaded up my car, and made the drive to my next duty station, Naval Air Station Meridian, Mississippi, for basic jet training.

4

I was beyond excited to report to NAS Meridian into Training Squadron Seven on November 30, 1969 to begin training in jets. I would be flying the T-2A Buckeye, a single-engine trainer, named the "Buckeye" from its state of design origin, Ohio, the "Buckeye" state. Once again, my training began in ground school, but I was required to learn far more than I had at my earlier schools. The T-2A Buckeye had a maximum takeoff weight of 9,916 pounds, which was over twice the weight of the T-34B, so while it did have a jet engine, it was underpowered with only 3,400 pounds of thrust. (I would get the opportunity to fly more powerful versions of the T-2 later on.) I made the Captain's List once again, and the entire class had "hero photos" made in front of a backdrop depicting the image of the jet.

This was also the first time I trained in a plane with an ejection seat, a major new area of expertise for all of us. We had trained in Pensacola on an ejection seat trainer where an explosive charge fired forcing us to ride up a rail to get a feel for how to best position our back and neck to minimize injury in an ejection. We learned right away that an ejection seat can't save a pilot in every circumstance.

Airplane attitude (its orientation relative to the Earth's horizon) and aircraft sink rate (how fast it's losing altitude) can make an ejection unsurvivable.

The shadow of the Vietnam War accelerated our training. The Navy needed pilots fast. My first flight in VT-7 was on December 11, 1970, a mere eleven days after I had first reported to the squadron. My instructor was LTJG Jim Gifford. He was a "plowback," a pilot who had finished pilot training, received his Navy Wings, and was then assigned back into Training Command as an instructor. The Air Force called them FAIPs, or "First Assignment Instructor Pilots."

My first flight in the T-2A was memorable, mainly because I had never flown a jet before. The procedure was to stop on the runway centerline, hold the brakes, and run the throttle to full power while timing how long the engine was taking to reach full power, referred to as "100 percent RPM." It wasn't difficult to hold the brakes at full power with so little thrust. The engine was required to reach 100 percent RPM in less than 18 seconds, which honestly felt like a very long time. If the engine took longer than 18 seconds, we would measure the time from 80 to 100 percent RPM, and if it was less than 15 seconds, we were officially good to go. I was surprised by the T-2A. Once I released the brakes, the airplane accelerated immediately to about one-third G, or one-third the pull of gravity pressing against your chest, but after liftoff, it just kept accelerating, right up to 250 knots (about 287 mph) and beyond. While the acceleration wasn't blindingly fast, the speed was impressive. LTJG Jim Gifford was a good instructor, and I flew with him five more times before I was allowed to take my leave for Christmas. By that time, I had flown nine hours in the T-2A.

I traveled by air back to California for Christmas in 1969 to visit my family for two days, and then on to Santa Barbara to marry my college sweetheart, Cathy Von Epps. It was a relatively small wedding

First jet solo flight, January 22,1970. Credit: R. E. Gray

attended by her mother and sister and my parents, brothers and sisters, and a few friends. My older brother, Jon, was my best man. There wasn't time for a traditional honeymoon, so we had to settle for a drive in her car back to Meridian, Mississippi. I needed to get right back into jet training because of the urgency of Vietnam. I checked out of the BOQ at NAS Meridian, and we moved into an apartment in town. Cathy had her teaching credential, so she applied for a job teaching in Meridian and was eventually hired to teach in an elementary school.

I began flying again on January 8, 1970, and on January 22, flew my first solo as a jet pilot in the T-2A. I had flown seven times with Jim Gifford and three times with Marine Captain Neff. Captain Neff was the pilot of the chase plane that accompanied me on my solo flight. One of my class members joined him to take photos. I departed from NAS Meridian, flew into the practice area, and did air work, including "dirtying up," or flying with the landing gear and flaps down. Captain Neff, having told me to simply ignore him, stayed with me the entire flight in a loose formation. My classmate shot a good photo of me in the overhead break before landing. That flight lasted one hour, and I made only one landing back at NAS Meridian.

I flew visual flights five more times after the first solo, but then it was time for simulated instrument training. These flights were flown under a hood that covered the inside of the rear canopy so pilots couldn't see outside, forcing them to fly only with information displayed on the instrument panel. These flights were known as "bag hops." There were ten basic instrument flights followed by a check ride, and then six radio instrument flights while doing cross-country navigation under the bag. The bag hops were challenging and weren't nearly as much fun as the visual reference flights. I completed the course on March 20, 1970, and that same day received a very big honor, the "Student of the Month" award bestowed by the squadron commanding officer, Commander Croom.

The celebration was short-lived, however. The next day, I transferred into Training Squadron Nine (VT-9) and begin formation training and night flying in the T-2A. These were located at NAS Meridian as well and shared the same large hangar with VT-7. Formation work consisted of nineteen sorties (the term for the dispatch of a single flight unit), the first flights in two-plane formations and later flights in four. Formation flying is a mandatory skill for tactical jet pilots, and while it was challenging at first, it eventually became almost routine. Almost…

Night flying in a jet was a new experience for me. I flew with an instructor only once before I was required to complete three solo flights. One interesting aspect of night flying are the "night noises," meaning we would hear things we had never noticed before. These otherwise normal sounds might be perceived by pilots as potential problems while flying at night. Our ground school instructor warned us about this ahead of time so we wouldn't be surprised.

I finished my final formation training flight on May 12, 1970, and immediately transitioned to the T-2C Buckeye the next day. This was the jet I wanted to fly! It was a twin-engine T-2 with a pair of smaller jets, each providing 2,950 pounds of thrust. Although the plane was 3,264 pounds heavier than the single-engine T-2A, in comparison, it was basically a hot-rod. Its top speed of 521 mph wasn't much greater than the T-2A at 492 mph, but the T-2C accelerated and climbed much faster.

With the completion of the course requirements of VT-9 at Meridian, I would now move into probably the most challenging and exciting phase of my training. I moved back to NAS Pensacola and checked into Training Squadron Four (VT-4) for my Air-to-Air Gunnery and Carrier Qualification. With the acceleration of the program due to Vietnam, my first flight in VT-4 in Pensacola was only twenty days after my last flight at Meridian on June 10.

I flew the T-2B Buckeye for this phase, which looked like the T-2C but used two J60-P-6 jet engines with 3,000 pounds thrust each, so it had all the same energy as the T-2C. In air-to-air gunnery, we flew a "squirrel-cage" pattern with four in the pattern at the same time. We each took turns shooting at the target, a banner affectionately dubbed "the rag."

The banner was towed by another T-2B on a 1,000-foot towline. The four-shooter formation rolled in one at a time, made a firing pass, then pulled up and onto a perch position until it was their turn to roll in again for another firing pass. Under each wing, the T-2B carried a .50-caliber machine gun pod. Like with paintball, each shooter had bullets filled with a different colored dye—black, red, green, and white. I flew my first gunnery pattern in the back seat, with my instructor sitting in the front. He had one flight to score as many hits on the banner as he could, and then I had ten flights where I was in the front seat to score. The loser was required to buy the winner his favorite bottle of alcohol. My instructor did not score any hits on the banner, so it was wide open for me to win that bottle. I managed three hits, quite good since most students didn't achieve any hits at all. But instead of asking for an entire bottle of scotch, I suggested that he and I go to the Officers' Club where he could buy us a couple of drinks, which I saw as more enjoyable than owning a new bottle all to myself.

My final gunnery flight was on June 22 followed by training to go to "the boat" on June 29. I had two flights that day for Field Carrier Landing Practice, also known as "bounce practice," with an instructor in the back seat. We flew out of Bronson Airfield, an outlying Navy field about six miles northwest of Pensacola. The runway had a carrier deck painted on it and a Landing Signal Officer standing beside the simulated deck. He graded all our landings, and we stayed in the landing pattern to achieve the greatest number of FCLPs possible. It was normal to make eight simulated carrier landings in a single 30- to 60-minute flight.

The students were grouped in teams of five, and we all wore matching ballcaps. Every carrier landing was graded, and the grades were "OK," worth four points, "Fair" for three points, "No Grade" for two points, a "Wave-Off" for one point, and a "Cut" pass for zero. There was also a very rare grade of "OK Underlined," which earned five points. We named our group of five "OK Underlined" and put that on our ballcaps, which in hindsight was a really arrogant thing to do. The senior member of our group was USMC Captain Tom Toth. He was a former F-4 Radar Intercept Officer going through transition training to become a pilot. We made twelve practice carrier landings at Bronson Field, and I made 87 approaches and landings prior to going to "the boat." In an amusing way, the aviators referred to the aircraft carrier as "the boat," which annoyed the shipboard officers who called it "the ship."

We flew our last airfield practice session on July 13, 1970, and were ready to "hit the boat." We only had to wait until the next day.

For the actual Carrier Qualification, we flew solo. The standing joke was that no instructor was crazy enough to ride along with a student for their first actual carrier landing. Five of us would join up on our instructor as the flight lead, fly out into the Gulf of Mexico, and rendezvous with the Navy's Training Carrier, the USS *Lexington* CVT-16.

Captain Toth from my team was offered the opportunity to go to the boat before us, but he held fast and chose to stay with our team. I was impressed at his team spirit and resolved to be like him in the future. The five "OK Underlineds" set out on July 14, 1970 to "attack" the ship for our Carrier Qualification. We would all be making two touch-and-go landings with our tailhook retracted, and then four arrested landings, or "traps," and four catapult launches. I made my first touch-and-go, and I'll never forget the image of the giant carrier and the towering island superstructure passing by me as I touched down and added full power to go around. After my second touch-and-go, I got a call from the Landing Signal Officer: "350,

First carrier landing on July 14, 1970. Credit: Cathy Gibson

drop your hook." I was about to become a Navy carrier pilot. I dropped the tailhook and reminded myself to simply fly the way I had in my FCLP sessions and bounces.

Landing on an aircraft carrier is one of the most challenging types of flying. I needed to be precisely on speed because of limits on the tailhook and the arresting wires. There was no flare for landing; we established a stabilized descent angle and flew the airplane into touchdown at that rate of descent. Immediately on feeling any indication of contact with the carrier, we went to 100 percent RPM in case of a "bolter," which was when we missed all the wires. Failing to go to 100 percent power was a major error known as "taking a cut in the gear," and it earned you a serious chewing out from the LSO. Our LSO, who had observed all our bounces, had flown out to join us on the carrier to be the LSO on the platform who would "wave us" during our first carrier landings.

I landed in the touchdown zone and immediately caught one of the arresting cables. I was yanked to a rapid stop, more abrupt than anything I had ever felt before. It felt somewhat like a controlled crash since we don't flare smoothly for landing. We touch down at a constant descent rate and then are immediately dragged to a stop by the arresting gear. It was a great feeling of accomplishment, but I wasn't finished. I needed to quickly locate the deck handler, a "yellow shirt," who gave me the hand signal to retract my hook while another deck crewman disengaged the cable. Another man put screens over the jet intakes, and another attached a tow bar to help steer me right onto the catapult for another circuit and another trap.

With three or four Gs of linear acceleration, my first catapult launch, or "cat shot" as it was known, was also something I had never felt before. The T-2B could only accelerate at about 0.45 G on its own, so this was nearly seven times the force I'd previously encountered. The entire experience put a huge smile on my face. After launch, I climbed up to pattern altitude, spotted the T-2 that I was to follow, and came back for a second trap. The maneuver was just as thrilling the second time around. My second "cat shot" was also equally exciting, but right after I was airborne, I got the call, "Clean up, and you are signal delta." That meant I needed to proceed to the delta pattern and join up with our instructor flight leader. The delta pattern is a circle around the carrier at 2,000 feet where we would find the leader, and all five of us were once again back in formation. It turned out that because the ship had been steaming south all day, it was getting too far away from Pensacola. We had to put the wind along the landing area, the angled deck, and so we had to return to Pensacola having completed only two of our four required carrier landings. Two days later, on July 16, we went back out to the *Lexington* for one more touch-and-go and our final two arrested landings. We had the advantage of having debriefed the first day's events and returned to the boat "older and wiser." When we all landed back at Pensacola after that second trip, we were fully carrier-qualified in the T-2B and had completed all our Navy Basic Training. We were now off to Advanced Training and even more instruction on the tactical uses of jet aircraft.

Advanced training in the jet pipeline occurred at one of two locations—either at NAS Chase Field in Beeville, Texas, or at NAS Kingsville, Texas. NAS Chase trained in three squadrons of TF-9J Cougars while Kingsville had two squadrons of TA-4J and TA-4F Skyhawks and one squadron of the TF-9s. The TF-9 aircraft were older airplanes and were underpowered compared to the TA-4, so of course, I wanted to fly the more powerful planes at NAS Kingsville.

Luckily, I got my wish. I was assigned to VT-23 and the speedy TA-4s.

The TA-4J was a two-seat modification of the A-4 Skyhawk built by Douglas Aircraft, a very high-performance jet capable of high transonic speeds of 670 mph, meaning it could almost fly faster than the speed of sound. It was lightweight and small but had a powerful J52-P8 engine with 9,300 pounds thrust. Known as "Heineman's Hot Rod" after its chief designer Ed Heineman, the TA-4J had a wing shape referred to as a "delta wing," similar to Greek delta, or the shape of a triangle.

The delta wing design, like other "swept wing" airplanes, gives the plane favorable drag characteristics in the transonic region, or Mach One. A delta wing requires a high angle of attack at slow speed to produce lift, meaning the aircraft must make landing approaches in the nose-high attitude characteristic of delta wing aircraft.

After being assigned to Kingsville, Cathy and I had to rush and check out of VT-4, move out of the apartment there, drive 759 miles in our two cars, find an apartment in Kingsville, and check in to VT-23. At the start of training, there was the usual ground school followed by some simulator sessions before any actual flying. I flew my first "hop," or sortie, in a TA-4J on August 19, 1970, thirty-four days after my final flight in Pensacola. My initial instructor was LTJG Roger Hull, also a plowback like Jim Gifford had been back in Meridian. He was very methodical and precise, and I was expected to act the same through all my training flights. The first phase was the transition into the TA-4J and TA-4F aircraft, and then right into instrument training in the rear seat under a hood after five transition flights. All the flying I did in September consisted of hooded flights, and twelve of the nineteen flights I did in October were also under a hood, culminating in my C-18X Instrument Check on October 24, 1970.

Now that I was instrument-rated, I moved into the most interesting phases of Advanced Training for my final three months. These phases included formation flying, low-level strike missions, air-to-ground and air-to-air gunnery, and eventually carrier qualification. The TA-4J carried two 20mm cannons with a hundred rounds per gun, and we fired them against the banner, as we had in Basic Training, and into the ground during strafing exercises. A new area of training was the dive-bomb delivery. We flew 40-degree dive-bombing runs against marked targets using Mark 76 practice bombs, which matched the ballistic characteristics of Mark 82 500-pound low-drag bombs, but with only a small smoke charge to indicate where they had landed.

The flight intensity increased throughout Advanced Training with an additional sixteen flights in November, twenty-seven in December, and twenty-one in January 1971. Fourteen of the flights in January were Field Carrier Landing Practice, bringing the grand total to eighty-two carrier approaches and landings at the Naval Auxiliary Landing Field, Alice Orange Grove. My final FCLP flight was on January 25, then it was back to the *Lexington* on January 28, 1971. To complete the Advanced Training syllabus, I made two touch-and-go landings, six arrested traps, and six catapult shots, but I had two "bolters" as well. These were two times that I missed all three arresting wires, returned to full power, and came back around for another try. I had completed carrier qualification in a swept-wing jet and had finished ninety-eight total sorties in Advanced Training. I was awarded my Navy Wings of Gold the following day, January 29, 1971, and Cathy pinned them onto my dress blues. Of course, Mom and Dad were there too.

Wing ceremony with wife Cathy. Credit: U.S. Navy

Now that I was a Designated Naval Aviator, it was time to leave the Training Command and join the Navy fleet. Prior to finishing Advanced Training, we each filled out another preference card for type of aircraft and duty station. We referred to it as the "dream sheet." I had done well throughout flight training, so I was awarded my first choice, which was the F-4 Phantom, based at NAS Miramar in San Diego. I would be moving back to where I had lived before joining the Navy and within a hundred miles of my parents and siblings. It had been a long journey through AOCS and Navy Flight Training, but the many late nights spent studying and the constant training had paid off. I would get to move back to California and check in to VF-121, "The Pacemakers," for Fleet Training in the F-4J Phantom, the best all-around fighter in the world in 1971.

After receiving my Navy Wings, we made the 1,400-mile drive from Kingsville to San Diego. Mom and Dad drove along with us in one of our cars while towing a trailer with two motorcycles. One was mine, a Honda CL-175 Scrambler, and the other belonged to one of my fellow Navy pilots, LTJG Scott Davis. Scott and I had become good friends and frequently rode our motorcycles together during our time in Kingsville. Scott would later go on to shoot down a MIG-21 in Vietnam the very next year. It was exciting to be headed for "Fightertown, USA" at NAS Miramar, California, the home of the Pacific Fleet Fighters.

Fighter Squadron 121 was the Replacement Air Group that trained pilots, Radar Intercept Officers, and maintenance crews on the F-4J Phantom. I swelled with joy when I checked into the squadron to begin flying the mighty F-4, only to be quickly deflated. There was a huge "pool" of pilots in the squadron awaiting their time to start flying, and it would be months before we could actually begin the training syllabus. My class, at the time consisting of about twenty-five pilots and RIOs, would also include three future astronauts.

Seven years later, in 1978, Jim VanHoften, Mike Lounge, and I would all be selected to the first Space Shuttle Class of astronauts. Of course, we didn't know that at the time.

While we waited, and to keep the class occupied, we were scheduled for a few training courses one or two weeks in length at nearby NAS North Island, covering Maintenance Officer training, Electronic Warfare, and Prisoner of War guidance. We were treated to Survival, Evasion, Resistance, and Escape training, or SERE School, as well. SERE School was an unforgettable experience in an aviator's career, but not for being enjoyable. The first three days were spent at Naval Base Coronado in San Diego for lectures and survival training at the beach. We had to begin capturing crabs to eat because we weren't provided with any rations. While we caught enough crabs in the rocks and the breakwater not to go hungry during those days, it was only a sample of what was to come next. We were bussed to Warner Springs in the mountains east of San Diego for forest survival and actual POW training. Food was minimal during those several days as prior classes had pretty much picked the forest clean of anything to eat. We did find a tree with a honeybee hive in it and got permission to cut it down. After a few stings, we shared honeycomb, which really hits the spot when you're starving in the woods. And just when you thought it couldn't get any worse, we started the evasion and POW training phase of SERE.

We were taken to the starting point of the evasion course and then released to travel about one mile to "Freedom Village." Waiting for us at the Village was a ham sandwich and an orange if we were able to travel the distance without being caught. While it may not sound like the greatest prize, at the time, it was good as gold. We were told that "enemy forces" would start from the opposite end of the course and move toward us with a mission to capture us. The entire exercise would unfold over three hours, followed by a siren signaling the time for all of us to come out of hiding and surrender.

I began moving up the first hill of the course when there was gunfire right on the opposite side of the hill. The first trainees were being captured. While the ammunition used was blanks, we didn't know that at the time. The enemy was just over our hill and waiting for us. We were advised, as part of survival best practices, to delay capture as long as possible, forestalling the inevitable beatings and abusive treatment of POW internment, so I immediately found some dense bushes, crawled into them, and settled in with the intent to last the three hours hidden. Several times, I was passed by enemy forces who would announce, "You have been captured, so come on out!" But I stayed put. When the siren finally sounded, I stood up, walked out, and thinking I was safe, approached a group of the enemy, only to be immediately slammed to the ground and roughed up a bit, "welcoming" me to the life of a POW.

I was then waterboarded—yes, actually waterboarded. I was strapped to a board so I couldn't move, my head was held motionless, a soaking wet towel placed over my nose and mouth, and water was constantly poured onto the towel. I tried holding my breath, but that didn't work. The enemy said, "Oh, we have a breath holder," and they simply stopped pouring the water until I tried to breathe again. I quickly sucked in a batch of air and water, but my years of competitive swimming and lifeguarding came into play, so I swallowed the water and inhaled the air. I did that for several minutes, but quickly realized they weren't going to stop until I panicked. So, I acted frantic, and they finally let me off the board. In the debrief after SERE School, they revealed that there had been a Navy corpsman with fingers on our necks checking our pulse the whole time, and when your heart rate began to climb for fear of death, that was their signal to stop. It was most unpleasant, and they used the threat of more waterboarding for the rest of our time as "POWs."

I was then ushered into a large wooden box—about four feet square—to spend my time until a series of interrogations that would go on all night. As a POW, we had been briefed that per the Geneva Convention, all we were required to reveal was our name, rank, serial number, and date of birth. Through some physical abuse and other intimidation tactics, the interrogations were intended to break us down so we would divulge more information. A few hours after sunrise we were called out of our boxes and told to stand at attention while the enemy flag was raised in the compound. We were extremely surprised when the American Flag was unfurled, and when they announced, "Welcome Back to the USA." Tears flowed from a number of the POWs. We had survived SERE School, but it still wasn't time to start flying the F-4.

I was finally able to do some flying by June 1971 when I went through intensive instrument training with squadron VF-126 using TA-4J and TA-4F Skyhawks. This was a precursor to flying the F-4 and was intended to make us familiar with the required instrument approaches to many of the southern California military bases in the event we needed to divert from NAS Miramar. It was very challenging, and my first bag hop (and they were all bag hops) was on June 4 after four months of no flight activity. The syllabus called for nine flights, and we had hoped to start flying the F-4 afterward, but that didn't happen. Although I didn't see it at the time, something good was heading my way. I received a call from my squadron to report to Commander Sam Leeds who was leading the F-14 Fleet Project Team preparing to accept the F-14 at NAS Miramar. Scott Davis, Steve Shrock, and I had been selected to be staff workers for that team since we all had technical degrees. Our time waiting around to start training in the F-4 was over. We spent the next four months with the initial cadre of aviators working to get everything ready at Miramar for the F-14. (Little did I know that what I thought was a delay in my career, would become a reward several years later when I would be asked to join this very fighter squadron.)

We finally started ground school in October 1971, and after eight months of waiting, I flew the F-4J Phantom II for the first time on November 3, 1971. I flew my first two sorties in the F-4 with a pilot in the rear seat instead of a RIO in case there needed to be some serious "pilot shit" learning that only another pilot could provide. The Navy's version of the F-4 didn't have flight controls or throttles in the rear seat, so it required a pilot to be patient and calm since he couldn't change anything the front seat pilot may or may not do. For my third flight and all remaining training flights, I flew with an Instructor RIO. My third flight was with Lieutenant Commander Roger McFillen as the RIO, with whom I would fly many years later in the F-14 Tomcat, for which the Navy is now famous through the *Top Gun* movie franchise.

It was an incredible thrill to fly the F-4. It was my first experience flying a jet equipped with afterburner, a technology that injects fuel into the exhaust flow from the jet engine and ignites it to increase thrust by 50 percent, and the extra power was certainly impressive! Engaging the afterburner also doubles fuel consumption, but I agree with the words I remember Scott Davis saying right after his first flight. "Those afterburners are worth every pound of fuel they use!" This was my first supersonic experience, flying faster than the speed of sound. My second flight in the F-4 called for a speed run out to Mach Two—twice the speed of sound. It had to be done in a "clean" airplane, meaning the plane did not carry the centerline fuel tank that limited it to Mach 1.6, trading out a significant amount of flight time for speed. The flight lasted only 1.3 hours. It took a lot of fuel to go Mach 2, but it earned me the F-4 Phantom "Mach 2" pin, which I still have.

After my first transition flights came my instrument and radar intercept flights against a target airplane. During these exercises, we practiced intercepting another jet head-on and simulated firing a radar-guided missile. After passing the target plane, we were told to engage from the six o'clock position behind it, a maneuver called a "stern conversion," and then simulate firing an infrared heat-seeking AIM-9 Sidewinder missile. I also flew an air-to-ground bombing phase, where we dropped the same MK-76 practice bombs that I had dropped during Advanced Training, but once delivered actual 500-pound MK-82 bombs in the Chocolate Mountain Restricted Area near the Salton Sea.

Between November and January, I flew the F-4 fifty times. The suddenly intense schedule was like drinking from a fire hose, and I loved every minute! I made it to the air-to-air combat phase in January 1972, starting with one-on-one combat, commonly known as "dogfighting." Following a number of those, I went into two-on-one dogfighting and flew my first on February 2, 1972, with RIO LT John Uelses, who was a legend in Naval aviation. He had been an enlisted Marine and had set the world pole vaulting record in 1962, becoming the first person ever to exceed sixteen feet. He'd later gone through Officer Candidate School to be a Naval officer and RIO. I didn't have a good feel for two-on-one tactics, so he awarded me the only "down" I've ever had—an unsatisfactory flight. I flew three subsequent flights after my "down," and then did a re-flight of two-on-one with Lt. Tony Bull, a British RIO exchanged into the US Navy from the Royal Air Force, who told me I'd done a fine job.

I flew another eighteen times in February, and on Leap Day, February 29, 1972, I finally began day practice for landing the Phantom on the carrier. I mention "day" because this would include "night traps" for the first time. Most of the pilots qualifying in the F-4 hadn't practiced carrier landings during their training, but instead after they had joined their operational squadrons. I had done well in the RAG (Replacement Air Group), except for that one "down," so I had been designated as a "Category Alpha," which meant I could be sent directly to Southeast Asia to join a squadron already involved in combat operations in the Gulf of Tonkin.

I flew eighteen more times in March 1972, and all but one flight was associated with carrier qualification. Thirteen of the flights were night runs, and I made 148 night approaches and landings preparing for day and night CQ. One of my most interesting flights was a night flight to Naval Auxiliary Landing Field San Clemente midway through the training for four FCLP approaches.

NALF San Clemente Island is located 85 miles west of NAS Miramar on the north end of the island. The four approaches began with a Carrier-Controlled Approach, a maneuver that depends on the radar controller's radioed heading and glide slope corrections to each pilot. The airfield was completely black except for the lights that marked the simulated carrier deck on the runway. Above the sea at night, the water and the sky are both black, and the only lights a pilot sees are those indicating the landing strip on the carrier. The NALF runs were a perfect simulation of this. Several of the pilots that flew that night told me they had never actually touched down on any of their approaches because the LSO had waved them off each time. I had made four successful landings but was still humbled by the notion of the darkness that awaited us on the carrier.

March 23, 1972, I made my first day of landings on the USS *Midway*—one touch-and-go, five catapult shots, and six arrested landings. The F-4 Phantom was a much larger and heavier aircraft than the TA-4J, so its approach speed was faster at around 170 mph, but it was solid and stable on approach, which was very helpful. I returned to the Midway on March 25 and made my first ten night landings, which marked the end of my F-4 training. I was now a fully-qualified Phantom pilot, so I checked out of my squadron and started packing my bags to leave for the Vietnam War.

5

The day had finally arrived. It was time to start the long journey to the Gulf of Tonkin to board the USS *Coral Sea* and Fighter Squadron 111. There were four of us designated Cat Alpha who were traveling together. We three pilots—Steve Shrock, Dick Gray, and myself, who had all known each other from our time together during flight training—were accompanied by a RIO by the name of Jack Obszarski. We flew commercially from San Diego to Oakland, and then made our way to Travis Air Force Base for our flight to Clark Air Base in the Philippines. The flight was on a chartered airliner with a stop in Honolulu to refuel and then on to Guam. Andersen AFB in Guam was home to more than 150 B-52 bombers at that time in 1972. With plenty of time to kill while we were waiting, we were able to watch the US Air Force B-52 Stratofortress bombers take off, heavily loaded with fuel for a round-trip to Vietnam, each packing 108 500-pound Mark 82 bombs. There was a steady stream of these planes departing and struggling for altitude under so much weight.

We continued our long journey and finally landed at Clark AB, but the next leg of the trip from Clark AB to NAS Cubi Point that evening was harrowing. The roads were one lane in each direction and were alternately paved and unpaved. We climbed into an Air Force vehicle to make the roughly forty-mile drive, which took two hours. Our Filipino civilian driver was in such a hurry to get back to Clark, he raced past other vehicles, most of which were moving slowly on the not-so-great-roads. We were exhausted from the long trip and were happy to arrive at the Bachelor Officers' Quarters at Cubi Point. We didn't have a way to continue that day, so we had to stay the night to catch our ride to Vietnam the next day.

We met two members of our squadron, a pilot named George Drummond and a RIO named Pete McManus, who were there to retrieve an airplane and return it back to the USS *Coral Sea*. Their F-4 wasn't ready yet, so they were spending the night at Cubi Point as well. They decided the four of us new guys needed to experience the city of Olongapo for the first time. It was quite the experience! We took a commercial on-base taxi to the main gate, then walked across the bridge over the Olongapo River and into town. The river, also serving as a sewer system, was a foul-smelling tributary dubbed the "Rio de Turds." Despite the danger of swimming in the water, there were always young Filipino kids in sampans with nets asking people passing by to toss them quarters. If they missed catching the coins in the net, they would dive in after them.

The dirt streets in Olongapo were festooned with bars, all of them advertising ladies of the night who were trying to make a living off the sailors who frequented them. Whenever you sat at a table, you had to leave an empty seat next to you so one of the girls could sit with you. They made commissions by having sailors buy them a "lady's drink." Those same sailors could also hire them from the bar for the night if they so desired. Of course, a happily married man, I was never tempted by this practice. We made our way back to base and spent the night in the BOQ. The following day, we climbed aboard an Air Force C-141 transport plane at the Cubi Point Airfield for the trip to Vietnam.

We flew to Cam Ranh Bay to refuel, offload some personnel and equipment, and load for the flight to Da Nang. Cam Ranh Bay lies on the southeastern coast of Vietnam about 180 miles northeast of Saigon. From there, we flew to Da Nang and landed in an active war zone. The specter of war was immediate with our first views of concertina wire and sandbags stacked against buildings and the steady stream of fighter and attack airplanes landing and departing. We made our way to the Navy side of Da Nang, which was far more primitive than the Air Force side. We had hoped to be able to go directly to our carrier, the USS *Coral Sea*, but we were told we couldn't leave that evening. We checked in to the humble BOQ on the Navy side which had sandbags covering the entire first floor of the building. A couple hours later, we saw one of our group of four leaving with all his luggage as he proudly announced, without irony or intent to render aid, "I found a ride out to the *Coral Sea*, so you guys enjoy the night here in Da Nang." He had a reputation for narcissism; this instance was a classic example.

The three of us remaining in Da Nang were at the mess tent eating dinner that evening when we struck up a conversation with some of the "old hands" based there. Naturally, we asked them about rocket attacks. Da Nang was renowned for rockets from the Viet Cong who nearly encircled the base. For protection, helicopter patrols flew every night, all night long, in search of the enemy. But the old hands told us, "Oh, you don't need to worry about rocket attacks. We haven't had an attack for five weeks."

Well, that jinxed us. About 1:00 a.m., we were awakened by the explosion of a rocket impact. I leaped out of bed and scrambled to put on a pair of my khaki uniform pants and get myself into the bunker next to the BOQ, shirtless. Like many Navy structures, the bunker was an extreme, "no-frills" type of structure with a dirt floor and a roof covered with sandbags, not concrete or steel. It was interesting that the air raid sirens hadn't sounded until after the rocket impact. I had heard that Da Nang had radar sensors that would spot the incoming rockets and alert the base before impact, but it was obvious that hadn't happened. There were about a dozen officers in the bunker with me, all waiting for the "all-clear" siren, which never came.

After an hour or so, I struck up a conversation with the young, enlisted Marine assigned to guard the bunker, and we talked about when the all-clear would come so we could go back to bed. He explained that the real threat at Da Nang was from Viet Cong "sappers" who would try to sneak into the base armed with hand grenades, tossing them into the bunkers, and turning them into "death traps." After hearing this and seeing that the guard was unarmed, I had no confidence in our safety and felt extremely uneasy about being in that bunker. After several hours, officers began leaving and going back into the BOQ, though we never did get the all-clear signal. I eventually gave up and went back to the BOQ myself, sleeping fitfully the rest of that short night. My first night in Vietnam was miserable and memorable for all the wrong reasons. I think those on the aircraft carrier felt sorry for us pilots who'd gotten waylaid because the next day, they sent the ship's helicopter into Da Nang to pick us up and return us to our squadrons. Of course, our squadrons also badly needed us due to the intense pace of combat missions.

I'll never forget how hot it was in the Gulf of Tonkin, even aboard the ship. I would learn to describe Southeast Asia as "the land where you're never cold." While the ship did have air conditioning in both the Ready Rooms and living quarters, it was never capable of getting to a reasonable temperature. We were sweating profusely by the time we had lugged all our bags and flight gear—helmets, boots, flight suits, etc.—to our squadron's spaces. We were then taken to our squadron's Ready Room to begin meeting the other aviators. I remember my feeling of embarrassment after shaking hands with the squadron commanding officer, CDR Bob Pearl. As much as I tried to wipe my hand dry, it remained wet, and he had to wipe off his hand afterwards. It was a bit of a whirlwind meeting other pilots and RIO's in the squadron because I didn't know any of them beforehand. One of the aviators I met was LT Chuck McNary. I remember him vividly because as I was walking to the front of the Ready Room, he was walking to the back, and I got a big smile from him under his huge handlebar mustache. I was sporting a mustache by that time, but it was perfectly within regulations. After that, I decided to grow mine out more fully to look like a real fighter pilot! I liked him right away because of the warm welcome he gave me. He said, "You must be one of our new guys. I'm Chuck McNary." From that moment on, he was my life-long friend. We are still in contact more than fifty years later.

Another aviator I met early on was the squadron Operations Officer, Lieutenant Commander Dave Cowles. The OpsO is the third most senior officer in a squadron after the CO and the Executive Officer. He was also warm and welcoming, and I still see him every other year at our VF-111 reunions. Right after we shook hands, he asked me, "Do you have a nickname?" All fighter pilots and RIOs go by callsigns in the air, so you never hear over the radio, "Hey, Jim. This is John." When decisions in the air must be made in fractions of a second, you want to immediately know who is being addressed. Something like, "Hey, Mauler. This is Gunner."

But I didn't know that yet. My name is Robert, and I had been "Bob" all my life. So I told Cowles, "Yes, Sir. It's Bob."

He looked at me sideways and said, "No, I mean a real nickname!"

I thought quickly, as a fighter pilot does, and said, "Well occasionally in the past, I've been called 'Hoot.'" (Of course, the famous cowboy movie star, "Hoot" Gibson, was to blame for the moniker in those days—if your last name was Gibson, you were likely to have been called "Hoot" at some point.)

BANG! Cowles loved the name, and from that moment on, it stuck. I've been "Hoot" for more than fifty years. That name went on the canopy of my F-4, on my squadron coffee cup, on my leather nametag for my flight suit, and it's been my callsign ever since. I have Cowles and that single interaction to thank for this formative moment in the development of my identity. The name rooted so firmly that eventually even my own squadron members had forgotten my actual name. (I did learn later, however, that my father had also been called "Hoot" during his time in the Army Air Corps.)

For the remainder of that day and well into the night, we were briefed by Ops Officer Weaver "Wingo" Simonsen, one of our senior RIOs, on squadron Ops rules, Air Wing doctrine, and USS *Coral Sea* rules. There was also the "small" bit of news that we were going right into combat, and we needed to know how to survive. This was challenging to listen to not only due to the risks involved, but also because I was so jet-lagged after the long days of traveling through fifteen time zones. This was life-saving information, and I could barely keep my eyes open. Finally, they said, "Let's quit for the night, and we will continue early tomorrow." After a day or two, we completed the rest of the briefings and were declared ready for combat. We also spent some time getting our flight gear in order, learning how to check out a Smith & Wesson .38 Special revolver for self-protection during missions in case we were shot down, and spending time in the cockpit of the F-4B because it was a different version of the Phantom from what I had flown in the RAG, the F-4J.

I was ready to go and wanted to go fly, but I was still quite apprehensive about combat missions. We had to wait several more days because all missions were strikes to the hottest and most heavily defended parts of North Vietnam such as Hanoi, Haiphong, Vinh, Nam Dinh, Than Hoa, and many others. Finally, on April 17, the OpsO said, "We are running our pilots ragged without you, so tomorrow you'll fly regardless of where the missions go." I had also never launched from a carrier at such high gross weights, loaded down with 3,000 pounds of Mark 82 bombs, two or four AIM-9 Sidewinders, and one or two AIM-7 Sparrow missiles. In addition, the USS *Coral Sea* was a Midway Class carrier, so it had shorter catapults, the very reason my squadron had F-4Bs rather than the heavier F-4Js. Since they were shorter, the catapult stroke would be that much more energetic, with higher Gs. I waited with trepidation to see what missions would come my way the following day.

As luck would have it, the Carrier and Air Wing 15 were given a bit of a break on April 18, 1972, and all the missions were to South Vietnam, a much lower-threat environment. I did launch in the same F-4B the Skipper was flying, which bore the names of pilot CDR Bob Pearl and his RIO, LT Gil Sliney, on the cockpit. This airplane was special in our squadron. Flown by LT Garry Weigand and LTJG Bill Freckleton, on March 6, 1972, the plane downed a MIG-17 of the North Vietnamese Air Force. On its left engine intake duct, the plane wore "MIG KILL" markings.

My Senior RIO for the first mission was Weaver "Wingo" Simonsen, also known as "Black Cloud" because at times he seemed be a jinx to others and unlucky to himself, but I had to put that reputation out of mind and focus. The Phantom could be a challenging airplane to fly from a carrier catapult launch because it came off the front end of the flight deck at about a zero-degree pitch angle but needed a 10-degree nose-up pitch in order to fly, and that wasn't the only issue. The Phantom had a "heavy nose," meaning the pilot had to yank the stick backward to get it to lift from zero degrees, but once it had an upward pitch, it needed significant pressure downward to

F-4B side number 201 catapult launch. Credit: Chuck McNary

stop the rising pitch angle. This could be really challenging at night because the maneuver had to be flown in the dark using the attitude gyroscope in the cockpit with no outside references. With my heavy load of ordnance combined with a heavy nose, I over-rotated by about 5 or 10 degrees for my first carrier launch in that heavy Phantom. Still, this was preferable to under-rotating which would have put the airplane immediately into the water.

The mission from there was to South Vietnam, where we met up with a Forward Air Controller, callsign Covey 515, who was supporting troops in contact with the Viet Cong forces and needed air support to repel the attack. We dropped our bombs in the location the FAC had pointed out to us, somewhere in the dense jungle, then made our way back to the carrier in the Gulf. My first launch in the squadron was less than perfect, as was my first carrier landing back aboard *Coral Sea.* I was supposed to fly a purely visual circling approach, then roll the plane to a wings-level attitude at about three-quarters of a mile from touchdown, then "fly the ball" to landing. For visual carrier landings, each ship had what is referred to as a "meatball," a bright light on which the pilot relies as a reference point to guide them into the landing. It turned out I mistook the reflection of the sun for the meatball, so I was too low to land. The Landing Signal Officer barked over the radio, "Come on! Get it up in the middle where you belong!" Once I corrected, I saw the actual ball and landed without issue, but I was awarded "No Grade" for my approach and landing, the lowest grade there is. I was off to a poor start, and I couldn't blame any of it on Black Cloud. From then on, my career had nowhere to go but up.

I flew another mission into South Vietnam two days later, this time working with another FAC, callsign "TUM 35," followed by a second mission. We frequently flew multiple missions in a single day. Senior RIO "Flags" Fontaine joined me for the second flight, a strike inside the Demilitarized Zone that separated North and South Vietnam. This was a high-threat environment due to the Easter Invasion of 1972, which placed 30,000 to 40,000 North Vietnamese Army troops, 200 tanks, long-range 130mm artillery guns, and air defense units into the DMZ in an attempt to topple the South Vietnamese government. The air defense units carried 57mm, radar-guided anti-aircraft artillery guns which produced large, gray explosions of flak when they detonated. I was the fourth aircraft in a four-ship formation led by the squadron CO to attack the tanks and the guns. When I watched the first three airplanes of my formation roll in for their bomb runs, I saw so much flak bursting around them, I grew concerned when it was my turn to roll in. This was the first time I had seen any defensive fire, and it was only my third combat sortie. I

F-4B Phantom II bombing run. Credit: U.S. Navy

remembered one of my USAF exchange instructors from the F-4 RAG who had spoken about how the Marines would jink back and forth during their bomb runs, in the attempt not to fly a predictable path, throwing off both the radar-guided and optically aimed guns. I decided this was the occasion for such a bomb run and rolled into the standard 40-degree dive angle, then jinked to the left, to the right, up, and down, until my RIO announced, "Track," at which point I steadied up and took precise aim at the target. A thousand feet of descent later, he called, "Stand by," and then, at the appropriate altitude of 6,000 feet above the ground, he called, "Mark," at which point, I hit the "pickle button" to drop all six of my Mark 82 bombs. This was followed by a five-G pullout, and we re-joined the flight and flew back to the carrier.

We went into the debriefing to discuss the targets and defensive fire. Toward the end of the briefing, Flags proceeded to say, "We had one of those screwed-up bomb runs where we were trying to get stabilized all the way down. We were left and right, up and down, but we hit the target. So good bombs."

I interjected, "No, that's not what I was doing! I was jinking!" All seven of my fellow aviators in the debriefing howled with laughter at the idea that I was jinking in a bomb run! I had already been named "Hoot," and from then on, I was "Hoot the Jinker" or just "Jinker."

Afterward, I was taken aside by the Ops officer, who said, "You are not to jink in a bomb run. We have gone through a lot of effort and risk to get you in place over a target, and you need to be as precise and stabilized as humanly possible. You will not jink in a bomb run again."

I replied, "Aye, aye, Sir," and resolved never to do it again, and I never did—except for my last combat sortie after fifty additional missions, but that's a story for later.

Cape Mui Ron in North Vietnam, known as "Crab," was one of

our landmarks, while Hanoi was known as "Bullseye." If our radar controllers needed to warn us of surface-to-air missiles or MIGs, referred to as "Bandits," in the air, they would be referenced to Crab or Bullseye. I got a radar warning call on one of my missions that stated, "Bandits. Crab 180 degrees at 10 miles," which really got my attention because that's exactly where I was. I spotted the MIG down low and dove to intercept but realized it was too small for a Bandit. I joined up close to it and saw it was a "Buffalo Hunter," one of our unmanned reconnaissance drones, so I refrained from shooting it down. I flew another mission on April 23, my fifth combat sortie, that was memorable because it was against a radar site at Cape Mui Ron and was my first mission into North Vietnam and a SAM envelope.

I was very apprehensive venturing into a SAM environment, mainly because of how lethal the missiles were—radar-guided, traveling at Mach Four, four times the speed of sound, and had a blast warhead of 350 pounds. The missile could be outmaneuvered by my Phantom, but a pilot had to perform the high-G maneuvering perfectly, or the missile would win. My airwing had suffered twelve downed aircraft on this single cruise, and the majority were due to SAMs. No SAMs were launched at us on this particular mission, but they always loomed large in the back of my mind. Apprehensive was the wrong word; I was downright scared. I flew the majority of my combat missions to North Vietnam and never had one shot at me, so I never got the opportunity to defeat one and build my confidence. So I lived in constant fear of them throughout all of my missions.

I had a very close call during my seventeenth mission. I was flying with LT Bob Geary as my RIO, and during the catapult shot, the time release mechanism of my ejection seat fired, which cut me loose from the seat. The springs, designed to push me and my parachute pack away from the seat, shoved me forward since all my seatbelts had been cut loose by the TRM. I managed to rotate and fly away from the water despite all the debris that was now loose in the cockpit, myself included. We climbed to altitude and called the ship saying I wanted to divert to Da Nang and land there instead of trying to do a carrier landing, which would have been far riskier since the deceleration of an arrested landing would have slammed me into the instrument panel. Somehow, the wording that made it to my squadron was garbled, and they thought I simply couldn't lock my shoulder straps. The radio call that came back to me was, "Your commanding officer says you are to bring that airplane back aboard the carrier." When I heard that, I thought to myself, "They surely don't care about my life at all." If I had to eject for any reason during that landing, it would have been fatal since I was already separated from the ejection seat.

As expected, when I landed and the arresting gear decelerated my airplane at four to five Gs, I was shoved up against the instrument panel, my parachute laying on top of me. I was barely able to raise my head high enough to see ahead of me to taxi out of the arresting gear while the Air Boss up in the tower was frantically calling, "Are you all right?" My RIO had to answer because I couldn't reach the switch to transmit over the radio. I was able to taxi to a spot to shut down. The plane captain was amazed at the mess that was my cockpit. Me, the parachute, and all the springs cluttered everything. My squadron CO felt awful for telling me to bring the airplane back to the carrier, but he hadn't been told about the actual problem. I was lucky I didn't have to eject from that airplane, so I think I wore out one of my guardian angels that day.

I had a very memorable day on June 3, 1972. I launched with LT Gil Sliney, one of our more senior RIOs. We were tasked with "Barrier Combat Air Patrol," or BARCAP, and these patrols were generally a little boring because we remained over the Gulf of Tonkin in a holding pattern for the entire flight to serve as protection for the Navy fleet in case MIGs launched to attack. The mission was scheduled to launch at 8:35 p.m., making it a night BARCAP. The flight was without incident until we returned to land on the *Coral Sea*. I flew a normal night precision approach to the carrier, with a controller providing course and glide slope guidance via radio transmissions. I received the final call from the controller, "You are at three-quarters of a mile, call the Ball," whereupon we made our "Ball Call," as usual. But then, the LSO called, "The ship is in a turn, wave it off." This was immediately followed by the Air Boss transmitting, "You are signal 'Bingo' to Da Nang. Da Nang is bearing 175 degrees at 140 miles."

As it turned out, I was "Trick or Treat" on the approach, meaning I either landed successfully aboard the ship, or I had to divert to an airfield because I was approaching the minimum fuel required to make it to the field if that's what I chose. A "Bingo Profile" is a demanding flying task because the amount of fuel remaining was always critical, and any errors would use excess fuel. The standard profile would arrive at the destination with only 1,200 pounds of fuel remaining, which for an F-4 Phantom was less than ten minutes of flight time. The procedure called for a climb straight ahead from the wave off, at 250 knots airspeed to 2,500 feet, then a turn to the desired heading and a climb at 400 knots and and Mach 0.86. For a 140-mile Bingo, the profile called for a climb to 35,000 feet, a brief cruise, and then an idle power descent at 55 miles to go. If all went according to plan, I would arrive at sea level for landing with 1,200 pounds of fuel remaining. This is the kind of math vital to aviation.

However, I had a significant problem. There was a huge thunderstorm directly in our path. I could either fly around the storm, which would greatly increase the distance we needed to fly, or I could try to fly over the top of it. The storm was massive, so I could see that I would run out of fuel going around it, so I took the second choice, but in doing so, I burned a lot more fuel climbing to about 43,000 feet. Once we were clear of the thunderstorm, I started an idle descent from 65 miles out. The weather was clear at Da Nang, so I had the lights of Runway 17 in sight right away in the long descent. Topping the storm had cost a lot of fuel, and we were still consuming fuel even in the idle descent. I was seeing only 900 pounds of fuel on the gauge as we were about to land, but there was yet another problem. I had 400 pounds of fuel trapped in the wings, so only 500 pounds was available for the engines in the fuselage tanks. When we touched down on the runway, I immediately shut off the left engine to save fuel. For operations from the carrier, we used very high tire pressures of 350 PSI, which made it easy to lock up the wheels and blow tires.

I decided to drop my tailhook to catch the midfield arresting cable used routinely at Da Nang. The cable made it easy to stop, and once we rolled backwards a little, I retracted the hook and started to hurry to parking so we wouldn't run out of fuel. I turned off the runway and was hustling along on the taxiway when I saw all the crash trucks hurrying toward me, blocking the way. I had to come to a stop and was immediately surrounded by the crash and rescue team. I was frantically trying to wave them away and managed to get one of them to come up on my boarding ladder. I yelled over the engine noise, "I'm about to run out of fuel! Get out of my way!" He hurried down and got everyone clear, and I was able to continue on, park, and shut down with very little fuel remaining. We landed at Da Nang at about 10:30 p.m., refueled, and returned to the *Coral Sea* at around 12:30 a.m. to finish a very long day.

My final combat sortie, and the only other time I jinked in a bomb run, was on June 30, 1972, and it was the last combat day of the cruise. There were two Alpha Strikes scheduled for the day, one early in the morning, and another in the afternoon. An Alpha Strike is a mass attack of thirty to forty aircraft against a heavily defended target in hopes that the large volume of attackers would overwhelm the defenders. I was assigned to the early Alpha Strike, and I do mean early! I have a copy of the flight schedule for that day, and the briefing was held at 3:45 a.m. We launched at 5:45 a.m. in the dark; sunrise wasn't until 6:16. It's interesting to note that I had been on five-minute alert the night before from 6:00 to 8:00 p.m., so I could not have gotten more than six and a half hours of sleep after a long day prior. Sleep was always at a premium aboard the carrier. Our target that day was the Patrol/Torpedo Boat base at Vinh Harbor, and the sun was just starting to rise as we approached Vinh.

I remember thinking, *We're so early, we're going to catch them asleep*. I watched as the strike leader rolled in on his bomb run, followed rapidly by the next batch of aircraft, and then, all of a sudden, the sky went black! The defenders were wide awake and waiting for us. There was so much flak in the air, it must have come from around a hundred AAA guns. The flak encompassed the entire target area, and I thought to myself, *There's no way we can fly through that and survive!* But the lead aircraft had completed his run, and subsequent attackers were finishing theirs, bottoming out, and heading back out into the Gulf.

I prepared to start my run as I pulled up over Vinh, but I was following two A-7 "Corsairs," and they were pitching down right into my way. Had I continued, we would have collided. I had to pitch up aggressively to miss them, so I was now the last airplane to roll in and the last remaining target for all those guns. I finally rolled in, and as I steadied in my bomb run, a stream of tracers, an explosive round that produces a bright visible trail, loomed in front of me, precisely along my flight path. The tracers are shot from 23mm high-rate-of-fire cannons, and they are impressive to see, especially when they are homing in on you! Regardless of my prior pledge, I jinked to the left away from them, and they followed me and were right in front of me again. I jinked up and to the right and did this the rest of the way down until it was time to release my bombs, with the tracers trying to home in on me the entire time. I pulled up and high-tailed it out of there, heading back to the ship. I never did find my flight leader, but the ship had a "Ready Deck" for us, meaning we could land whenever we arrived back at the boat. It had been a short mission, only an hour long. My RIO on this mission had the callsign "CVAN," an abbreviation of his full name, Clark Van Nostrand, and he never complained once that I was jinking in a bomb run. He'd seen all the same tracers I had and must have agreed with my maneuvers. Neither of us ever told the OpsO that I had jinked again.

We finished our debriefing, then several of us, including Mike Guenther, callsign "Mauler," headed down to the officers' wardroom to have lunch. All of us who had flown the morning Alpha Strike were done for the rest of the cruise. After that day, the USS *Coral Sea* and Air Wing 15 sailed back to California. "Mauler" was an old hand in the Vietnam business. He had made at least four prior deployments to Vietnam and combat operations. He had started as an attack pilot, flying attack aircraft such as the A-4 Skyhawk, which was a bomber, not a fighter. Somehow, he had managed to change communities and join the fighters, almost unheard of in Naval aviation. He had flown MIG Combat Air Patrol on that morning's Alpha Strike. They were the fighters called to engage the MIGs if they came up to attack the strike force, although we in the F-4 could also serve as MIGCAP once we had dropped our bombs. But at this stage of the Vietnam War, we felt that the North Vietnamese had learned the adage, "You don't eat yellow snow or fuck with the gray F-4s!" The gray Navy fighters had decimated the MIGs in 1972 due in large part to the training that "TOPGUN" had instilled into our Navy fighter tactics. So it was rare that the MIGs would engage us at all.

As we were entering the officers' wardroom, the aviators assigned to the last remaining combat mission of the cruise were somberly having lunch before going into harm's way. When Mauler passed through the door, he grabbed the handle and flung it open, causing it to crash against the wall, announcing our arrival with a bang. The aviators having lunch all stopped eating and looked our way as Mauler stopped in place, stretched his arms to the side and announced loudly, "Guys, wouldn't it be shitty to get shot down this afternoon?"

If I had been one of those going out for that last mission, I would have probably bitten right through my fork. Mauler was adept at gallows humor.

The final Alpha Strike turned out to be a walk in the park. There had been no real threat, and every aircrew returned safely. My own final combat mission had been the most intense barrage of flak and gunfire I had ever seen. The entire cruise had been a costly deployment for the USS *Coral Sea*. In the ship's nine-month cruise, the airwing had suffered twelve downed aircraft and eighteen aviators in those planes. Six aviators were recovered, six became POWs, two, including the Air Wing Commander, were killed in action (KIA), and four were listed as missing in action (MIA). However, the four MIAs never returned and were likely KIA. There were four additional aircraft lost in operational accidents with eight aircrew recovered, but four KIAs. I had joined the airwing about four months into its deployment, and nine of the aircraft shot down had happened while I was in the airwing, six of them on days when I'd flown missions.

I had one additional flight that cruise, but it didn't happen for sixteen more days. I rode the ship back to California, and we bypassed Hawaii on the way home because we were expected to have a short turnaround. After arriving back in San Diego, we were due to deploy right back to Vietnam seven months later because in 1972, the war had grown to its highest intensity since 1967-'68. We sailed on a great circle route back toward NAS Alameda in San Francisco Bay, the USS *Coral Sea's* home port, and the route took us far north in the Pacific Ocean. We were able to experience some refreshingly cold weather after spending months sweltering.

We launched from the carrier when we were about 150 miles from the northern California coast. I was flying the F-4B, and my RIO was Bill "Farkle" Freckleton who had been with Garry Weigand to down the MIG-17 back in March. We had a flyable airplane, but many things weren't working. We had no radio and no Tactical Air Navigation, which was our only navigation aid, so we would fly as a wingman alongside "Slick" Burns, whose plane was fully operational. After we launched from the boat, we flew for about a hundred miles with nothing in view but clouds and ocean. I'll never forget the moment I first spotted land ahead of us, because I had a "lemur," also known as a "cold shot of piss to the heart"—a kind of startled sense of doom. Then I thought to myself, wait, this isn't North Vietnam, it's California. It was then that I realized how tense I had been for all my combat missions. I had buried those feelings and refused to admit my fear. We coasted inland near Big Sur and flew the rest of the way to Miramar Naval Air Station in San Diego to finally land on American soil July 16, 1972. My combat cruise was over. Mom and Dad were there to greet me, along with Cathy. I'll never forget when Dad walked up to me, gave me a big hug, and said, "You will never know how, for the last six months, I wished I had never taught you how to fly." I still get teary-eyed thinking of that moment. I was 25 years old, and my father's greatest fear was losing me.

6

With the cruise over, we were pleased to settle back into stateside life back in San Diego at NAS Miramar. The San Diego summer was in full swing—a true delight, especially compared to where we had just come from—rarely hot, with blue skies and warm temperatures as a rule. We used to describe San Diego as "another average day in paradise." We were able to take a week of leave after the cruise, but then it was right back to squadron activities because we were heading back to Vietnam in six months. The squadron had a big surprise in stock for me. I was given a "plum assignment," that is, a highly prestigious post, in operations as a Weapons Training Officer.

This was usually given to far more senior and accomplished aviators, so I was quite surprised by it, as was Ed Downing who had been the prior WTO. I remember him saying something like, "Weapons training? Really?" He was a fairly senior lieutenant and an experienced aviator who was in the process of leaving VF-111 for a different shore assignment. Ed was also our squadron's Landing Signal Officer, and he had been the controlling LSO for my first landing on the *Coral Sea* when he'd awarded me a "No-Grade" for my bad approach. Every carrier landing grade is graphed on the "Greenie Board" displayed on the wall in the squadron's Ready Room for all the world to see, even those of the CO and XO if they are pilots. It was possible to go into any squadron's Ready Room and look in on how all their pilots were doing. The intent of all this visibility was to instill the highest level of professionalism in every pilot when it came to carrier landings. Screw up or act out, and all of your peers would know about it, in full Technicolor—OKs were marked with a green square, Fairs with a yellow, No-Grade with brown, Wave-Offs in white, and Cut Passes in red. It was easy to spot trends. I myself can only recall earning a single OK Underline (the A+ of carrier landings awarded five points, if you'll remember), but I fortunately had never received a Cut Pass on any carrier.

My flying must have been decent enough in the squadron to be awarded the Weapons Training job because that position also required my attendance to the new Navy Fighter Weapons School. A fighter squadron was allowed to send only one aircrew (pilot and RIO) to NFWS per year, so it was a real honor when I was chosen to be the one pilot. Aviators later shortened the name of the NFWS to TOPGUN. Most Americans don't recognize the name, "Navy Fighter Weapons School," but nearly everyone now knows TOPGUN after two very successful movies by that name starring none other than action superhero Tom Cruise.

TOPGUN was created after a report was published on the unacceptable number of Navy combat losses during the Vietnam air war through 1968 by Navy Captain Frank Ault, who led the investigation. The Ault Report found many performance deficiencies along with their root causes and ultimately recommended the need for an advanced course in fighter tactics. The study was initiated by the Chief of Naval Operations, Admiral Tom Moorer, who was disturbed by the dismal performance of Navy air-to-air missiles in dogfights

TOPGUN hangar at Miramar Naval Air Station. Credit: U.S. Navy

with North Vietnamese fighter jets. The kill rates of these missiles had been a very poor 9.2 percent for the AIM-7 Sparrow, 9.2 percent for the AIM-4 Falcon, and 18 percent for the AIM-9 Sidewinder. After the Korean War, the United States Military had concluded that airborne radar and radar-guided air-to-air missiles made dogfighting and guns obsolete. Air Force and Navy fighters had become "interceptors" that would achieve air-to-air kills from a greater range through radar. The Vietnam experience had shown that dogfighting was in fact still a vital tactic that needed to be re-introduced.

TOPGUN had been established in 1969 as part of Fighter Squadron VF-121, the same F-4 Replacement Air Group at NAS Miramar that I had trained in. It would take three years for the Navy to begin seeing the results of the TOPGUN program. Before 1968, combined Navy and Air Force fighter kill ratios in the Vietnam War had been about 2.5 MIG kills for every American aircraft shot down. Following the implementation of TOPGUN, the Navy's kill ratio improved to 12:1 when the air war resumed in 1972. I was selected to fly in TOPGUN around this time. I was told years later that TOPGUN wouldn't have accepted a pilot like me, then only a Lieutenant Junior Grade, and lacking the experience required for advanced training. But I had been picked by the new VF-111 Ops Officer, LCDR Jim "Cobra" Ruliffson, one of the founding members of TOPGUN. I was approved for TOPGUN training because he had selected me.

Jim Ruliffson was my boss, directly over me, and I learned a lot from him. He also asked me to develop several training graphics and other materials during our turnaround before re-deployment back to Vietnam. One of these was a multi-page document covering flights from Miramar to the east into restricted areas north of the Salton Sea and to Yuma, Arizona, complete with flight routing, communication frequencies, and all the parameters to follow. When I submitted it to him for review, he went though it in detail, handed it back to me, and said, "Looks good. Go ahead and print it." I knew he could have done it better and could have made many improvements to it, but he didn't. That taught me to be as thorough as possible. It also showed me that as a leader, it isn't necessary to make a myriad of changes based on personal taste unless it's to fix something that truly needs correcting.

My RIO for the course was LTJG Joe Gatewood, and the two of us were the only LTJGs in the class, which started late September 1972. There were three aircrews from the east coast squadrons, who flew from NAS Oceana at Virginia Beach. The Skipper of TOPGUN was LCDR Ronald "Mugs" McKeown, who had shot down two MIG-17s on May 23, 1972, the same day I had also flown two combat missions. Mugs had been awarded the Navy Cross for that action, our Nation's second-highest award behind the Medal of Honor. There was another Navy Cross winner in TOPGUN, LT Randy "Duke" Cunningham, who had downed a MIG-21 in January 1972, a MIG-17 on May 8, and then three MIG-17s on May 10 to become the first Ace of the Vietnam War, a pilot who had downed five or more enemy aircraft. Becoming an Ace was just as much a matter of opportunity as it was skill. For example, I had flown a mission to Cam Pha in North Vietnam the same day as Duke but had not seen any MIGs at all, but other Navy fighter pilots had shot down seven in another location, and without suffering any losses.

The syllabus for TOPGUN consisted of spending half the day in classes studying enemy tactics, aircraft types, and air-to-air missiles, and making comparisons of aircraft performance. We spent the remainder of the day in simulated combat against TOPGUN instructors flying aircraft types comparable to MIGs. We trained to dogfight in different configurations—one-on-one, two-on-one, four-on-four, and many-vs-many. My first dogfight in TOPGUN was a one-vs-one in my F-4B Phantom against none other than the Ace, Duke himself, who was flying a stripped-down A-4 Skyhawk called a "Mongoose," with some modifications to simulate the performance of a MIG-17.

The MIG-17 and the Mongoose had a much lighter wing load than my F-4, so I couldn't turn as tightly in a dogfight. I had to use the superior power of the F-4 by fighting in the vertical and avoiding a level competition. While Duke had to stay level to gain an advantage, I had to stay in the vertical and try not to turn with him. The outcome of the sortie was a draw—neither of us "shot" the other down. I had been very apprehensive about going up against the MIG Ace who had far more experience than I did. From my perspective, fighting him to a standoff was a huge victory!

My RIO and I were the only student aircrew with actual combat experience, which proved to be very useful for our final exercise, an Alpha Strike to a bombing range on San Clemente Island 74 miles off the California coast. We TOPGUN students served as fighter cover while escorting a large number of strike aircraft loaded with Mark 76 practice bombs. We were completely successful. Not a single one of the aircraft we were escorting was "shot down." We graduated from

TOPGUN on October 20, 1972, and rejoined our squadron preparing to go back to Vietnam.

After squadron-level and coordinated airwing training at NAS Fallon, we were declared combat-ready once again and prepared to leave for Southeast Asia on February 5, 1973. We had packed our gear and were ready for another eight-month deployment when we were informed on Friday, February 2, 1973, that a cease-fire had been signed six days earlier and our departure date had been delayed to March 9. We were granted another month at home in San Diego prior to sailing back to Vietnam, but we saw no more combat in 1973. The only tactical operations we conducted were photo reconnaissance escort missions with very limited overflights of South Vietnam. Halfway through the cruise, I became the Skipper's pilot. CDR Tom Markley was now the CO, and as a RIO, he selected me to fly for him. I was both honored and flattered to be chosen as the CO's pilot, and we got along great. He was a fine leader and treated me as an equal, though I wasn't. I always called him "Sir," "Skipper," or "Commander." I was a mere lieutenant, and he was two ranks my senior.

I remember he and I flew one mission to carry some air recon films to Thailand. On July 17, 1973, we launched from the carrier, coasted in over Da Nang and flew through South Vietnam, across Laos, and skirted the northern part of Cambodia to Udorn, Thailand, where the USAF was using the air base to launch recon aircraft like the RF-4s. The mission was without incident, and we returned to the *Coral Sea* that same day. This cruise was not without some controversy, however. We had received a new XO who had come to us from the East Coast Navy, whom I'll call "John." He was a Navy Commander like our CO, but with him came an attitude that made our lives difficult for several months. He was a pilot, and thus the senior pilot in the squadron, but since I was the only TOPGUN pilot in the unit, he had an issue with me. He was also gunning for our MIG-killer, LT

Garry Weigand, and it took me several years to finally figure out why.

My first run-in with John was after he and I flew against each other in a one-on-one dogfight, both in our F-4Bs. We separated by about four miles and turned in head-on toward each other. When we were about two miles apart, he suddenly dove down in altitude. An old axiom in dogfighting since World War I has always been to engage with an altitude advantage, so I was confused by his move. Then he started an aggressive pull-up so that when we passed each other, he had achieved 90 degrees of vertical angle against me, so with another 90 degrees, he would be on my six and able to simulate firing a missile. Immediately, I was at a huge disadvantage, but in the ensuing dogfight, I outmaneuvered him and reversed all his gains. We hit our minimum fuel level at that point, so I wasn't able to actually shoot him down, and thus, the dogfight finished in a draw.

His behavior when we got back to our Ready Room was pathetic and went against everything that TOPGUN taught about debriefing dogfights. He walked over to me and pretended to rip my TOPGUN patch off my flight suit saying, "You call yourself a TOPGUN graduate? You don't deserve to be wearing this patch!" I attempted to calmly debrief the situation and pointed out that I had reversed all his initial gain, but he wasn't hearing any of it. TOPGUN had taught me that a debrief needed to be done without emotion and focus on what had happened and what lessons could be learned. He attacked Weigand in much the same way, and in doing so, alienated virtually every pilot in the squadron. He was a loose cannon for quite some time during the cruise until his poor behavior suddenly stopped. It turned out that the CO, CDR Tom Markley, had pulled him aside and told him, "You are messing up my squadron, and I want it to stop. You're not going to take over command of this squadron after me without my endorsement."

XO John had taken a shot right between the eyes from the CO, and he had to change his attitude and rhetoric if he hoped to upgrade to squadron commander.

I figured out some time later why his attitude had been so bad toward us in the first place. It was interesting that the RIOs in the unit seemed to have no problem with him, and even seemed to like him. The RIOs were of no threat to him or his ego. Pilots had trouble because of his inflated sense of self-worth, and as the senior ranking pilot in the squadron, he felt like he should have the reputation of "top stick," or best pilot. It really bothered him that Weigand and I had that reputation instead, so he had made us his targets.

As the cruise was drawing to a close, we were in port at Subic Bay for a few days. An event occurred that would greatly change my career as a fighter pilot and a future astronaut. My CO and my RIO, CDR Tom Markley and I were in the Cubi Point Bar having a drink of some kind and out of the blue he asked me, "Hoot, how would you like to make another cruise?"

My first thought was, *Oh no! Not another one!* I had been aboard the USS *Coral Sea* for about twelve of the previous nineteen months. I said something like, "Gee, I don't know Skipper, I'd need to think about it."

Then he said, "…in F-14 Tomcats." The Navy had been bringing into the fleet the next major new fighter, the F-14 Tomcat, and the first two operational squadrons, VF-1 and VF-2, were forming up. The Tomcat was a quantum leap in fighter plane capability and complexity, and some senior pilots and RIOs had already been assigned, but many in command felt that the new technology required experienced pilots. Because it was a complicated airplane, the Navy wasn't ready to relinquish the Tomcat to pilots fresh out of training, so a request had gone out to every squadron CO to nominate one pilot who had completed at least one cruise.

Of course, I agreed to be his nominee and became one of six

pilots, three from west coast squadrons and three from the east coast, to join the first F-14 squadrons. My time with the F-14 cadre back in 1971 had paid off because CDR Sam Leeds selected me to join his squadron, VF-1, "The Wolfpack." I left the USS *Coral Sea* and VF-111 shortly after my last F-4B flight on October 14, 1973, and traveled back to San Diego and NAS Miramar to begin training with VF-124, the F-14 RAG. The day I boarded the C-1 carrier that would fly me to Cubi Point, the Skipper, my RIO and my friend, CDR Tom Markley, came to the ship's flight deck to say goodbye. I was touched by his consideration. As I was about to board the plane, I heard over the flight deck PA the announcement, "Lieutenant Gibson, departing."

The F-14 was a major improvement over the F-4. It had a variable-sweep wing, meaning the angle of the wings could be adjusted from 20 to 68 degrees, from the cockpit. The forward 20-degree sweep was optimized for takeoff and landing, loitering, and long-range cruising while the 68-degree sweep made the F-14 a more efficient airplane at high supersonic speeds up to Mach 2.4. The afterburning turbofan engines were more economical than the F-4's afterburning turbojets, and consumed a third less fuel during normal flight, though they did use more fuel when the afterburner was engaged. The plane had a very sophisticated radar and weapons system to boot and could carry the AIM-54 Phoenix, AIM-7 Sparrow, and the AIM-9 Sidewinder missiles. It incorporated the M-61 Vulcan cannon, a 20mm, six-barrel Gatling gun that could fire a hundred rounds per second. (You read that right—per second!) We had learned from flying the F-4 in Vietnam that a fighter jet should have a gun, and this was one hell of a gun.

In late October 1973, I checked in for training, and I was thrilled. The squadron had put together an abbreviated syllabus for the six pilots who had been selected to join the first two F-14 squadrons. A standard RAG syllabus would normally be six months or longer, but we started ground school in November, and by the end of the month, I had flown my first flight in the F-14. That flight was on November 26, 1973, and I went on to fly twelve more times, finishing on January 3, 1974.

My first two flights had LCDR Mike Guenther "Mauler," my good friend from VF-111, sitting in the rear seat. By that time, he had become a pilot instructor in the Tomcat, and he had pulled some strings for the opportunity to fly with me during my first two familiarization flights. Just like the Phantom, the "Cat" was configured without controls in the rear seat, so normally, instructor pilots hoped to avoid the first two "Fam Flights" with a new pilot, but he wanted to fly with me, and nothing was stopping him.

I'll never forget that first flight in the Tomcat. I remember accelerating along the runway and reaching rotate speed. I started to apply aft stick, and almost instantly, the airplane lifted off the ground and was flying. I wasn't aware that my pitch attitude had noticeably changed, but I was airborne immediately. By comparison, the F-4 would rotate to about 10 degrees nose-up and hesitate before lifting off. Similar to a delta wing, it needed to start generating enough lift to take off, so it would be nose-high. But there was no hesitation in the F-14, and the take-off speed was much lower at around 155 mph. Compared to the F-4's 180 mph, that meant I could be in the air much faster.

The abbreviated training included a few basic tactical missions, a night flying component, and instrument training through January 3, 1974, then I left VF-124 and joined my squadron, VF-1. Since fleet introduction of the Tomcat was such a great assignment, VF-1 was top-heavy with senior aviators. I was at the very bottom as the lowest-ranking pilot and was paired with RIO LTJG Ted Wills, callsign "Termite," probably due to his smaller stature.

Termite was a fine RIO, and we got along very well. Due to my junior rank, I wasn't a flight leader, so we were paired up with LCDR Cleck "Bear" Irvin and RIO LCDR "Moon" Mullins as our flight lead. I started flying eight days after checking in. I flew six times in January with Termite then commercially to Long Island to pick up one of our new airplanes from Calverton, where Grumman, the manufacturer of the F-14, had its final assembly plant. I traveled there and flew back to San Diego in the brand-new Tomcat with RIO LTJG Dale Gardner, who would ultimately become an Astronaut Mission Specialist on the space shuttle after he and I were both selected to the first class in 1978.

I flew often with the squadron as we geared up to take the F-14 on its first deployment to Southeast Asia. We did a lot of one-on-one and two-on-two air-to-air combat training against A-4 Skyhawks, F-4 Phantoms, and T-38 Talons. It was great to be flying a fighter that could really turn! The Tomcat could out-turn any of our adversaries, which made dogfights far simpler. We also did air-to-air gunnery against a banner, and I found the F-14's gun to be very lethal.

We had a real-time gunsight that combined radar ranging, an inertial navigation system with an accelerometer and gyroscope for precise orientation, and an air data computer with extremely accurate air speed and altitude data. The combination of these parameters meant that if you calculated for a bullet's time of flight, and if you were coordinated and smooth on the controls, you couldn't miss. I earned some serious fame and accolades the day I put 55 rounds in the rag. Our "Ordies" in the ordnance shop were so impressed that they kept the banner and hung it up in the hangar with the words, "Hoot's Shoot!" on it in huge letters. We had a beer call with our maintenance folks after that, and Petty Officer First Class J.D. Waits loudly proclaimed a toast: "To the best gunner in the squadron, Hoot Gibson!"

In April 1974, the entire airwing deployed to NAS Fallon, Nevada, for coordinated air wing exercises. These would be Alpha Strikes against marked targets with more than thirty aircraft participating. The airwing had A-7 Corsair and A-6 Intruder attack aircraft, A-5 Vigilante reconnaissance planes, E-2 Hawkeye early warning radar aircraft, H-3 search-and-rescue helicopters, and the F-14 squadrons for fighter cover. We flew multiple times each day in Fallon, but I only flew one night sortie the whole time I was there, which left my evenings open for trips to the Officers' Club for quite a few nights out.

At the O Club, essentially the bar and meeting place for Navy officers, we all drank too much and acted like a bunch of college frat boys, but you must understand that a squadron is in fact very fraternal by the nature of the job and mission. You had to trust your fellow officers as you would trust a brother, and late-night hijinks make for strong fellowship. We didn't necessarily drink often or heavily in our normal lives, and never during missions.

To offer another example of the peculiarities of our community, we kept a running log of mistakes and funny events that happened throughout our time at NAS Fallon, and toward the end, we convened a kangaroo court for laughs. LT Dan Pentecost, one of our most capable fighter pilots who also possessed a distinguished demeanor, served as our judge. Each member of the squadron was called to the witness dock in turn to answer for errors or actions that had been amusingly recorded in the log. Unofficial fines were levied, but mostly good-natured ridicule was handed out as "punishment." At one point in the trial, one of the squadron divisions decided to streak through the courtroom fully naked. Later, the squadron XO, a Navy commander, was wrongfully accused of a misdeed and judged innocent. He addressed the court, saying, "Now, with the court's permission, I will 'moon' the accusers." Pentecost replied, "You may proceed," and we watched our XO stand on a chair for all to see, drop his pants, and face his behind at his accusers, who also had to pay a fine in addition to the humiliation. Fraternal hijinks, indeed.

The next month, we began day and night Field Carrier Landing Practice in preparation for our next cruise in June. Throughout the month of May, I flew nine sorties, doing thirty simulated carrier landings during the day and thirty-nine at night. This was the first time any Navy aircrews qualified the F-14 Tomcat for carrier landings, other than test pilots. We were part of Air Wing 14, and our ship, the USS *Enterprise*, was the pride of the fleet at the time, and the Navy's first nuclear-powered aircraft carrier. I had only been accustomed to Midway-class carriers, and with the nickname of "Big E," it was indeed a big boat.

I flew to the ship five different days in early June, making thirteen traps during the day and six at night. The entire squadron successfully qualified, which didn't always happen on the first attempt, but in our case, with so many senior and experienced aviators, it would have been a surprise if the squadron hadn't. Grumman Aircraft Corporation, who had built the F-14, was proud of us, and sent us each a printed certification. The F-14 was a good airplane for carrier

F-14A landing aboard USS Enterprise. Credit: Hoot Gibson

operations due to its large variable-angle wing and slow approach speed on landing. The only downside was that the TF-30 turbofan engines had a slow "spool-up" time relative to the F-4's turbojets, which responded instantly.

In August, we spent more than two weeks aboard the USS *Enterprise* flying coordinated air wing exercises, and I made another dozen carrier landings and catapults. I flew my Tomcat in September to NAS Alameda, from which it would be hoisted aboard the *Enterprise*. We departed from Alameda several days later and sailed westbound toward Hawaii.

We conducted flight operations in the Hawaiian Islands over the next six days, and I flew seven sorties including the first-ever landing of an F-14 Tomcat in the islands. On September 24, I flew into Marine Corps Air Station Kaneohe Bay with RIO LCDR Roger McFillen. After spending a night at Kaneohe and having a few beers with the Marines at the O Club, we were the envy of our squadron.

The airbase was beautiful and home to the Marines' F-4 Phantom squadrons, and they were excited to see the new F-14 fighter jet. It seemed like the entire base had turned out to watch us depart, so of course, I had to put on a bit of a show. I did a low transition, accelerating to more than 460 mph in full afterburner, swept the wings to aft position, then pulled up into a vertical climb out of sight.

I did some other exciting flying while we were operating in Hawaii. Kaneohe kept a squadron of AV-8A Harriers, and we flew simulated air combat against them. The Harrier is unique in that it was the only jet at the time that could take off and land vertically, relying on vectored thrust nozzles that can direct the jet exhaust downward during takeoff instead of backward, but the orientation of these engines can also be adjusted mid-flight. The Harrier has thrust greater than its weight, which makes both a powerful fighter and a capable attack aircraft.

The Marine squadron had a real TOPGUN named Major Harry Blott, and two of us from VF-1, LCDR Dave "Bunky" Bjerke and I, flew against him in a one-on-one dogfight. Bunky was a former TOPGUN instructor and renowned as a skilled tactician, but I don't think I rose to that same level. I fought three engagements against Blott, and all three ended up the same way—I was gaining on him because I could outturn him, but whenever I nearly pulled into a firing position behind him, he would yank his jet nozzles into the vertical position and essentially come to a stop in midair. But I couldn't stop in the Tomcat, so he would immediately fall into gunning position behind me and "shoot me down." Bunky flew against him in a high-speed fight that neither of them could win, but my designs to beat him in a turning fight had left me groveling in the dirt. When the *Enterprise* docked for a final night in Hawaii, I was able to debrief with MAJ Blott. He told me I had impressed him with the Tomcat's turn capability. "That's great," I said, "but I was still 'shot down' all three fights!"

However, I did exceptionally well in another challenge while we were in Hawaii. The squadron flew practice gunnery hops against "the dart," a hard target towed behind an A-4 Skyhawk on a 1000-foot cable. The A-4 would stream the dart out at 20,000 feet of altitude, then dive into a four-G descending turn. Two F-14s would alternate rolling in, firing at the dart with our 20mm Gatling gun, then pull up to allow the other F-14 to roll in. I managed to hit the dart with a 50-round burst, and it instantly disintegrated into a hail of aluminum honeycomb that I had to dodge to keep from hitting. Once again, the real-time gunsight of the F-14 was lethal! I was a star again because only one other pilot scored a kill on the dart—none other than LT Dan Pentecost, the judge in our kangaroo court who had authorized our XO to moon us. Pentecost and I were awarded the coveted "Wolfpack Dart Killer" patch on our flight suits as a result of our sharpshooting.

My F-14A side number 114 over the South China Sea. Credit: Ted Wills

In future battles against the dart, I would score two more times.

The carrier arrived in Subic Bay, the Philippines, in early October, and we were back in the vicinity of the Cubi Point Officers' Club high up on the hill above the carrier pier. I flew four FCLP approaches at Cubi Point on October 20, and then we were back out to sea doing flight operations. We transited into the Gulf of Tonkin, the first carrier to return since the cease-fire. It nearly caused an international incident because North Vietnam took offense, accused us of saber-rattling, and said our presence represented a brazen provocation. We did fly sorties in the Gulf but never ventured over land at any time. Never a team to pass up a good opportunity, the carrier had a crew patch made which was appropriately titled, "Brazen Provocateur" and included the phrase, "About 50 Saber-Rattling Missions."

By the end of the year, I had flown twenty-four sorties since arriving in Southeast Asia. I was flying night FCLP approaches on January 2, 1975 when I heard the call, "Aircraft in the water!" I hurried offshore to the vicinity of a search-and-rescue in progress and learned that the plane was one of my squadron F-14 Tomcats, and that LCDR Skip Giles and LCDR Roger McFillen were in the water west of Subic Bay awaiting a rescue helicopter. LT Bob Vincent was their wingman, and he had remained above their position to vector the helicopter to them for a successful rescue. They described to the squadron that they had experienced a "thump-bang," and that their "Fire Warning" indicator had lit up. In less then two minutes, the airplane had become engulfed in fire and had gone out of control, and they had ejected. The carrier departed from Cubi Point and Subic Bay shortly after, and was planning an around-the-world cruise. I flew two more sorties while we were under way. The carrier passed through the Strait of Malacca twelve days later, and we were doing flight operations when a second F-14 from my squadron caught fire after a "thump-bang" and loss of control. LCDR Dave Bjerke and LT Jerry Kowlok also successfully ejected and were rescued. It was apparent that the F-14 had a problem, and we were grounded.

Brazen Provocator patch. Credit: Hoot Gibson

The carrier continued into the Indian Ocean, and the Navy Safety Center studied the F-14s' symptoms and arrived at the conclusion that one of the first three compressor stages in the engines had failed and ejected fan blades that had punctured the airplane's fuel tanks, leading to fiery explosions in both cases. The blades had failed due to corrosion in the salt water environment. The TF-30 engine had been used successfully in Air Force F-111 Aardvarks, so some of the testing had been eliminated when the engine was selected for the F-14, including its susceptibility to salt water. We were directed to scan all the fan blades in the first three stages of every engine with eddy current testers to detect microscopic cracks. The task required hours of testing to clear a single airplane, so I didn't fly for eighteen days. I flew only four times in the month of February 1975, but twelve times in March.

Meanwhile, the situation in Vietnam was becoming extremely bleak. North Vietnamese forces were moving into South Vietnam, and province after province was being overrun. It was clear that the end was approaching for South Vietnam. The *Enterprise's* cruise was extended to remain in the Gulf of Tonkin and cover the fall of Saigon. I flew four times in April 1975 prior to the last day of the Vietnem War, April 29, 1975.

I flew Combat Air Patrol over Saigon to defend against any aerial intervention by North Vietnamese forces. I saw no actual combat, but I was credited with one more combat mission. I didn't realize it at the time, but April 29 would also mark my final carrier landing. From the Gulf of Tonkin, the *Enterprise* sailed to Subic Bay, and on the way, I flew an F-14 from the carrier to NAS Cubi Point. We departed the Philippines and sailed back to Hawaii for one day, then we headed for the west coast of California.

7

I flew one final time from USS *Enterprise* on May 19, 1975, to fly back to NAS Miramar with LTJG Dale Gardner. I knew that my time in Fighter Squadron One was growing short because I had been chosen to serve as an instructor for the F-14 Replacement Air Group. This had been part of the plan the whole time—we six pilots would make the F-14's first cruise and return to the RAG with actual fleet knowledge. But I had another, much larger target in mind. I really didn't want to leave VF-1, but I felt the aviators in the RAG were especially protective of their positions and way of doing things and would not listen to the advice of a mere six pilots, and I wanted to get on track to become a test pilot like my dad, the hero of my life.

Back in 1974, before I left for my cruise aboard the *Enterprise*, my Tomcat squadron got a visit from Astronauts John Young, Gene Cernan, Joe Engle, and Dick Truly, who flew to NAS Miramar in their NASA T-38 Talon jet trainers to get a look at the shiny, new F-14 Tomcat. I was selected to show them the airplane and then fly a sortie with Engle in his T-38. While showing them my F-14, they told me about the new space shuttle that would be flying in the early 1980s. I was immediately fascinated by the space shuttle, an airplane that would fly to space as a rocket, operate for weeks at a time, and then fly a gliding reentry to land on a runway. I now saw a new path for my career. It could fly higher and faster than I ever had in my F-14 Tomcat, and I remember thinking, *I've got to get into one of these!* I knew that if I hoped to fly the shuttle as a pilot and commander, I would need to be a graduate of Test Pilot School (TPS).

I applied just as the *Enterprise's* cruise was ending. I would be leaving sea duty and going to shore duty, and TPS was shore duty. But I failed to be selected for the December 1975 class, and there were only two classes per year, one in July and the other in December. It was a mystery to me as to why I wasn't selected with my fleet experience in two different fighters and my exceptional results on my officer fitness reports. The Air Wing Commander, CDR "Smoke" Wilson, had also given me his highest recommendation of all the pilots he had endorsed for TPS.

It turned out that the Bureau of Naval Personnel had decided that F-14 training was so expensive and valuable, once someone was trained in the Tomcat, they weren't going to let him move out. But Smoke had been the operations officer at TPS, and one of his former students, Bob Johnson, was now the school's commander, so Smoke gave him a call, then told me to call him directly. Johnson had me send my application package directly to him, bypassing the Bureau of Personnel, which is relatively unheard of. Then he drove from NAS Patuxent River to Washington, D.C., dropped my application on the detailer's desk, and said, "Your policy is preventing me from seeing an applicant like this." That cleared the logjam. I was scheduled to begin in July 1976.

I still transferred to the F-14 RAG in September 1975, but they didn't know what to do with me. Most of the new pilots in the RAG at that time had no F-14 experience, so they had entered the Instructor-in-Training (IUT) syllabus. I had logged ninety F-14 carrier landings and had hundreds of hours in the Tomcat, so there was no need for me to go through the IUT syllabus. Thus, I was ignored and didn't fly very much for the first several months. I finally asked the operations officer if I could be scheduled more frequently, and he did get me more flying time as a flight leader on gunnery flights against the banner, which I particularly enjoyed. I was also assigned to do three lectures in the ground school portion of the training, which I also liked. My collateral job in the squadron was in Instructional Systems Development, working on the next generation of F-14 simulators, a challenging and rewarding education for me.

I spent nine months in the F-14 RAG and detached at the end of May 1976. I sold my home in San Diego, and my wife Cathy and I drove her car to NAS Patuxent River, Maryland. I had my 1955 Porsche Continental Coupe shipped to Maryland because I wasn't sure it would make it all the way from California to the east coast. I stayed at Patuxent River for a few days with LT Kevin Dwyer, a good friend from my Tomcat squadron, and then found a new house under construction and contracted to buy it. It wouldn't be finished for about a month, so I rented a Hopewell Manor trailer waiting for the house to be completed. I checked into TPS and dove into the training.

I experienced a wonderful, life-changing event right after starting TPS in July. My daughter, Julie Christie Gibson, was born on July 24 and became the first baby born in our class. I'll never forget the feeling of love that overwhelmed me when she arrived. I remember saying to myself, *I thought I knew what love was before, but now I really know what it feels like!*

TPS was the most demanding course of instruction I have ever experienced. It was more difficult than aeronautical engineering had been in college and more challenging than astronaut training would

Hoot holding newborn daughter Julie. Credit: Cathy Gibson

be several years later. We had classroom instruction for half the day, then flew the other half. While it was strenuous, I was fascinated with it. I had dreamed of being a test pilot, and now it was time to sink or swim. We were learning how to write technical flight test reports, and we were required to submit one every week. We did aircraft evaluations on flying qualities and performance, stall and departure characteristics, and a variety of other aspects. In my year of TPS, I flew eighteen different aircraft, and I was truly in pilot Heaven! It wasn't all fame and glory, however. I had some dismal moments, as well, when my reports came back bleeding with red ink after being reviewed by an instructor, and there were times I thought I was falling short of expectations. There was a correct format for technical reports, and we were in TPS to learn how to plan, conduct, and report on flight testing. It was sometimes frustrating, but I never learned as much in a single year as I did in TPS.

The members of the class became a band of brothers. There were twenty-one pilots, five Naval Flight Officers, two civilians, and two engineers. And we had one pilot from the Royal Netherlands Air Force and an engineer from the German Air Force, so aviation-wise, we were a fairly diverse group. We all faced the same difficulties and challenges and succeeded together, save one of us, an engineer who was not able to keep up with the pace and was dropped in the first half of the year.

We were all given a final assignment at TPS, a graduation exercise. We were to conduct a Naval Preliminary Evaluation of an aircraft that we had not yet flown. The airplane was assigned in early May, and we would be allowed four flights and/or six flight hours to conduct as much testing as we could. The first portion was to prepare a flight test plan and matrix of the evaluations to be done and submit it to the TPS instructor monitoring and evaluating you. My evaluator was LCDR Mike Smith, who had flown the A-6 Intruder in the fleet and was a highly respected instructor. He had been one of my instructors at TPS and had given me several helpings of red ink on some of my reports. I was assigned to a very exciting airplane for my NPE, the Air Force's F-101B Voodoo.

The Voodoo was a supersonic Century Series fighter designed as an interceptor capable of a rapid climb to altitude and the high-speed intercept of incoming bombers. It had high-thrust engines for climb and speed but small wings. It was not originally intended to be used for dogfighting, but it certainly excelled as an interceptor, flying at Mach 1.85. It had two J-57 afterburning engines, delivering 16,900 pounds of thrust, and the plane's thrust-to-weight ratio was 0.74, allowing it to accelerate at nearly .75G. The airplane had been loaned to us by the 107th Fighter Interceptor Group out of Niagara Falls, and since I had flown a TPS T-38A Talon there, I was allowed to fly the F-101 simulator before the actual plane, which gave me a bit of an edge.

It had been a year since I'd flown an F-14, so I was excited to fly the F-101 and experience that much acceleration and rate of climb. I found that the time to climb to 35,000 feet from brake release was two minutes, twenty-seven seconds. That included takeoff, acceleration to 400 knots (about 460 mph)—which took forty-four seconds—and the pitch up into a nearly vertical climb for another 103 seconds to reach 35,000 feet. The climb rate, once established at 400 knots, was 20,388 feet per minute. The relatively small wing and heavy wing loading meant final approach speeds of 175 to 185 knots (about 201 to 213 mph). Minimum speeds to stay within traffic patterns on descent approach to the runway were between 220 to 230 knots (or about 253 to 265 mph), resulting in an unusually wide pattern. Any airplane during landing must enter a pre-set flight path around the landing strip, similar to a funnel, as they reduce power and slow down, and in the F-101's case, it was easy to overshoot the runway lining up for landing.

Based on four flights totaling 4.9 hours, I produced a ninety-seven-page technical report. The two longest flights I'd made were only 1.3 hours in duration due to the way those afterburning engines swallowed fuel. LCDR Mike Smith gave my technical report an excellent score, which put me in the running for the Navy Preliminary Evaluation Award at graduation. In my debriefing with Smith, I mentioned this detail, and he replied, "You don't need to be worried about that." Without saying the words, I knew I wasn't getting the award, but I shouldn't have felt disappointed in retrospect, given where my career was heading.

I should mention something else about LCDR Smith. He left NAS Patuxent River just before graduation to return to the fleet and join an A-6 squadron. He would join NASA several years later and become a space shuttle pilot in the astronaut class after mine. Sadly, his first space flight on the Space Shuttle *Challenger* in January 1986 would result in disaster. Mike Smith and the other six astronauts who perished in the explosion during launch that day were all dear friends of mine, and I will cherish those relationships for the rest of my life.

Test Pilot School graduation ceremony. Credit: U.S. Navy

Graduation from TPS was an extremely rewarding experience after all the stress. The ceremony consisted of a formal banquet in full military dress uniform, and I was so pleased that Mom and Dad had traveled all the way from California for the occasion. It wound up being a big night for me, so I was very happy they were there. First, we were presented our diplomas by the Commander of the Naval Air Test Center, Admiral Foxgrover. I noticed I was seated across the banquet table from Captain L. Wayne Smith, who was Commander of the Strike Aircraft Test Directorate, where I would be working next. Then the awards were presented, including the NPE Award and the Outstanding Student Award. The NPE Award went to LT Jim Keen, a good friend from the Aircraft Systems Group, of which I was also a member. Then came time for the Outstanding Student Award. I'll never forget the words of Mr. Les Shaw, the president of the Patuxent River Council of the Navy League, saying, "The outstanding student of Class 71 is Lieutenant Robert L. 'Hoot' Gibson." There was a standing ovation, and I remember sitting in shock. I had no idea this was going to happen. Captain Smith reached across the table to shake my hand, and I was thrilled to death that Mom and Dad had been there to be part of it. It was one of the most impressive awards I'd ever been given. Test Pilot School was extremely competitive, and selection was difficult, but it was an even greater honor to be named the outstanding student of my class. I had been doing some extra tutoring for my class members about flying qualities, and fellow student LCDR Dick Scott shook my hand and said, "There is justice," which showed me just how much he had appreciated it. That gave me just as much satisfaction as winning the award.

My time at TPS had come to an end, and I was assigned to the Strike Aircraft Test Directorate, the division that performed flight testing of fighter and attack aircraft. "Strike" was divided into specialties of carrier suitability, ordnance testing, and flying qualities and performance. I was assigned to FQ&P, which was what I had hoped for since it would involve climbing into the cockpit. I was fortunate to join Strike at the time Admiral Foxgrover had directed only pilots with fleet experience to fly his F-14 Tomcats. Only one other fleet pilot was assigned to Patuxent River then, LT Kevin Dwyer, so I stepped into a great assignment—the initial testing of new technology for the F-14, the Tactical Air Reconnaissance Pod System, or TARPS.

The TARPS was a large sensor pod mounted in the "tunnel" between the engines with three camera bays that could be used for reconnaissance. At seventeen feet long, it was the largest external store ever flown on an F-14. Wind tunnel testing of the configuration had been cut to save funds, so the flight testing was high-risk until I could gather data. The tunnel of the F-14 was known to produce strange effects. Back in the testing phase, bombs dropped from the Tomcat had been observed moving sideways after release, hanging up in the tunnel, and trailing behind the airplane. Obviously, there was some uncertainty about the aerodynamics. Because of previous F-14 accidents at the Test Center, the flight test plan was carefully scrutinized and testing closely monitored. It was great to be flying a Tomcat again, and I had several flights to refamiliarize myself with the airplane before the TARPS test.

I had an excellent RIO, LT Larry Baucom, and an excellent flight test engineer, Bob Webster, who had the largest role in preparing the plans. Bob was also watching over us in mission control, keeping an eye on the Real Time Data System where all the telemetry from the airplane was displayed. I made several high-speed taxi tests to 60 knots and 100 knots on the runway to identify any noticeable stability or drag issues. On the first TARPS flight, a TA-4J chase plane was assisting me. During take-off, I left the landing gear and flaps down until I reached a higher altitude. Then I raised the flaps and checked to be sure there were no problems with stability or control before raising the landing gear. The first flight was very conservative. I only flew to a speed of 250 knots and stayed below 2.5 Gs. After several days of data analysis, we continued to fly, steadily increasing the maximum speed and G-loading of the aircraft with the TARPS.

To remedy the lack of wind tunnel testing, we placed yarn tufts in the tunnel area of the F-14 as well as all over the TARPS itself to visualize the airflow. I was able to do some of the initial flight testing

F-14A TARPS test flight. Credit: U.S. Navy

over the Chesapeake Bay, but I needed to expand the flight envelope of the TARPS out to Mach 1.65 and 6.5 Gs. I flew the first supersonic test flight offshore over the Atlantic Ocean and made supersonic wind-up turns at several Gs. By the time I landed, the operations duty officer was waiting for me. He said, "Captain Smith needs to see you right away." I was in trouble.

It turned out I had "boomed" Ocean City, Maryland, pretty badly. In flying a high-G, supersonic turn, I had inadvertently focused the shock waves from sonic booms together and fired them toward Ocean City. I was legal where I was flying, but the designated area was only about four miles off the Atlantic coast. I was ordered to do all the rest of the supersonic testing 30 nautical miles offshore.

It was nearing the end of the year in 1977, so the air and water were cold with winter conditions. NAS Patuxent River didn't have a search and rescue helicopter, but they were making do with a CH-46 helicopter which had very limited range and time on station, that is, time hovering over a target. After flying from Patuxent River to the Atlantic coast, the plan was that the CH-46 would land and shut down to conserve fuel. If Larry and I needed rescuing from the ocean during a test flight, the helicopters would start their engines and fly thirty miles out to the warning area. However, they would only have less than thirty minutes of fuel remaining to actually search for us. It was a less-than-ideal situation and posed significant risk, but we had to adopt the Navy-standard can-do attitude or fail to do the testing. The good news was that we might not even need rescue because we wouldn't be able to survive that long in the cold air and water anyway.

The final two test flights of the TARPS were on December 2 and 3, 1977, and were long-duration flights. I had yet to achieve data points from all the highest speeds out to Mach 1.65 and G-loadings up to 6.5 Gs. These flights needed a lot of afterburner and used a ton of fuel, so we refueled on the wing with the help of a Marine KC-130 tanker out of MCAS Cherry Point. I was qualified for air-to-air refueling in the F-14, but I had never tanked from a C-130. The aircraft had an extremely long refueling hose, twice the length of other tankers I had previously refueled from. Turbulence or small perturbations by the tanker made the hose move around much more than I had seen before. I needed three refuelings on each of the two December flights, so by the end of those two sorties, I was fully qualified. The two flights totaled 5.2 hours, the test was complete, and we had verified the aerodynamic and structural flight envelopes of the F-14/TARPS combination. The only minor anomaly we discovered was that we would run out of nose-down trim capability at airspeeds above 510 knots (587 mph), meaning at those speeds, the plane required constant pilot input to remain on a steady course.

I had several other projects while I was at Strike. There had been an incident in the fleet where a crew reported they had lost virtually all roll control power in the airplane. The Tomcat did not have ailerons for roll control like most aircraft. It used spoilers on each wing that deflected air upward, reducing lift on that wing, and differential tail deflection of the horizontal tails. With the wings swept all the way forward, the spoilers provided 75 percent of the roll control power. It was suspected that the incident had been caused by an electrical failure of the spoilers, so I was asked to do flight testing with inoperative spoilers to find solutions to the problem. Larry Baucom and I flew a Tomcat outfitted with a feature to disable the spoilers once we were at a safe altitude and could attempt to use differential tail deflection and engine thrust for roll control. It was alarming how marginal the roll control was with only differential tail and without the spoilers. We found, however, that differential engine thrust was very powerful and could be used to augment the roll control, so we provided that information to the fleet.

While we were doing this testing, it became apparent that differential engine thrust could get a crew into serious trouble because it was powerful and could cause large changes along both the pitch and roll axis. This was a fact that had been ignored in the flight manual for the airplane, and in fact, the manual said the Tomcat was essentially a centerline thrust airplane. This ignored the fact that the engines were eight feet apart and could each produce 20,800 pounds of thrust. I could see that the flight manual needed to be rewritten to establish normal cautions for multi-engine airplanes, such as, "avoid turns into the dead engine." This particular characteristic of the F-14 had caused a fatal crash in 1977. A crew had to shut down their left engine after takeoff and then made a turn toward the dead engine and needed afterburner thrust on the right engine which drove the Tomcat out of control to the left. They both ejected, but neither one survived. It was a personal tragedy for me because the RIO was a dear friend, LT Steve Miller, who had served in VF-1 with me and was one of my roommates aboard USS *Enterprise*. I attended Steve's funeral at NAS Oceana, Virginia, and it seemed like the entire airbase had turned out for the service. I tried to talk to Steve's wife, Jan, afterward, but I was too choked up. I did a major rewrite of the Naval Air Training and Operating Procedures Manual, known as "the F-14 Bible," for the Tomcat covering single-engine procedures. These remained the standard for the rest of the F-14 program.

I was working on something else major in 1977 while flying as a test pilot. NASA had issued a call to both the military and the general public to recruit a new team for the space shuttle. This was exciting news! NASA had asked the Air Force and Navy to do a screening and send a list of pilot and non-pilot candidates, forty-five of each, to the NASA selection board. I applied and made the pilot list from the Navy just as NASA was preparing to do the first gliding test flights of the first space shuttle, also named *Enterprise*, at Edwards Air Force Base in California. My mom and dad had driven all the way from Westminster, California, to Palmdale on September 17, 1976 to watch the rollout of *Enterprise*. I was on the phone with Dad and asked him why they had come all the way there for that. I'll never forget his answer. "Because I know someday you are going to be flying these," he said. I was only in my third month of Test Pilot School at the time and didn't dare to dream, but Mom and Dad had always been lifelong fans of my career. The first glide flight of *Enterprise* began on August 12, 1977, when it was released from the back of a modified Boeing 747.

Enterprise was released at 24,100 feet altitude and only took five minutes and twenty-one seconds to descend to Rogers Dry Lake for landing. I vividly remember watching the flight on television because NASA had invited me to come to the Johnson Space Center in Houston the following week to be interviewed for the upcoming astronaut selection. I was excited to be traveling to Texas two days after the first space shuttle landing test, on Sunday, August 14, 1977. I was in the second group of twenty pilots selected for physical tests and the interview with the board. NASA had us all staying in the Ramada Inn in Clear Lake City near JSC. We met with George Abbey, the Director of Flight Operations, and Duane Ross, who managed the selection process, that Sunday evening and were issued our detailed schedules for the week. We underwent extensive Class 1 physicals all week, including several exams I had never experienced, the interview with the selection board, and interviews with two different psychiatrists. One was with Terry McGuire, the "nice guy," and the other was a psychiatrist who asked frustrating questions to evaluate how well we could handle pressure. McGuire was a delightful, smiling, fatherly sort of person, and I enjoyed meeting him. I was actually okay with the other psychiatrist, as well, and performed fairly well during his line of questioning. One of my fellow test pilots at Patuxent River had warned me, "Don't try to 'shit' the shrink," so I spilled my guts on everything they asked me about. McGuire said at the end of my interview, "You are a lot more honest than most people."

Late in our interview week, all twenty of us candidates and the selection board met for a social event at Pete's Cajun Restaurant, a favorite hangout near JSC, and I got into a conversation that gave me a glimmer of hope. One of the other pilots had asked one of the board members, "How many Air Force and how many Navy pilots are you going to select?"

"We don't have any quotas like that," the board member said. "What we are looking for are pilots who have had to perform in stressful situations, which to us means flight testing, combat, and carrier landings." I thought to myself, *Oh, gosh! I have all three!* But the truth was, so did the other nineteen candidates.

I had a brief discussion that evening with Astronaut Ed Gibson, who had spent eighty-four days in space aboard Skylab. He saw my name tag and said, "We can't have two Gibsons here. It would be too confusing." Fortunately, he was joking.

The selection board was chaired by George Abbey and included Chief Astronaut John Young, Astronaut Joe Kerwin, Duane Ross, Joe Atkinson from Equal Opportunity, and several other participants. I thought of the interview as a one-vs-many dogfight, with me against them, but actually, it wasn't a fight at all. The board went out of their way to try to make every candidate feel comfortable. Maybe I would call it more of a high-stress encounter. I was seated at the center of a long, green table across from Abbey, and the other eight or so participants asked me questions for about an hour and a half. They probed my knowledge on aircraft flying qualities and capabilities, questioned me on how I would lead in certain situations, and even asked me what I thought of the United States giving the Panama Canal back to Panama. One of the pilot astronauts on the board asked how I compared the flying qualities of the F-4 Phantom to the F-14 Tomcat. I tactfully said the Tomcat was better but was careful not to trash the Phantom. This had been the right tactic on my part. I found out later that the board members had asked questions that might embarrass other members of the board. In my case, board member, John Young, had been one of the original test pilots for the Phantom, and they had tried to corner me into saying something negative about the Phantom. Fortunately for me, I hadn't given them anything to use against Young.

I remember being a bit embarrassed when one of the board members asked what I thought I was good at. Even today, I get a bit uncomfortable when someone complements me, and there I was, forced to brag on myself, though I was reluctant. I managed to mention that I had performed fairly well in air-to-air gunnery, in carrier landings, and in-flight testing. Then I finished my "bragging" with a very level-headed statement. I said, "I guess I'd say that when it comes to a precision flying task, I think I can learn to do it as well as anyone." I didn't try to say I was the best at anything, which I'm not, and apparently, that was a good answer.

I would learn many years later, after reading through a summary of the selection process for the 1978 cohort, that 40 percent of the selection was based on background and experience, while 60 percent was based on the interview. When I served on astronaut selection boards myself, I would find out just how easy it was to spot a thinly veiled ego. Typically, a selection board will spend another half-hour deliberating a candidate after their interview. Should a board member announce something to the effect of, "I think I was seeing a thinly veiled ego," that would mean the kiss of death for that candidate. Another board member or two likely had seen the same thing, and we couldn't select that person to continue. We had enough big egos in the astronaut corps.

After my interview, I returned to NAS Patuxent River and resumed flight testing. Several days later, one of my fellow test pilots asked me, "What do you think your chances are of being selected?"

I said, "Zero!" I was feeling a bit dejected after seeing the other nineteen impressive pilots I had interviewed against, test pilots I'd read about and heard of for years in the Navy, and I couldn't see how I was competitive with any of them. The experience ended up teaching me a lesson—don't ever give up, and don't ever write yourself off from anything. NASA had received 7,778 qualified applications, had interviewed eighty pilots and 128 mission specialist applicants, and had selected fifteen pilots and twenty specialists. I waited months for an answer. Then 1977 came to an end, and there had still been no word. January 1978 arrived, and I was busily flying our accelerated service test in the same Tomcat to put as much flight time in on an F-14 as possible, ensuring that we retained the most-tested plane and engines in the Navy and to identify any aging or reliability issues in the airplane before fleet squadrons would see it. On January 16, I was scheduled for a three-hour AST flight before heading to Orlando for a meeting to develop an F-14 simulator. I arrived a little late to work because Pat O'Neil, another test pilot, had asked if I could give him a ride that morning.

That's when I found a fateful note on my message board. Fortunately, I was in good physical condition and didn't have a heart attack when I read it. I called George Abbey, as the note advised, and he picked up and asked, "Are you still interested in flying the space shuttle?"

It was hard to contain my excitement. He played with me a little, as he was known to do, and finally said, "Well, okay. If you're not against it, then we'd like to select you for this astronaut class."

I think I fumbled around and stuttered something like, "This has to be the greatest day of my life!"

Abbey then told me to keep it confidential for the time being but that I could tell the world later that day, after the press release was out. I was higher than cloud nine—maybe on cloud ten or more.

I went through my day as planned. During the three-hour AST flight, I told my RIO, Larry Baucom, my good news. He and I left later that day and flew on an airline to Orlando for the simulator meeting and to do the "flight test" of the new simulator to verify that it modeled the F-14 accurately. In the meeting, an old friend from NAS Miramar, LT "Beaver" Logan, broached the subject of how long I planned to remain at Patuxent River, and I said "only until June."

"Are you returning to NAS Miramar?" he asked.

"No," I replied. "Moving to Houston."

"Getting out of the Navy?"

"Going to NASA."

The entire room erupted with congratulations, and I'm sure my face was bright red with embarrassment.

Later that day, Larry Baucom joked, "It didn't take you any time at all to brag about being an astronaut!" From him, a classic Navy aviator always prepared for a good-natured ribbing, I wouldn't have expected anything less.

My life accelerated when I returned to Patuxent River from those meetings in Orlando. There were three aviators at Patuxent River selected for the space shuttle, LT John Creighton, Marine Corps Captain Jim Buchli, and me. For a time, we were treated as the "heroes of the base," and Captain Smith held a ceremony in his office to honor us. We were presented with a proclamation from the City Council, and Admiral Foxgrover let my daughter Julie, then eighteen months old, hold his F-14 model.

NASA asked all thirty-five members of my astronaut class to come to Houston the last week of January for initial briefings and to meet our fellow astronauts. I'll never forget the words of the JSC public affairs chief. "I want you all to know that from now on, you are all public people," he said.

I would be at Patuxent River for only four more months. It was time to sell the house I owned, start packing up, and prepare to move to Texas. I was able to return to TPS in April and May to fly the T-38 Talon, and I managed to make twelve flights before my departure. My final Tomcat flight was in my TARPS bird on May 30, 1978, with RIO Baucom. Then, Cathy, Julie, and I began the drive to Texas in June in our two cars to begin our amazing adventure into space.

8

Full of enthusiasm for my new life as an astronaut, I arrived in Houston and checked into the Johnson Space Center (JSC) on June 29, but I was immediately informed that I was only an astronaut candidate, or an ASCAN. (Yes, it's meant to sound the way it does.) Apparently, past NASA selections had turned out to be unsuitable, so we were placed on probationary status for two years while we were being evaluated. NASA's leadership felt it would be easier to dump a probationary ASCAN than someone who had been named an astronaut. We were the largest astronaut class that NASA had ever selected, and we were the first astronaut selection in nine years. It was also the first selection that included women and minority candidates. We had six women, three African-Americans, and one Asian-American. NASA held an introduction in the Teague auditorium and then presented us to JSC and to the world.

Following my arrival to JSC that day, I was badged and then headed for the third floor of Building Four where the astronaut corps was located. I had studied our class roster, so I quickly recognized the first two ASCANs I'd seen when I'd arrived on the floor, Dick

Astronaut class of 1978. Credit: NASA

Scobee and Judy Resnik. I was paired up with the Asian-American candidate, Ellison Onizuka, and we were assigned to an office on the third floor, one of the only offices without windows to the outside. Ellison and I became dear friends. We were together in that office for our first four and a half years at NASA, and we truly enjoyed each other's company. He was born in Kona District, Hawaii, and was of Japanese ancestry. Every member of our class had been assigned to work with a senior astronaut for our first three months, and I was detailed to USMC Colonel Jack Lousma, who had flown a fifty-nine-day mission on Skylab 2 five years earlier.

Our 1978 class gave ourselves the somewhat whimsical name, "The Thirty-Five New Guys," or TFNG for short. The "FNG" portion of our name was a call-back to a common unofficial title in the military for new, and often clumsy, members joining a squadron—Fucking New Guys. I believe Judy Resnik participated in the design of our class patch that depicted the numeral "35" and our year.

We sat through many briefings and toured all around the Johnson Space Center to learn how the center functioned. We traveled to California to visit Rockwell at Downey where the Space Shuttle *Columbia* was being built for the first launch. We traveled to Florida, as well, to see the Kennedy Space Center and the shuttle launch pads. We sat through lectures by some of the world's most renowned scientists and trained in the NASA T-38A aircraft, a high-performance, supersonic training jet that could fly to Mach 1.6. It had tandem seating similar to the space shuttle's configuration, and to most other two-seater jets—one behind the other. The pilots were assigned to qualify in the plane, and the mission specialists were assigned to train in the back seat as crewmembers. The pilots were budgeted to fly fifteen

NASA T-38A Talon aircraft. Credit: Hoot Gibson

flight hours per month, which was normally enough time for our purposes. The jet cruised around 39,000 feet at 0.9 Mach, or about 622 mph, so it was fast but didn't carry enough fuel for more than about two hours of flight time. For example, a flight from Ellington Air Force Base in Houston to California would take about three hours, but we would need a fuel stop in El Paso, Texas.

The training process for the pilots was demanding, and the T-38's lack of visibility of the runway made for challenging landing approaches during instrument flight training "under the bag." The jet also had a high approach speed of 155 knots (178 mph) at minimum fuel, and that approach speed was even faster with more fuel remaining. Our instructor pilots worked us hard because once we'd passed our check rides, we were left to supervise ourselves in further training flights. We were expected to exercise good judgment regarding fuel reserves and weather conditions. Our experienced instructor pilots were all excellent teachers. I flew more than twenty hours in July to complete my T-38 qualification.

My entire class was enthusiastic about becoming astronauts. Early in our training, I remember wondering what we all had in common. We had arrived at NASA from all the military services and from all different walks of life. It took me a year to finally realize we were all simply nice people who were easy to get along with.

Everything about my NASA training on space and the space shuttle was progressing well, and I was enjoying it. We took in briefings from every surviving former astronaut who had flown in space, including the Apollo 11 crew, Neil Armstrong, Michael Collins, and Buzz Aldrin, who had been the first people to land on the Moon. Their stories and tales of the early space program fascinated us. The renowned scientists' briefing taught us about subjects I had always been interested in—geology, astronomy, oceanography, and meteorology—and how we would be photographing these from space in several years.

While my life at NASA was swimming along, things at home had gone from bad to incurable. My training and collateral jobs required a lot of travel and time away from home, and my marriage had suffered in my absence. My relationship with Cathy had deteriorated so badly that in December 1978, she filed for divorce. I was forced to move out of our house, and in July of the following year, while I was in Florida preparing for Space Shuttle *Columbia's* maiden flight, Cathy packed up the house and took my daughter, Julie, to live with her in California. Julie was three years old at the time and had moved more than 1,000 miles away from me. It was, and still is, one of the biggest heartbreaks of my life. I flew to California in my T-38 as often as possible so I wouldn't totally lose my connection to Julie. I am so very thankful that we have remained close all our lives despite the separation.

The women in our class, who called themselves "The Six," were Anna Fisher, Shannon Lucid, Judy Resnik, Sally Ride, Rhea Seddon, and Kathy Sullivan. Lucid and Seddon were licensed pilots, but none of them had logged any time in high-performance jets. I remember how new and odd a woman's voice coming in over the radio seemed to me in 1978, but NASA took great pride in them and care in their training. They and the other mission specialists who were new to the world of jet flight were trained by NASA instructor pilots before they were released to fly with the astronaut candidate pilots in our class. I flew several times with Judy Resnik, Sally Ride, and Rhea Seddon in our first year at NASA.

In early 1979, in a group of three T-38s, we did some interesting flying to Montana to observe a total solar eclipse on February 26. I had the idea to chase the eclipse as it moved from west to east, and it was an all-class experience including Dick Scobee, Steve Hawley, Mike Coats, "Pinky" Nelson, Sally Ride, and myself. The chief astronaut, John Young, decreed an astronomer needed to fly in each plane, so Hawley, Pinky, and Ride filled those roles. Hawley flew with Scobee, "Pinky" with Coats, and I with Ride. The six of us worked together planning our ground track to make sure we would remain within the region of totality, and I made all the arrangements with Malmstrom Air Force Base in Great Falls, Montana, for the support we would need for the mission.

We flew to Malmstrom, and the Air Force gave us an alert hangar in which to park our three T-38s, and air traffic control cleared us to fly in a block altitude, that is, any altitude within a range, along our planned route. On the day of the eclipse, we launched all three aircraft and flew separated so the pilots could focus on the eclipse rather than remaining in tight formation. I flew the lead plane, and as we raced along beneath the eclipse at Mach 0.9, about 622 mph, I would shoot a frame about every thirty seconds or so on my Nikon F Photomic camera, complete with a 300mm lens and a pistol grip. Since the Moon's shadow along an eclipse's ground track moves between 1,100 and 5,000 mph, we could only keep up for so long, even flying at near the speed of sound. We experienced more than four minutes of totality,

Total solar eclipse on February 26, 1979. Credit: Hoot Gibson

a significant difference when compared to the two minutes and forty-five seconds of totality experienced on the ground, according to records in the Old Farmer's Almanac. We continued to the east after the eclipse ended, flew past Mount Rushmore, and landed at Ellsworth Air Force Base to refuel. We returned to Ellington, and home.

In my first six months at JSC, I had the great pleasure of meeting one of the original engineers who had helped establish the Space Task Group in the late 1950s—John W. Kiker, one of the world's leading experts in parachutes who had been instrumental in the design of the Mercury, Gemini, and Apollo spacecraft. Like myself, John was a devoted and capable modeler of radio-controlled airplanes. To prove to NASA that the space shuttle could be launched from the back of a modified Boeing 747, named simply a Shuttle Carrier Aircraft, Kiker had built and flown an RC model of the combination. His model successfully demonstrated the separation of the shuttle from the SCA, and his singular contribution to the Space Shuttle Program had earned him a Presidential Citation from President Jimmy Carter in 1978.

The day I met him, I had brought in a model I had constructed of the F-16 Fighting Falcon, also called the Viper, to show Astronaut Joe Engle. Someone called Kiker, and he came all the way across the Space Center to Building Four just to see it. After that day, we grew to become dear friends for twenty-eight years and flew our RC model airplanes many times together on the radar range's paved runway.

From 1979 to 1980, I was assigned to several teams. I helped troubleshoot displays on the space shuttle, I worked bugs out of flight simulator software and displays, and I participated in the Shuttle Avionics Integration Laboratory (SAIL) to verify the software and electronic systems for first flight. The SAIL had a functioning system of orbiter computers and electronics along with a full cargo bay set of wiring. And I flew simulated missions to examine shuttle hardware

John Kiker's shuttle and 747 models. Credit: Hoot Gibson

and software operation. We worked long hours in the SAIL and sometimes experienced delays trying to get the real hardware to operate properly with the simulation systems. Our job of thoroughly debugging the software and computers for every launch was critical to mission success. It was long, tedious work, and testing was often delayed, so much so, we frequently referred to the lab as "SNAIL" instead. The experience was indispensable in that we'd become experts in the operation of shuttle computer systems, but, siloed in a separate building, sometimes we couldn't help but wonder whether we had been forgotten by our management team and the rest of the astronauts. Still, I remember leaving the lab late at night, my mind still churning over how much I had learned about shuttle operations, and thinking this was the best place on Earth to work.

After my first year, I was appointed lead astronaut in SAIL, and I managed all the scheduling for the team of astronauts who flew the simulated missions during software and hardware interface verification runs. I was promoted to that position over several astronauts senior to me, and I learned many lessons in leadership, the first being not to act like a boss, but as a team leader and compatriot. In the words of World War I Flying Ace Oswald Boelcke, "You can win the men's confidence if you associate with them naturally and do not try to play the high and mighty superior."

I also worked for more than a year in the Aircraft Operations Division (AOD) as Deputy Chief. Joe Algranti was Division Chief, and he was excellent. He had so much experience managing complex aircraft operations, I learned just by watching him. One small problem was that he also loved to fly, so he would often leave on multiple-day missions. As his deputy, I was left behind at Ellington Field to keep the day-to-day functions running. He was also a very strict manager, so it frequently fell on me to smooth things over with the workers at AOD. We managed thirty T-38 jets, a KC-135 "Zero G" airplane, four Shuttle Training Aircraft, several helicopters, and the Super Guppy oversized transport plane. One of my many jobs was keeping the peace between the maintenance division, quality assurance, and engineering. Soothing hurt feelings was excellent management experience and critical for keeping the division running smoothly. It kept me away from Building Four, however, and I frequently felt like I was laboring unnoticed and under-appreciated in the forgotten corners of the Johnson Space Center. I had several assignments at both AOD and SAIL and did my best to be productive and hardworking, which paid off in the long run. In spite of my despair, I came to find out my work had never gone unnoticed. In fact, all of the TFNGs had done very well; instead of remaining ASCANs for the full two years we'd been told were required, NASA promoted all of us to full astronaut status after our first year!

But even though we were officially astronauts, we all knew you weren't the real deal until you got into space.

I had another extremely significant and happy life change that occurred during my early years at NASA. It involved one of America's first female astronauts, Rhea Seddon. We often flew in the T-38s together and enjoyed it, other than this one time in shuttle chase practice when I flamed out both engines, effectively turning the T-38 into a glider. We dated over the span of several years and became very close, and on February 16, 1981, I asked her to marry me. We had gone out to dinner in Kemah, Texas, on the waterfront of Clear Lake and walked out on one of the piers admiring the shrimp boats. There was one named "Rhea," and she thanked me for arranging to have a shrimp boat there with her name on it.

First six American women astronauts. Credit: NASA

Standing by that boat in the night under the stars I asked her, "Well, are you going to marry me?"

Without hesitation, she gave an equally matter-of-fact response. "Sure!"

We didn't share the news with anyone right away. We waited two months until after STS-1, the first Space Shuttle, *Columbia*, had launched successfully on Sunday, April 12, 1981. I stood up in an all-astronauts meeting Monday morning and announced that Rhea and I were engaged to be married on May 30, 1981. It was the first time that two American astronauts were about to marry. The press took notice, and it received a significant amount of unanticipated press coverage.

9

I'd gotten my first taste of flying as a shuttle chase pilot in March 1979 when the Shuttle *Columbia* was passing through Houston on the back of NASA's Boeing 747 Shuttle Carrier Aircraft (SCA) on its way to Cape Canaveral. Astronaut Dave Walker and I flew a T-38 and joined up on the SCA and shuttle when they made a low pass over JSC. I'll never forget how impressed I was, flying next to such a gargantuan assemblage of aviation. The SCA continued to Florida and arrived at the Kennedy Space Center the next day.

I campaigned to be part of the shuttle chase team for STS-1 and was assigned Chase Four. The other three pilots were Jon McBride in Chase One, Dick Gray in Chase Two, and Dave Walker in Chase Three, all of us in T-38s. Chase One would join close, just to the right of the shuttle, give a check of airspeed and altitude, and then call out height above touchdown as a backup for the radar altimeter in *Columbia*. Chase Two would fly off the orbiter's left wing at a thousand-foot lateral distance with a TV cameraman in the rear seat. Chase Three and Four would be holding at the low-energy initial point and would do these same tasks if the shuttle came in at lower-than-ideal speed and altitude and re-route to the low-energy runway for landing.

All four chase pilots were Navy fighter pilots, and the planning and training necessary to rendezvous with the shuttle landing at Edwards Air Force Base on STS-1 was both challenging and exciting. First, we needed to pick a ground reference point at an altitude of 35,000 feet. At this altitude, *Columbia* would be coming in slow enough for us to match its speed. I found a small, dry lakebed just to the east of Rogers Dry Lake that *Columbia* would fly over on the way to land on Lakebed Runway 23. We named it "Mushroom" after its shape, and it became the initial point (IP) from which we flew a six-minute pattern waiting for the shuttle. We would arrive at Mushroom and make a one-and-a-half-minute turn to a downwind leg, fly for one minute, make another one-and-a-half-minute turn toward the IP, and then a final one-minute leg to arrive at exactly the moment the shuttle arrived. We needed to fly at an airspeed of 300 knots at that altitude, but needed to slow to 280 knots to lower our landing gear and generate enough drag to stay with *Columbia*. In addition to the landing gear, we needed flaps set manually to 40 degrees, engines at idle RPM, and speed brakes deployed. We flew planes outfitted with NASA-modified speed brakes 50 percent larger than normal and landing gear bay doors taken from the F-5, allowing them to open at higher speeds.

The technique for arriving at the IP to join with the shuttle was to fly at 300 knots in the pattern, then pitch up at the IP to slow down, lower landing gear immediately, set flaps, accelerate back to 300 knots, then extend speed brakes to stabilize on the shuttle. We practiced the maneuver using one of the T-38s to simulate the shuttle, which would fly west from Edwards AFB about forty miles to the small city of Tehachapi, and return along the shuttle ground track to the IP, descending from 40,000 feet while the chase birds were holding. Chase One and Chase Two would then join on the T-38 at 35,000 feet, and the three would fly down to make a simulated touchdown on Lakebed Runway 23.

We flew chase practice at Edwards for all normal shuttle landings, at Kennedy Space Center for the possibility of a Return To Launch Site abort, in which case the shuttle would return and land back at Cape Canaveral, and at White Sands Missile Range in the event of an abort after the shuttle had reached orbit, called the Abort-

NASA T-38A chase practice. Credit: NASA

Once-Around, or AOA, site. We also got an opportunity to practice the rendezvous timing on a Mach 3 target—an Air Force SR-71 Blackbird. NASA scheduled the high-altitude spy plane to fly from the Pacific Ocean toward Edwards along the shuttle's ground track to verify that base operations could follow a beacon at high speed, and the chase team flew its usual drill. After the SR-71 had passed over Edwards and our timing was successfully verified, the SR-71 crew invited us to join them for a flight back to Palmdale, where they practiced several low approaches to the runway without touching down. It was exciting to fly on the wing of a Blackbird, the plane that set the record for high-altitude sustained flight at 85,068 feet in July 1976, which it still holds to this day. Even the U-2 Dragon Lady, currently in service, can't fly that high.

We did so much chase practice because, all things considered, it was an extremely high-risk maneuver with high stakes for any failure. Precision was key. Traveling at slow speed in the T-38 at the join-up altitude of 35,000 feet, any minor pitch or rudder excursion as the nose landing gear was coming down could cause an airflow disturbance that almost always resulted in a compressor stall and ultimately a dual-engine flameout, or failure of both engines. If this happened, without the immediate intervention of pulling back on the throttle to the point of cutoff, excess fuel in the engines would soak the ignitors, preventing them from restarting. If this happened, the plane had to descend to 26,000 feet, the highest altitude with enough air for the engines to reignite, and from 35,000 feet, it was a long wait while struggling to breathe. The engines also powered the generators for

Chase practice with an SR-71 Blackbird. Credit: NASA

cabin pressurization, so oxygen masks would go to higher pressure, and the sudden decompression would cause your lungs to expand, making it difficult to exhale. In these conditions, a pilot could easily lose consciousness. Essentially, during the join-up maneuver, the slightest deviation off-course could trigger a cascade of effects that could make the T-38 fall out of the sky and kill the pilot before hitting the ground.

I experienced two such flameouts during chase practice, one of them while Mission Specialist Rhea Seddon was my passenger, and needless to say, my future wife wasn't pleased with me at all. (Remember, this was before we had announced our engagement.) I did recover both engines on both occasions, and I wasn't the only pilot to experience dual engine flameouts during chase practice. But no one experienced any injuries or physiological issues.

After a couple years of practice, we were finally prepared to launch *Columbia* for the first time on April 10, 1981. The crew consisted of John Young as shuttle commander making his fifth trip to space, and shuttle pilot Bob Crippen on his first space flight. I deployed to El Paso to be in place to fly chase if an AOA abort happened to White Sands. There was a lot of excitement for the first launch, so much so that I was "fished," or lured, into making an unauthorized high-performance takeoff from Ellington Field.

My crew chief told me, "Story Musgrave won the cool takeoff contest this morning when he did a low transition in full afterburner and then went straight up!"

I said to myself, *Oh yeah? Watch this*. I asked departure control for an unrestricted climb, but they told me no; I needed to level off at an altitude of 2,000 feet. I decided I could still go vertical, so I accelerated in full afterburner to the end of the runway, went vertical, and immediately rolled inverted and pulled down to level off at 2,000 feet.

Later, in El Paso, I received a phone call from A.J. Roy, one of the senior pilots at AOD. "Hoot, did you take off this morning at about 9:30?" he asked me.

"Yes, sir," I answered.

"Mr. Algranti was driving to work at 9:30," he said, "and saw one of our T-38s flying inverted over highway three. He told me to find out who it was and ground him."

I should have retorted with, "Why is he only coming to work at 9:30?" but that would have been a further lapse in judgement. Instead, I held my tongue. I had to call Joe Algranti, the Directorate Chief, but he let me off the hook because I was necessary for STS-1 support. Just as I'd done in high school, I had dodged a bullet. I should have been grounded for showing off.

The launch attempt on April 10 was scrubbed due to synchronization issues between the four primary computers and the fifth backup computer. I flew more chase practices over the next couple of days, and *Columbia* finally launched on April 12. The launch was flawless, and immediately after the shuttle was established in orbit, I took off in Chase Four alongside Dave Walker in Chase Three to be in place at Edwards in the event of an abort-to-landing after *Columbia's* seventh orbit. Chase One and Two had been in Florida in case an RTLS abort were required during launch, but since it had gone off without a hitch, they flew back to Edwards to join us.

The chase team was on alert for an unexpected landing should one be necessary, but the planned landing day was April 14. Thousands of spectators showed up on landing day, and the desert air was thick with excitement. *Columbia* would be approaching from the west and would pass over Rogers Dry Lake and then fly a left descending turn to line up on Lakebed Runway 23.

When it was time to take off for *Columbia's* landing, all four chase planes taxied in formation to Runway 22 at Edwards, which immediately got us into trouble. It turned out that Jon McBride, pilot

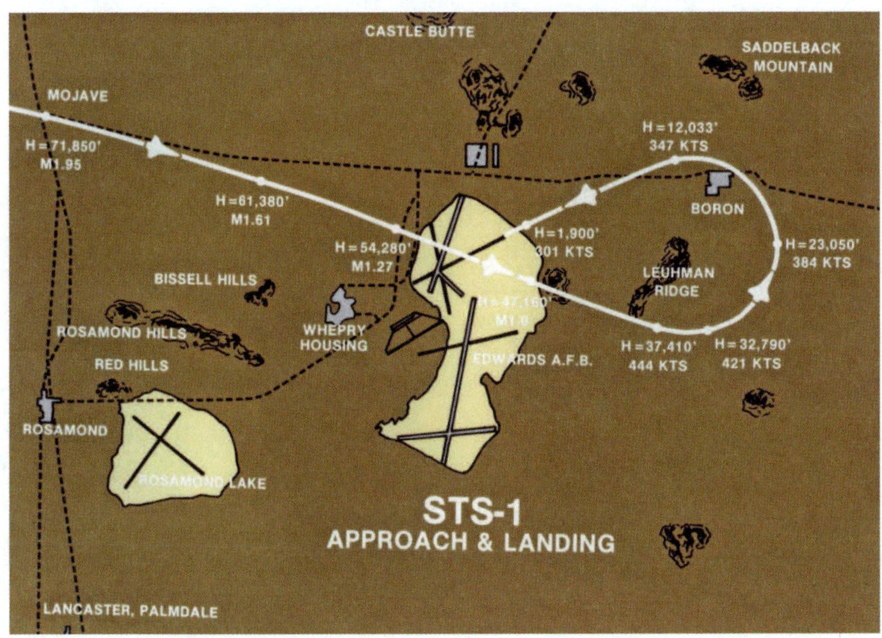

Columbia's STS-1 approach path. Credit: NASA

of Chase One, had been in the Officer's Club talking with the base general. The general had told him we were to halt our formation taxiing because it would set a bad example for his Air Force pilots at the base. When I found out about it, I was surprised the general wasn't confident his pilots could safely do formation taxiing. But we did it anyway, and we looked really cool, all four of our NASA T-38s taxiing in formation amid all the excitement of STS-1 returning to land. Suffice it to say the general was very displeased.

Chases One and Two were at the IP south of Leuhman Ridge at 35,000 feet to join on *Columbia*, and I was with Chase Three to the west at the low-energy IP. Chase One and Two joined up with *Columbia* at about 15,000 feet and Jon McBride gave them the airspeed and altitude check and called height above touchdown for their main gear and nose gear. It was good that the chase planes were there because the radar altimeter in *Columbia* locked onto the shuttle nose gear when it deployed and gave the same ten-foot reading the rest of the way to touchdown. We were allowed to remain at Edwards after the landing so we could be there for the huge celebration of the first flight of the space shuttle.

The next day, all four chase planes took off from Edwards to fly back to Houston. We made it as far as the Arizona border when air traffic control told us we could not continue at an altitude of 41,000 feet because their radar was down. We quickly computed and decided we could descend to low altitude and fly using visual flight rules en route to Luke Air Force Base, refuel there, and continue to El Paso to refuel again before returning to Houston. We rarely ever flew the T-38s at low altitude because the fuel consumption was much higher, but it was nice to be able to do that just that once.

When we were back at JSC, we were notified that we four pilots were grounded because we had overflown our fifteen-hour monthly budget and we were to be "walking" for the next couple of months until our average was back to normal. There had been several issues that we had to work out with Frontier Control—our Vandenburg Air Force Base radar controllers for STS-1—and those had caused us to exceed our allotted flight time. I returned to work at SAIL and flew only once in May and once in June, and it turned out I was the only one of the four pilots who had done as he had been told, but because I had followed orders, I was the only pilot from the STS-1 chase team assigned to chase again for STS-2 launching in November 1981. I was given three new pilots to train—Dick Covey, Loren Shriver, and Ken Baker. Two astronauts joined my team in the rear seats, Kathy Sullivan with me and Jeff Hoffman with Dick Covey. Our two photographers were Bob Gray with Ken Baker in Chase Two, and Terry Slezak with Loren Shriver in Chase Four.

Since we had overflown our flight time by so much for STS-1, I immediately put together a training syllabus for my team to get the new pilots trained for RTLS at Kennedy Space Center, AOA landing at White Sands, and of course the planned landing at Edwards. I took my syllabus plan to Director of Flight Operations George Abbey to explain to him how we would do all the training and stay within our budgeted flight time, and the answer was communication. I would send a memo to all astronauts any time the chase team was going to deploy to the landing sites for chase practice to alert them that we would be taking a few T-38s away from home base for three or four days so that they would be able to plan around it.

August through October, we trained at all three of the potential landing sites, and in early November 1981, with Kathy Sullivan and I in Chase One and Ken Baker and Bob Gray in Chase Two, we deployed to KSC for a launch attempt. Both chase planes were airborne on November 4 for a launch attempt, but it was aborted because of a malfunction in an Auxiliary Power Unit. We returned to Houston and deployed again for the next launch attempt on November 12. Chase One and Two launched anticipating STS-2 success. Chase Three and Four had been deployed to El Paso to cover the AOA possibility. I positioned Chase Two closer to the launch pad so that Bob Gray could capture the launch on television, which would be broadcast to the ground. *Columbia* successfully launched for the second time on what was planned to be a five-day mission. Both chase planes landed to refuel, and then we headed for Edwards AFB for the planned landing.

Four hours and forty-five minutes into the mission, Fuel Cell One on *Columbia* failed, and the flight was downgraded to a minimum-duration flight. The three orbiter fuel cells provided critical electrical power, so the mission was planning to land only two days later instead of the scheduled five. The crew of *Columbia* was still able to accomplish most of the objectives set for the flight, including the first deployment of the Remote Manipulator System, the shuttle's robot arm.

On November 14, I took off from Edwards in Chase Two and entered the six-minute holding pattern at 35,000 feet near the Mushroom as we waited for the call from Mission Control and adjusted our pattern to coincide with the shuttle's arrival at the IP. The most significant call from Mission Control was, "Chase, stand by for a mark at Mach nine. Stand by… MARK, Mach nine." This meant *Columbia* was nine minutes from the IP, decelerating at one Mach per minute. I hit the IP with one six-minute holding pattern to go and steadied up on the final leg to the intercept. I saw *Columbia* the first

Columbia STS-2 initial approach. Credit: NASA

time when they were at about Mach four, and the intercept was going very well. I arrived at the IP on time and felt like I would be joined up at 35,000 feet, slightly to the left of the shuttle and closing in. I dropped the landing gear and configured for the chase, and the next thing I saw was the entire top side of *Columbia* as Joe Engle, the pilot, made a steep left turn and pulled about 2.5 Gs. I was immediately passing nearly head-on to him as he shot past me. I raised the flaps, went to 100 percent RPM, and pulled about four Gs. While trying to make the impossible turn, I was lagging behind and racing to catch up. So much for joining at 35,000 feet.

As I was about to join up underneath, Engle called on the radio. "Chase," he said, "we are at 230 knots at 21,000 feet."

I replied, "Roger. We are about to be with you at 19,000." I delayed below *Columbia* so Kathy Sullivan could get photos of the underside, one of our primary reasons for chasing the shuttle. If there were any tile damage, we needed to know whether it had occurred on reentry or from debris thrown up by the landing gear. Sullivan took several photos of the bottom of the shuttle showing minimal tile damage prior to landing.

I stabilized on *Columbia* on the right side and noticed they were quite slow. Engle was flying at 210 knots because they had lost

STS-2 *Columbia* outer glide slope. Credit: NASA

energy and were working to stretch their glide to reach the runway. I provided an airspeed and altitude check, which Engle acknowledged and agreed with according to his instruments. We settled onto the final straight-in leg toward the runway, but I was starting to become anxious about their slow speed. They needed a higher speed in the final dive to be able to flare for landing, that is, to pull up to minimize the sink rate at touchdown. I called out, "7,000 feet, 220 knots," and at that point, Engle went into a steeper dive angle and said they were accelerating. They didn't reach the normal airspeed of 300 knots for the pullout, but they did manage to flare for the landing and touched down at a normal airspeed of 197 knots with a sink rate of only one foot per second. They made it to the runway, but only by about 780 feet.

The debrief with Joe Engle and Richard Truly was held on December 20, 1981, with all the astronauts in attendance. The debrief

STS-2 *Columbia* landing. Credit: NASA

revealed what had happened in the final moments of the flight and why they had gone so low on energy. They had experienced high jet stream winds out of the west at 35,000 to 40,000 feet, so the plan had been to make a tighter left turn when intercepting the Heading Alignment Circle, the turn that places the orbiter on the final straight-in for landing. Engle was to make that turn very tight and then cut across the HAC and not go as far away from the runway as the HAC would have taken them otherwise. That was why I had met them nearly head-on inside the HAC turn. After making the tight turn, which bled off energy, they then proceeded to do a planned speed brake sweep, which had further decreased their energy. Engle stated that things hadn't looked correct out the window, so he had then switched flight control back into AUTO mode, and the orbiter had flown all the way back out to the normal HAC distance, which had reduced their energy even more. Engle said they were flying only 220 knots at 10,000 feet and had only picked up to 270 or 280 knots for the final pullout and flare for landing. All of this explains why they just barely made it to the runway threshold.

Engle and I were next-door neighbors living on the same cul-de-sac. After we all arrived back in Houston following the landing, I walked over to talk to him that evening and told him I had the rendezvous nailed until he had made that high-G turn. An Air Force officer, he said to me, "You didn't think I was going to let a Navy pilot get on my six, did you?" Fighter pilots never seem to grow up or get over their rivalries.

After my exciting times with chase for STS-1 and STS-2, I went back to work at SAIL and AOD for several more years in support of STS-3 and subsequent missions, but there was a very significant event that occurred four months after STS-2. On March 19, 1982, the crews for STS-7, STS-8, and STS-9 were announced by George Abbey, and for the first time, members of the TFNG class were assigned to fly. Rick Hauck, John Fabian, and Sally Ride were named to STS-7, which would result in Ride being the first American woman to fly in space. Dan Brandenstein, Dale Gardner, and Guy Bluford would fly on STS-8, making Guy the first African-American to go to space. STS-9 included Brewster Shaw and several of the astronauts who had been part of the corps for years as well as several European astronauts.

This called for a big celebration, and a large group of the astronaut corps went to The Atrium that evening to celebrate. Rhea and I were not part of the first members of our class to be assigned, but we wanted to be part of the celebration for our fellow TFNGs. I admit I felt a little disappointed even though, as the youngest pilot in our class, I didn't expect to be assigned early. But Rhea and I were going to be there to celebrate our crews and be happy for our friends in the class.

I told Steve Hawley, "Hey, let's go talk to George Abbey," and he made the mistake of agreeing to go with me.

We walked over to Abbey, and I said, "George, Steve and I wanted to tell you that you really messed up today."

Suddenly, Steve wished he hadn't accompanied me. I could see it in the look on his face.

George grinned and said, "Oh, how's that?"

"You didn't pick us!"

George gave us a big smile, and we all enjoyed the evening extremely well.

However, there were several of our classmates who hadn't showed up for the celebration that evening. The next day, Rhea and I talked to one such astronaut I won't name here. Rhea said, "We missed you at the celebration last night."

The astronaut replied, "I didn't see anything to celebrate about." That left us speechless.

I saw another member of our class at the astronaut gym, and he was on a rant. "I'm not going to waste the rest of my life hanging around here!" he complained. "I'll go back to my community and save what's left of my career!"

Yet another member of our class was overheard saying, "This is bullshit!"

It still amazes me to this day that in such a small group of deeply accomplished people as our astronaut class, anyone could feel they deserved to be the first ones named to fly, rather than their peers, and I can only guess that it must have been due to inflated egos. I believe it's important to never let your ego get in your way.

Rhea and I celebrated the birth of our son on July 26, 1982, and named him "Paul" after my dad. It was not an easy birth, however, and it would be three days before Paul began to improve. Rhea had been in labor for more than fourteen hours, and the baby was showing signs of distress. The surgeon said, "We are going to need to take this baby out now." Paul was born via C-section and had severe lung problems. He had meconium aspiration syndrome which resulted in a coating inside his lungs, and he was barely getting enough oxygen, even with aid. He took his first flight at about four hours old in a medical helicopter from the Clear Lake Hospital to Herman Hospital in downtown Houston, one of the world's best neo-natal care facilities. For the next three days, Dr. Gene Adcock and his teams gradually cleared Paul's lungs and saved his life. It was one of the most stressful times of my life, commuting between Herman Hospital downtown and Clear Lake Hospital, where Rhea was recovering from surgery. I would stand worrying beside Paul's bassinet, where he was heavily sedated and being treated with saltwater pumped into and back out of his lungs to remove the meconium. I would talk to him for long periods of time, hoping that he might recognize my voice. His nurses told me they saw improvement after each of my sessions with him, and I really hoped that was true. Rhea was finally released from Clear Lake Hospital, and she flew on the Life Flight helicopter to Herman Hospital. Meanwhile, our story had leaked, and the media became interested and requested a press conference with us and Dr. Adcock. At this press conference, journalists dubbed Paul "the first US Astrotot."

Rhea and Hoot and baby Paul press conference. Credit: NASA

Soon after I brought Rhea and Paul home from the hospital, we moved into a different house, which created additional turmoil on top of the new baby and Rhea's recovery. We had a lot of help from the astronaut corps, however, because the secretaries had put out the word that the "Ace Moving Company" was needed. Several dozen astronauts showed up in their pickup trucks and moved us into the new house in a single day. Rhea showed up to work the Monday after she was back at home for the all-astronauts meeting to show it would take more than a challenging delivery to slow down a woman astronaut!

10

I had been working at Ellington Air Force Base at the NASA Aircraft Operations Directorate as the Deputy Chief for more than a year when I was asked to stop by headquarters to see George Abbey, Director of Flight Crew Operations, in February 1983. The work at AOD was very important because we managed more than forty NASA aircraft, but like my work at SAIL, it was a low-visibility assignment, and few, if any, of the astronauts knew what the job involved. I showed up at George's office, and after being ushered into his inner sanctum, he asked me to take a seat at his large table alongside Astronaut Vance Brand. Vance had been at NASA for many years and had flown in space on the Apollo-Soyuz docking mission in 1975, and then again as the commander of STS-5 in 1982. It wasn't unusual to be one of several astronauts sitting in Abbey's office, and I didn't think anything of it at the time.

Abbey got right down to business. "You've been out at AOD for about a year now," he said. "Have you given any thought to what you'd like to do next?"

After working in relative obscurity in two different positions, I said, "Well, I guess everyone would like to be a CAPCOM, so maybe I could do that next." Capsule Communicator was a very visible job always held by an astronaut in Mission Control. They are the ones talking directly to the space shuttle while in orbit. I wasn't at all expecting what Abbey asked next.

"Do you have any interest in any of the upcoming flights?"

I was momentarily speechless, but I managed to stutter, "Well, yes, I'd be interested in doing that."

In his typical understated manner, Abbey said, "Okay. If you're not against it, then maybe you and Mr. Brand here would like to go fly STS-11."

I was stunned. After four and a half years, the moment I'd been waiting for, all of a sudden, had arrived. I was being named to my first shuttle flight. Abbey asked me to keep it quiet for a while, but he said I could tell the world after the press release was out in another day or two.

I walked out of his office in a daze, and I realized then that I really hadn't been invisible at all. I was being rewarded for working in several very important jobs with little or no recognition, but obviously, Abbey had been watching. I was the youngest pilot in my astronaut class, and I had assumed I wouldn't fly early, but I was now destined to be the fourth pilot out of my class of fifteen to go to space. It was a wonderful payback for all the long hours of effort with little acclaim or feedback.

What a dramatic mission STS-11 was expected to be! Eight days long, the fourth flight of the Space Shuttle *Challenger*, and the tenth shuttle launch, and it was scheduled to fly at the end of January 1984. It was a five-member crew consisting of Vance Brand as Commander, Bruce McCandless, Ron McNair, and Bob Stewart as mission specialists, and myself as the pilot. The two pilots on a shuttle flight are the commander, and the pilot, whose real position is to serve as the copilot. For many years, I've been fond of a saying—astronauts are such prima donnas, no one is willing to be called a copilot. There would be two commercial communication satellites aboard our flight that we would deploy from an orbit 160 nautical miles above Earth, and they would each fire a perigee kick motor rocket to boost themselves into geostationary orbit over the Earth's equator at an altitude of 22,236 miles. At that altitude, a satellite orbits in twenty-four hours, so it appears stationary, and an antenna on the ground can remain aimed at it at all times.

The mission would also include several planned Extravehicular Activities, including a feat that no human had ever done before—an untethered spacewalk. Bruce McCandless and Bob Stewart would free-fly the Manned Maneuvering Unit from *Challenger* out to a distance of 330 feet from the shuttle. The MMU was a large rocket pack that used compressed nitrogen thrusters to maneuver while maintaining orientation with the earth. The EVAs also required the Remote Manipulator System, the robot arm capable of grappling objects such as satellites, be on board, since the end effector, the grappling "hand," also carried a TV camera.

The normal training template for a spaceflight was to begin one year before the mission, and we were already behind, so we dove into training right away. I still needed to keep performing my duties at AOD until the end of March, so my workload grew tremendously. There were countless briefings, simulator sessions, and flight training. I was already checked out in the Shuttle Training Aircraft, so I was prepared to move into the mission-specific course. The STA was by far our best landing trainer, a Grumman Gulfstream II extensively modified to make it fly like a space shuttle. The landing flaps were modified so that they could increase and decrease lift, the engines altered so they could produce reverse thrust inflight to mimic the drag on a shuttle, and the left cockpit rendered to match the shuttle's same instruments and heads-up display.

An instructor/safety pilot flew in the right seat, and the simulation pilot flew in the left seat using a shuttle control stick and throttle/speed brake control. The instructor would fly the STA to various altitudes and distances from a runway and engage the shuttle simulation through a computer while the astronaut pilot would fly the

Shuttle Training Aircraft simulating landing approach. Credit: NASA

plane to a simulated landing. Since the actual shuttle was so tall, the STA's wheels were twenty-six feet off the ground, and the pilot's eye height thirty-five feet. The actual flightpath for shuttle approaches would use a dive angle between 20 and 22 degrees because of the shuttle's large amount of drag.

Most of the STA sessions were flown at the White Sands Missile Range, which made for a great day of flying. We would fly a NASA T-38 from Ellington Field in Houston to the El Paso International Airport, where NASA kept a detachment. We boarded an STA for a training session, flew up to WSMR, and after ten practice shuttle approaches, returned to El Paso, climbed back into the T-38, and returned to Houston. It was possible to do all of that in about two-thirds of a day, so there was still time remaining for other scheduled events. Time was always critical, and as the launch drew closer, the schedules became even more demanding. In the final stretch before the launch, a sixty-hour work week wasn't unusual.

Each shuttle flight crew was assigned a dedicated training team to work with through all flight training events put together by the training manager—a team lead and six or more experts in the individual systems of the shuttle, who operated the simulators and would input malfunctions to challenge the crew. Some were stand-alone simulations where it was only the training team and the crew, while others were integrated sims that included all Mission Control Center personnel and sometimes even external groups like satellite manufacturers. Many of the sims were only four hours long, but some integrated sims ran for up to thirty-two hours, exercising the flight crew as well MCC to prepare the entire company for flight.

As mission pilot, I was second in command and trained to land the shuttle in case a malfunction prevented Vance Brand from making the landing. The mission commander was always the one to perform the landing, and throughout the shuttle program, there was never an automatic landing. I was trained to operate the robotic arm along with Ron McNair. All crew members trained in photography, which made for some excellent photos of the flight.

I remember leading the project to develop our crew emblem and mission patch, a task I very much enjoyed. It was my great honor to work with renowned aviation and space artist Bob McCall, who had painted several of the huge murals in the National Air & Space Museum in Washington, D.C., as well as others at the Johnson Space Center in Houston. I made several trips to his home in Phoenix to get it done. I developed a rough sketch in cooperation with the rest

STS-11 crew. Credit: NASA

of the crew and provided some of those to Bob. He then produced a brilliant work of art that became our crew emblem. The patch memorialized several of the major events of our flight, the satellite deployments, the untethered EVAs, and our planned first landing at the Kennedy Space Center runway. We also managed to schedule a crew portrait photo during our busy training events. In that time, STS-11 had been re-named STS 41-B.

After training for nearly a year, we went into quarantine on January 27, 1984, seven days prior to launch. Quarantine was in place as an attempt to keep the crews separated from anyone who might be carrying an illness, and anyone who was in contact with the crew had to pass a primary contact physical administered by our doctors in flight medicine. It was an exciting milestone to be seven days from launch, but the excitement really grew three days before. That would be the day we said goodbye to our training team, headed to Ellington Field, climbed into our T-38s, and flew to Cape Canaveral. Our hectic pace of training was over, and we had a few days to rest a little and get ready to go to space. We still had several briefings to attend each day, including updates on vehicle status and the state of the weather around the world, in the event we had to abort into a foreign land. There was also time to relax, which was a much-needed change of pace.

When NASA first acquired the land that became the Kennedy Space Center at Cape Canaveral, the few homes located there were all dismantled but one, The Beach House. We were allowed to be there each of our final three days on Earth, and we hosted parties with qualified spouses and children. Children had to be at least fifteen years old, and they and the spouses had to be designated primary contacts. We had a larger party two days before launch that included our parents and guests. This was our only opportunity to be with them.

There was an event that always happened the night before launch, called "night viewing." About 12 hours prior to liftoff, the Rotating Service Structure that protected the shuttle rolled back, leaving *Challenger* in full view. High-intensity xenon lights lit up the vehicle, which made for a grand and memorable sight for our launch guests. Our Commander, Vance Brand, surprised us all by saying, "We are going to night viewing." I was surprised because there were hundreds of people there for the event, yet we were still in quarantine. I expected a madhouse, and it was. When our guests spotted us, we were swarmed. NASA security did their best to keep them at least fifteen feet away, but they were only partially successful. On the positive side, I was able to at least say a distant "hello" to many of my guests who were not primary contacts. My family, including Mom, Dad, and all my siblings, had traveled all the way from California to watch me go to space. I'd been able to see Mom and Dad at The Beach House, but this fifteen-foot distance was the only time I could see the faces of my brothers and sisters before launch.

On February 3, 1984, we were awakened at 4:00 a.m. to take off at 8:00. Events the morning of launch had been carefully planned, and after a brief video opportunity at breakfast, we had a final weather briefing that told us we had beautiful weather both in Florida and at our primary Trans-Atlantic Landing Site in Dakar, Senegal. We suited up in only a treated cotton flight suit and flight boots and headed for the crew van to take us to launch pad 39A.

When we arrived at Space Shuttle *Challenger*, our vehicle had come alive, making noises I had never heard previously. This was my first experience with a shuttle on the launch pad ready to fly. The huge external tank had been filled with four-and-a-half-million gallons of liquid hydrogen and liquid oxygen, and the "stack" was hissing and clanking with thermal expansion and contraction resulting from the extreme temperatures. As the liquid oxygen and hydrogen boiled off into gasses, they vented, making it seem like our shuttle was a breathing giant. It seemed very lonely on the launch pad because only a small closeout crew was there to assist us with ingress to the shuttle, strapping us in, and then closing up the shuttle for launch. Anyone else was at the three-and-a-half-mile roadblock ready to assist in an emergency.

For a nominal satellite launch like ours, we would enter the vehicle and strap into our seats two hours and ten minutes prior to liftoff. We had an Astronaut Support Person (ASP) in addition to the closeout crew who double-checked all our communication and oxygen connections and our seat straps. The ASP would then power on our thruster drivers, configure some of our rocket engine valves, and put our ascent cue cards in place by the commander and pilot's seats. The ASP would then leave the cabin along with the closeout crew and the crew would configure all the vehicle systems from that point on. There were communication checks with the Launch Control Center and Mission Control, a cabin leak check, and activation of the water boilers that would cool the hydraulic power units called APUs, or Auxiliary Power Units. The Backup Flight Computer was synchronized with the four primary General-Purpose Computers at fifty-two minutes before liftoff. At thirty minutes prior to liftoff, the primary computers and the backup computer were loaded with OPS 1 software for launch configuration after having been processed earlier on the ground in OPS 9. At twenty-six minutes before liftoff, I prepared for ignition by configuring several switches on my right console R2 that provided helium to the space shuttle's three main engines. At T-minus nine minutes, the launch countdown timer was paused for a ten-minute hold for a final weather update from MCC and to clear up any remaining problems. After the wait, the LCC and MCC gave the call, "Go for Launch," and the countdown timer resumed.

By that point, we were all very busy, and I had many configuration changes to make as the pilot. I configured the Alternating Current Bus Sensors at T-minus eight minutes, the crew access arm retracted at T-minus seven minutes, and then I became *really* busy at T-minus six minutes doing the APU pre-start. When we had first begun our training, this checklist had been described as the "pilot nightmare." I had to verify the positions of twenty-eight switches, activate nine more, and then verify that I had three APU/HYD RDY indications, meaning the APUs were ready to be started. I had sixty seconds to complete that before it was time to start the APUs at T-minus five minutes. I then started the three APUs, verified they were all running and that our hydraulic pressures were all in the LO green, move the HYD MN PUMP PRESS switches to NORM, verify the HYD PRESS HI green and the HYD PRESS light off, and report to LCC and MCC that everything was complete. The pressure was on the pilots because a delay in completing the hydraulic power-up would interrupt the Space Shuttle Main Engine (SSME) gimbal checks at T-minus 3:25 and would cause a countdown delay. This brings into play another unofficial astronaut's motto: "Better dead than look bad!"

The entire world is watching the pilot, and thank Heaven, I didn't mess it up. The gimbal check moves the SSMEs, and we could feel them moving due to their very large mass. We closed our helmet visors at T-minus four minutes and cleared any remaining Caution and Warning messages. At launch minus 31 seconds, LCC called, "GLS is 'Go' for Auto Sequence Start," meaning the Ground Launch Sequencer is ready to command SSME start, and the shuttle is controlling the countdown.

At T-minus six seconds, the shuttle engines begin lighting, and by the end of "five, four, three, two, one, zero," they are at full blast and producing 1,125,000 pounds of thrust. Since the shuttle is mounted above the ET and the boosters, this causes the stack to bend at the Solid Rocket Boosters (SRBs), and the nose of the ET moves about fifteen inches, then bends back to vertical when the SRBs ignite at T-0. The noise from the SSME's ignition is deafening—so loud, in fact, that there isn't a noticeable increase in noise level when the boosters light and add their six million pounds of thrust. My noise sensors were already maxed out. The command to ignite the SRBs at T-0 is sent simultaneously with the command to fire the explosive bolts holding the boosters and the entire stack, so they had better both ignite. The booster rockets reach their full thrust in three-tenths of a second, altogether creating a combined 7.5 million pounds of thrust to push the shuttle's 4.5 million pounds of weight upward. The immediate acceleration is close to two Gs. I was accustomed to watching the launch tower gantry slide past me as I lifted off in the simulator, but it seemed like it was moving more than twice as fast in actual flight.

Liftoff of STS 41-B/ STS-11. Credit: NASA

In an instant, we were pushing beyond two Gs of acceleration, burning propellant at an incredible rate of a million pounds of solid fuel per minute and 3,000 pounds of liquid fuel per second. About seven seconds after liftoff, we were clear of the launch tower, and the stack entered into the roll maneuver—90 degrees of roll to the right. CDR Brand called, "Roll pitch program, Houston," and the CAPCOM replied, "Roger roll, *Challenger*." Vance and I both switched our attitude indicators to local-vertical-local-horizontal mode once we reached 180 degrees of roll. At 0.6 Mach and 30 seconds, we checked that the SSMEs reduced thrust to 75 percent chamber pressure to limit our maximum dynamic pressure to 676 pounds-per-square-foot at Mach 1.55, 60 seconds after liftoff. We verified that the main engines came back up to 100 percent pressure at 1.3 Mach. The solid boosters and aerodynamic turbulence made the flight very noisy and rough for the first two minutes. For the remainder of the launch, we relied on our Ascent Cue Cards, quick reference guides listing launch procedures, checklists, and other information.

I will never forget watching my Mach meter passing through Mach 3.0 and thinking to myself, *I've never even been at Mach 3.0 before, and now here I am, accelerating through it in a climb! This rocket has some power!*

The next major event was SRB separation, which was preceded by a computer message that read "Pc < 50," meaning the chamber pressure in the SRBs was less than 50 PSI. They separated at two minutes, 7.92 seconds after liftoff, designated as 2:07.92 MET (Mission Elapsed Time). The large, explosive bolts went off, two of them situated very near the cabin, to cut the SRBs loose from their attachment points at the external tank. Then the separation rockets at the nose and tail of each SRB fired, pushing the boosters away from the external tank and the shuttle. All of these explosive events made SRB separation feel like a train wreck. The rocket plumes from the separation motors fired in front of the cockpit windows and left a coating of soot on the forward windscreens.

From that point on, things were noticeably smoother. Vance looked over at me and said, "Electric Drive," which was how it felt riding on the SSMEs the rest of the way to Main Engine Cut-Off. The aerodynamic affects were gone since we are above most of the atmosphere, and the main engines were running with minimal vibration, so it was very smooth.

Our acceleration dropped to one G without the SRBs thrusting, but we were continuing to burn 3,000 pounds of fuel per second, so our G level continued to increase after SRB separation due to our reducing weight. In addition to our mass and weight decreasing, the thrust from the SSMEs increased from 375,000 pounds each at sea level to 475,000 pounds at vacuum, so we were over two Gs by 6:20 MET. Around 7:20 MET, we reached three Gs, and the SSMEs were throttled back to maintain three Gs until fine count, when they were throttled down to 75 percent in anticipation of cutoff. Cutoff then occurred on-speed at 25,670 feet per second at 8:41.42 MET.

We suddenly went from more than two Gs to zero G! Everything was floating next to us in the cabin. Our checklists were dangling at the ends of their tethers, anything not fastened down rose upward, and I got the biggest smile on my face that I've ever had. I remember thinking, *Wow, that was fun! Let's do that again!*

Launch had been stressful because I'd been all keyed up preparing for malfunctions to happen and readying myself to spring into action to resolve any problem. But everything was just fine. We flew the entire launch with no anomalies of any kind.

Now, we still had plenty of work to do. External tank separation happened eighteen seconds after engine cutoff, and we fired a small separation burn to distance ourselves from the tank, which would disintegrate during reentry, the pieces splashing down in the southern

Indian Ocean. It was noisy because we were now controlling the orbiter's attitude with the Primary Reaction Control System (RCS) thrusters, which had 900 pounds of thrust. It sounded like cannons when they fired in 40-millisecond pulses.

Unless we wanted to follow the tank down and reenter the atmosphere with it, we needed to do a burn almost immediately. We were in a sub-orbital trajectory at that point, meaning we were going to reach a high point called apogee within about three or four minutes. Without another burn, we would begin to fall back to Earth, so we had to do it right. We needed to calculate the burn, maneuver *Challenger* to the burn attitude, and be ready to execute the burn when we saw a flashing "EXEC" on our display. The burn was 150 seconds in duration and raised our apogee to 160 nautical miles. We coasted uphill toward OMS-2 at 45:24.6 MET, when we did a second burn of 124.8 seconds to arrive in a circular orbit at 160 NM. CDR Brand was the only one of us who had previously been to space. He welcomed us to orbit saying, "Welcome to space, rookies! You are now real astronauts!"

External tank separation. Credit: NASA

11

Once we established a safe orbit, we went down the checklist to prepare for post-orbital insertion. We transitioned the computers to the OPS 2 orbit software, opened the payload bay doors, and initiated operation of the radiators mounted inside. This allowed us to stop using our flash evaporators, which had been boiling water away to vacuum, cooling our cabin and orbiter electrical and electronic components. Over the radio, Mission Control gave us, "Go for orbit ops."

We folded and stowed all seats. In weightless orbit, we had no need to sit. They would remain stowed until reentry preparation eight days later. We transitioned to the Vernier Reaction Control System thrusters, which only had twenty-five pounds of thrust and were completely silent, a welcome change from the 900 pounds thrust from the large PRCS thrusters. We stowed our Post-Insertion Checklists and went to our Crew Activity Plan, which would guide us for the remainder of the mission.

Our first action in the plan was to align the three Inertial Measurement Units using the two star trackers. We maneuvered to an attitude that placed a navigation star in each star tracker. These stars were a pair that were 90 degrees apart. The Guidance Navigation & Control computer then computed the angle between the stars, and any angle error in the Inertial Measurement Units (IMUs) was corrected by aligning them. It was critical that we had the most accurate shuttle attitude possible for the deployment of our first satellite, a Westar 6 Hughes 376 communication satellite for Western Union. It would be boosted to geosynchronous altitude of 22,236 miles by a rocket booster called the Payload Assist Module (PAM).

We entered the PAM Deploy Checklist at forty minutes prior to deployment and maneuvered to the required attitude. The satellite

Satellite deployment from cargo bay. Credit: NASA

would be ejected from the payload bay in a retrograde direction, opposite the shuttle's direction of travel. We turned on the floodlights in the cargo bay, prepared all the film and TV cameras, and started the mechanical sequence at fifteen minutes prior to deployment. This spun the PAM and the satellite on a turntable at fifty revolutions per minute to keep it stabilized along its longitudinal axis after release. Gyroscopes work the same way. The PAM moved out of the cargo bay, and we performed a separation burn with a single Orbital Maneuvering System (OMS) engine. Twenty-nine minutes later, we maneuvered *Challenger* to a window protection attitude to shield the shuttle's windows from the effects of the PAM burn. We closed the sunshields for the Westar enclosure to preserve the electronic components form harsh temperatures.

Everything about the procedures and the deployment of the satellite was perfectly normal. I verified that the attitude of the shuttle was correct, and we returned to the Crew Activity Plan for the remainder of the day.

The PAM burn, also referred to as the Perigee Kick Motor, occurred on time, but we couldn't see it because we were facing away to protect our windows from the exhaust. We began pre-sleep activities that included a number of checks and IMU alignments prior to the planned eight-hour sleep period. It was during pre-sleep that Mission Control called and asked several unusual questions. "Did the satellite attitude look correct when it left? Did you see any wobble or anything abnormal?"

I keyed the microphone and said, "Does this mean you can't find it?"

CAPCOM replied, "Yes, we don't know where it went." Suddenly, it seemed we had lost a $100 million satellite.

We had our first sleep period, then began our post-sleep activities. Mission Control told us they had located our wayward Westar 6 in a low orbit, functioning correctly, but at a useless altitude. The PAM booster had failed at some point in the burn, leaving our satellite too low in space. We were scheduled to deploy our second satellite on Day 2, another Hughes 376/PAM combination called Palapa B2, for Indonesia. The deployment was placed on hold to provide time for Mission Control and the satellite company to study what had happened.

We were waiting to do the Palapa deployment while the mission management team was trying to decide when, and if, it would happen. In the meantime, they decided to proceed with the rendezvous evaluation we were scheduled for. We would exercise the shuttle rendezvous radar and software for the first time using the Integrated Rendezvous Target (IRT), an inflatable mylar balloon deployed from our cargo bay that would inflate after we released it. The IRT had several hundred pounds of lead weight inside to give it some mass, so of course, we referred to it as the lead balloon. It was released by a spring that propelled it away from our cargo bay. We watched it for a long time, and it failed to inflate to its planned two-meter diameter. We had pretty much given up on it, when suddenly, it exploded.

Our MS2, Bob Stewart, keyed the microphone and told Mission Control, "Houston, it just blew up!"

Half of Mission Control celebrated, thinking we meant inflated, while the other half said, "Oh, no! It just blew up!" To clear up their dilemma, they asked us what we meant, and to their dismay, we specified. We were not able to do the entire rendezvous system checkout because of this failure, but we did exercise portions of the software and the radar after the IRT deployed.

Days later, the decision was made to go ahead with the Palapa deployment. Mission Control and the engineers decided (or at least hoped) the PAM malfunction had been a random failure. We deployed the satellite and had configured the elbow TV camera on the robot arm to watch the Perigee Kick Motors burn. We saw the burn for about thirty seconds and then watched the rocket plume expand and extinguish, indicating the rocket nozzle had failed and separated. Our Palapa/PAM had suffered the same random failure as the Westar 6 and was also in a low orbit. Our lead balloon had failed, we had $200 million of marooned satellites in orbit, and the onboard toilet was going to fail in another day or two. It seemed we were totally snake-bit during our first three days in space. The two satellites would ultimately be rescued later that year by shuttle mission STS 51-A and returned to Earth for refurbishment. Both would make it back to space aboard expendable rockets.

Our fortunes were about to change for the better when time came to prepare for our Extravehicular Activities (EVA). To begin, we had to initiate a procedure that hadn't been done before. We reduced our cabin pressure from sea level pressure of 14.7 PSI to 10.2 PSI, the new protocol to help prevent "the bends" in our two EVA crewmen who would be at a much lower 4.7 PSI in their spacesuits. Bruce McCandless and Bob Stewart did an oxygen pre-breathe, and then we stayed at 10.2 PSI throughout the EVAs for the next several days. The procedure was to reduce the amount of nitrogen in their bodies that causes decompression sickness, a buildup of nitrogen in the joints, lungs, and brain, a condition familiar to SCUBA divers.

The first EVA occurred on February 7th and lasted nearly six hours. We were all very excited to make history. Bruce was the first to fly the Manned Maneuvering Unit away from *Challenger* while Bob worked on experiments in the orbiter's payload bay. I was at the shuttle's overhead windows that faced in the direction Bruce was moving, away from us. I was armed with a 70mm Hasselblad camera and a 100mm lens to film the EVA. While I wasn't the only one who could operate the camera, I was the only one who had nothing else to do. The Hasselblad was a manual camera, all settings controlled by the photographer. Film speed, shutter speed, F-stop, and focus all had to be correct to make for a captivating picture. I'll never forget looking through the viewfinder for the first time and seeing the image of Bruce. I didn't press the shutter button. I simply said to myself, *I can't believe what a cool image this is! If I don't mess it up, I could have it on the cover of* Aviation Week *magazine!* In fact, from of the

Bruce McCandless flying the Manned Maneuvering Unit. Credit: NASA

rest of the EVAs, I captured images that would appear on three.

While the EVA crewmen were translating to and from the shuttle, they couldn't use more than one foot per second of speed relative to the shuttle or they would excite orbital mechanics. That meant that if they slowed too much, they wouldn't translate aft of the orbiter; they would descend below our orbit altitude. They would then be flying a lower and shorter orbit around the earth, causing them to fly out in front of the shuttle. Since McCandless flew out farther than 300 feet, it took more than five minutes at one FPS, so I had plenty of time in between pictures. The following photo was taken when he was out near the end of the translation.

McCandless at 300 feet of separation. Credit: NASA

12

It was time to come home, and we were anticipating our return. We would end a 2,870,000-mile journey at Cape Canaveral, making the first space shuttle landing at the Kennedy Space Center runway, and that day would prove challenging.

Other missions had hoped to land in Florida and save the costly shuttle transit from California, but the weather had always interfered. For us, it looked promising, and we started preparations on February 10, 1984, the day before reentry. We powered up the hydraulics by starting an Auxiliary Power Unit and performed a detailed check of the Flight Control System in addition to a hot firing of the Reaction Control System to verify their performance. We did a complete cabin reconfiguration and stowed all the items we had used during the mission.

We started post-sleep activities at seven days, sixteen hours MET, performed an IMU alignment, and maneuvered *Challenger* to a tail-sun attitude. Pointing the shuttle's tail at the sun chilled all the shuttle tiles topside and bottom, before they would encounter the extreme heat of reentry. In preparation for payload bay doors closing, we stopped the flow of coolant through the radiators and only used the flash evaporators to handle the cabin and electronic thermal loads. At seven days, nineteen hours, we left the CAP for the final time and started the procedures listed in the Deorbit Preparation Checklist. We entered that checklist at 3.5 hours before the deorbit burn and immediately started a timer counting down to the deorbit burn time of ignition, or TIG, scheduled at seven days, twenty-two hours, sixteen minutes. The timing of this burn was critical, so it was imperative we kept aware of our status within the procedure.

We configured the shuttle computers, stowed the KU-band antenna, and opened the sunshields for the satellite enclosures. Mission Control gave us the "Go for payload bay door closing," and we closed the doors. We maneuvered to an IMU align attitude, did the alignment, then did a second maneuver into an IMU alignment verification attitude to ensure the accuracy of the initial alignment. Reentry navigation was extremely critical. Then we maneuvered to the deorbit burn attitude. We reinstalled the MS seats at TIG-2:25 and put on our reentry harnesses and anti-G suits. At TIG-2:05, we transitioned the shuttle computers to OPS-3 software for reentry. Verification of all the orbiter switches began at 1.5 hours before the burn, followed by a crew review of all the entry procedures. The commander and I strapped into our seats an hour before the deorbit ignition.

We switched to the Entry Checklist forty-six minutes prior to the burn, and Mission Control sent final updates to our deorbit burn as well as a latest shuttle state vector, our position and velocity. We verified the landing site data for the Kennedy Space Center, including runway selection and altimeter setting. We configured the OMS engines for the burn and closed all the payload bay vent doors. Fifteen minutes before the burn, Mission Control gave us the "Go for deorbit burn." We started a single APU at TIG-5 to ensure we would have hydraulic power for the entry. We armed the OMS engines at TIG-2, and at fifteen seconds prior to the burn, the "EXEC" flashed on our display. We pressed the "EXEC" button, which gave the computers the go-ahead for the burn. Both OMS engines ignited and fired for 168 seconds. It was completely silent during the burn, and no one said a single word as we monitored the burn through countdown to cutoff. After the OMS engines shut down, the cockpit remained silent for another thirty seconds. I broke the silence with the words, "Well, I guess we're going to make the first KSC landing."

The burn had changed our flight path and put us in a trajectory that would encounter the top of Earth's atmosphere at 400,000 feet of altitude at an angle of 1.2 degrees and a velocity of 25,752 feet per second. At that point, defined as Entry Interface, we would be 4,762 miles from touchdown. We still had thirty more minutes of weightlessness as we descended from our orbit altitude of about 150 nautical miles to the EI, and we were committed to landing since we had used the remainder of our OMS propellants. We maneuvered

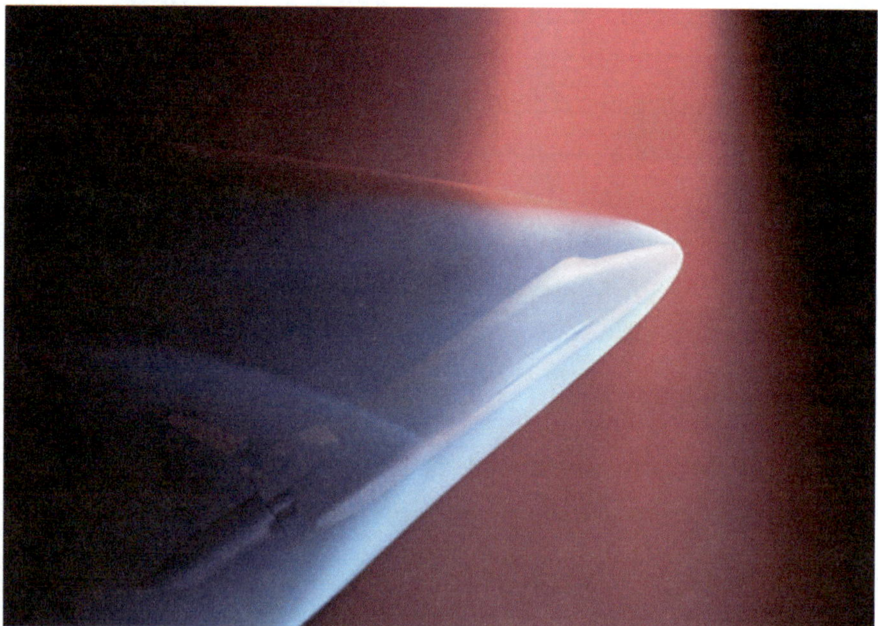

Shuttle model in Mach 25 wind tunnel test. Credit: NASA

Challenger to our EI attitude, 40 degrees nose-high, wings level, and orbiter nose aligned with our velocity vector. There would be no RCS thruster burns from the forward array during reentry, so we performed a forward Reaction Control System (RCS) dump for one minute and twenty-one seconds to lighten our weight and adjust the orbiter's center of gravity. We started seeing the effects of the atmosphere as we approached the EI because the air, while thin, was reflecting the light from our aft thrusters. We inflated our G-suits prior to EI and changed to our Entry Maneuvers Cue Cards for the duration of the reentry.

Fiery glow during reentry. Credit: NASA

We hit the atmosphere at Mach 25, and the shock wave around the shuttle reached a temperature of 6,000 degrees, causing the atoms of oxygen and nitrogen in the air to dissociate into a glowing plasma around the orbiter. We flew through this reentry "fire" outside our windows for fifteen minutes.

We used the Entry Maneuvers Cue Cards during the remainder of the flight through reentry and landing. These gave us checks to verify through the final moments of the mission, such as remaining RCS fuel. Our flight path during reentry had been described as a series of S-Turns during the descent and deceleration before landing. While an airplane may fly S-Turns to dissipate energy on approach to landing, the space shuttle must do S-Turns for an entirely different reason.

We encountered the atmosphere with wings level at 40 degrees Alpha, but the atmosphere was so thin at that altitude that we generated very little lift initially. When we reached a dynamic pressure of ten pounds per square foot and a drag of four feet per second squared, the shuttle was producing lift equal to our weight. If we kept everything the same, our lift would quickly become greater than our weight, and we would "skip off" the top of the atmosphere. To prevent that from occurring, we rolled into a right bank angle of 68 degrees to make our vertical component of lift equal to our weight, or one G.

By adjusting the bank angle, the orbiter controls the rate of descent while still locking the attack angle at 40 degrees Alpha. We were in a turn, but since our speed was so great and our G level only at 1.57 Gs, the result was a very slow turn rate. Our speed at EI was 25,957 feet per second in a descent angle of -1.2 degrees, with 4,762 miles to go until landing. We crossed the west coast of Baja at Mach 22 still in the right bank angle of about 60 degrees. By then, we had turned to a heading that was 10.5 degrees to the right of the KSC runway, and at Mach 13, we did the first roll reversal to a left bank angle.

We continued doing S-turns until we entered the region called Terminal Area Energy Management when we rolled to wings level just north of Orlando. From that point, we flew directly to a point where we intercepted an overhead circle of 301 degrees to line up with Landing Runway 15. At Mach 10, the reentry fire began to dissipate.

We had been in the dark for fifteen minutes, so the amount of fire and heating had been very apparent. I still remember thinking to myself when we came out of the fire at Mach 10, *I can't believe anything man-made can fly through something like this and survive! But I'm sure glad we can.*

We flew the reentry in auto flight mode, with *Challenger* making all the maneuvers and controlling our trajectory all the way down to just under Mach 1. Then CDR Brand shifted to manual control and

Challenger from NASA chase plane. Credit: NASA

took over Control Stick Steering mode for shuttle pitch and roll. I was glad that I didn't need to make the landing, because after eight days of weightlessness, I felt crushed by our G loads. Brand flew the entire 301-degree left turn. We experienced a maximum of 1.59 Gs around the turn to line up with the runway and rolled to wings-level at 10,000 feet in a glide slope of 19 degrees. The equivalent airspeed increased to a maximum of 292 knots until "preflare," when Brand initiated a 1.4 G pullup to intercept a 1.5-degree inner glide slope, decreasing our speed by more than 100 knots for the landing. Brand made a picture-perfect landing 1,930 feet down the runway with a sink rate of two feet per second. Braking and rollout used another 10,807 feet for a total landing distance of 12,737 feet of runway. Runway 15 was 15,000 feet long and 300 feet wide. Talk about precision.

Landing roll of *Challenger* STS 41-B. Credit: NASA

The crew had been very quiet during the manual flight portion of the approach and landing, making only mandatory calls. When CDR Brand called Mission Control and reported, "Houston, *Challenger*. Wheels stop," I shouted over the intercom, "Way to go, Vance!" and all our crewmates chimed in with cheers for our commander.

After we had exited the shuttle, it was pointed out to us that we had taken damage to our left OMS pod. The ice ball that had formed at the water dump nozzles had dislodged during the heat of reentry and impacted the pod. The damage had caused a burn-through of the OMS pod. While most of the OMS fuel had been depleted, there was still a significant amount of RCS fuel remaining, which could have caused a catastrophic explosion during reentry. Yet, we had survived. My first space flight was complete. I was a real, flown astronaut! We had prevailed over several setbacks and had experienced an amazing number of triumphs. It was obvious that our guardian angels had been watching over us.

13

My post-flight appearances went on for the rest of February and most of March. Then I received a note to go see Director of Flight Operations George Abbey. He had told me earlier that I had performed well on my first trip to space, and that he was eager to assign me as a mission commander, so going into the meeting, I thought the outcome would be similar to our meeting in which he had surprised me with my assignment to STS-11. With a skip in my step, I went to his office in Building One to hear what I thought would be news about my first command. But after a few minutes of talking, he revealed I was not being assigned to another flight, but was set to return to Ellington Field and serve as Deputy Chief of Aircraft Operations Directorate for a second tour. I had mixed feelings about this because while I had been effective on my first tour and was well-liked at the AOD, I had really hoped for the big prize of shuttle commander. No one ever before had been assigned to a second tour at the AOD, so it was apparent Abbey was pleased with my work. I was back on duty at Ellington Field by April of 1984, where I worked for about another year.

In this time, Rhea and I celebrated another big event in our lives. She was assigned to her first space flight, STS 41-E, scheduled to launch in August of 1984, making Rhea the third American woman to fly in space after Sally Ride and Judy Resnik.

Rhea's STS 51-D crew. Credit: NASA

Sadly, unfortunate circumstances delayed her mission. On June 26, 1984, the flight before Rhea's, STS 41-D, experienced a launch pad shutdown at four seconds before liftoff. The three main engines had been in the ignition sequence when a valve malfunction in engine three triggered an abort, shutting off all engines.

The launch was delayed two months, pushing all other missions back, too, in a kind of ripple effect. Rhea was re-assigned to flight STS 51-D, set to launch in 1985. This was a major disappointment for her, and her morale was the lowest I had ever seen. There wasn't anything I could do to help her feel better. In the interim, two other women moved ahead of Rhea, and she would end up being the fifth

American woman to fly in space. Sally Ride would fly a second mission before Rhea ever flew her first. The dust finally settled, and missions were combined. Several Payload Specialists were added to Rhea's flight, including Charlie Walker and Senator Jake Garn. Jake was the chairman of the Senate Space Subcommittee, and he had lobbied successfully to fly on the shuttle.

STS 51-D liftoff. Credit: NASA

Discovery blown tire. Credit: NASA

It was a good crew, and I would have the opportunity to see space flight from a different perspective, that of a spouse instead of a crew member. Rhea's flight was finally scheduled for March 19, 1985, but was then delayed again due to damage to a shuttle payload bay door. They finally launched aboard the Shuttle *Discovery* on April 12, 1985, the fourth anniversary of the STS-1 launch and the twenty-fourth anniversary of the first space flight by Russian cosmonaut Yuri Gagarin.

During the mission, Rhea successfully used the Remote Manipulator System to flip the switch to deploy a satellite, a feat Sally Ride and Judy Resnik, who considered themselves RMS experts, doubted was possible. However, the satellite wouldn't activate, and *Discovery* blew a tire on landing. In spite of these issues, the mission was considered a success.

14

In October 1984, I was finally assigned to fly as mission commander, scheduled for a launch in August 1985, and an excellent group of astronauts would join me. Sometimes, I can't help but wonder whether Director Abbey hadn't assigned me such a good crew to watch over me during my first command. Regardless, I couldn't have been happier with his selection. The Pilot was Marine Corps Lt Col Charlie Bolden, who had been selected in the 1980 astronaut class and had flown A-6 Intruders. He was a Vietnam veteran, a Test Pilot School graduate, and he would be making his first space flight. Mission Specialist One was George "Pinky" Nelson, selected from my class in 1978. He had a PhD in astronomy, had flown on STS 41-C, had experience as an EVA crewmember, and had flown the Manned Maneuvering Unit when his crew successfully rescued the Solar Max satellite. Mission Specialist Two was Steve Hawley, who had a PhD in astronomy and astrophysics and was also from my 1978 class. He had flown on STS 41-D and had experienced the launch pad engine shutdown. Franklin Chang-Diaz was from the 1980 class along with Charlie Bolden and had a PhD in Applied Plasma Physics. He was making his first space flight. We were the youngest complete crew to fly. None of us were even forty years old. I was the youngest pilot in my 1978 astronaut class and was the fourth one from my class assigned to command a mission. All those years of laboring at SAIL and the AOD in important but relatively invisible assignments had earned me this adventure.

Our mission went through a number of revisions before we flew. We were initially scheduled to deploy the first satellite owned by American Satellite Corporation, ASC-1. We were to deploy it at about 160 nautical miles of altitude, and it would boost itself to 22,300 miles for a geostationary orbit at 81 degrees west longitude. Our launch date slipped later, and ASC-1 was instead deployed from STS 51-I in August 1985 after my crew's launch was pushed to December. We were next assigned to a mission designated STS 51-L, which would be launching a Tracking and Data Relay Satellite. But problems with the Inertial Upper Stage booster rocket for the TDRS caused STS 51-L to be delayed until after my flight, and my crew was given instead a mission to deploy an RCA Satcom Ku-1 satellite, designated STS 61-C. We were also carrying a Marshall Space Flight Center Materials Science Laboratory MSL-2 in the cargo bay as well as a Get-Away-Special bridge assembly, some student experiments, protein crystal growth, and an infrared TV camera experiment (IRIE) replacing one of the shuttle cargo bay TV cameras. We had two Payload Specialists assigned to fly with us, Bob Cenker, an RCA engineer, and initially Greg Jarvis, who was an engineer for Hughes Aircraft. Cenker was involved in the IRIE, but while he worked for RCA, he was not involved in the deployment of the satellite. We would use the IRIE camera to examine patches of the Earth like the Andes Mountains as well as airborne targets. Jarvis would be doing studies of fluid behavior in simulated satellite fuel tanks in the weightless environment. Greg had been initially assigned to fly in April 1985 on my wife's first flight, but he had been pushed from that mission to allow room for Senator Garn to be placed on it. We had trained with Jarvis and had progressed far enough together to have made our crew emblem and crew photo with him. We all liked Greg and enjoyed working with him, but he was pushed from his assigned flight again in late 1985, this time replaced by Congressman Bill Nelson. He was moved from 61-C to 51-L, the tragic *Challenger* launch on January 28, 1986. Congressman Nelson was added to our crew late, but he worked diligently to make up for it.

STS 61-C crew. Credit: NASA

I took the lead in developing the crew emblem for the mission and took my drawing to Director Abbey for approval, but I was astounded when he told me it wasn't good at all. I'd had no difficulty getting the crew emblem for my first mission approved, maybe because I had tapped famed aviation and space artist Bob McCall for help.

I asked Abbey why he didn't like it, and he replied, "You need to have a dragon on it."

"A dragon!" I said, "Why a dragon?"

"Because no one has ever put a dragon on their patch before," he said.

I thought he was kidding, which he was known to do, but this time he meant it. I slinked back over to Building Four with my sketch. I made him an emblem with a dragon and my crew in the Shuttle *Columbia* blasting the Russian Space Station and brought it back over to him in Building One. I asked, "How's this, George?" but of course, it wouldn't do.

Astronomer Steve Hawley came up with another solution, which would ultimately become our patch—use the constellation Draco, the dragon. It wasn't what Abbey had imagined, but it was in fact a dragon. We had outfoxed him, which was difficult to do, and he didn't like being outfoxed. Reluctantly, he went along with it.

We were an extremely harmonious crew, and everyone enjoyed each other's company from the mission's start to finish. We would all go for crew runs together, and we became infamous for one of them. We would leave the astronaut gym and run out through the west NASA gate, around Johnson Space Center on the north side, and then back into it through the east gate. There was no gate on the north side, so it made for about a four-mile run. We were halfway through our run when a big thunderstorm moved in on top of us. We still had to complete the run to the east gate to get back to the gym, when the head of Life Sciences, Dr. Carolyn Huntoon, drove past us while we were all soaking wet. She called Abbey as soon as she was back in her office and asked, "Don't your astronauts have enough sense not to go out running in a thunderstorm?"

It was the entire crew, all seven of us, so we were lucky not to have been struck by lightning. Congressman Nelson was an interesting addition to the crew and he really enjoyed being part of the Space Shuttle Program. He told me that he had not been a runner before 61-C, but it was a life-changing experience for him, and he continued to be a runner from then on. He would also go on to become a United States Senator after our mission and then later, the NASA Administrator.

We went through the same intense training schedule as we had for my first flight—assignment to a crew followed by a solid year of training. December 1985 finally arrived, and we were scheduled to launch on the 18th, so we entered quarantine at JSC on the 11th and then flew to KSC three days later. We had a launch time of 6:55 a.m., so we started shifting our wakeup times in quarantine to 1 a.m. It made a good start for the day to go for a run, so we did that while we were in Houston. It was always a large media event when a crew arrived at the Cape for launch, and I spoke on behalf of the crew.

Our launch schedule slipped back one day because of excessive work needed in *Columbia's* aft compartment, so December 19 would now become the big day. We left the crew quarters about 3:00 a.m. to board the crew van heading for the launch pad.

My first launch on *Challenger* had seen a picture-perfect countdown and clean launch with no anomalies. This mission would turn out to be an entirely different situation. We boarded *Columbia* and started the countdown. Our families went out onto the roof of the Launch Control Center at T-minus nine minutes (later, we learned the weather was freezing up there). We would have been the coldest launch to date, had we actually launched that day. But we couldn't.

I was looking directly at our onboard countdown clock when it hit fourteen seconds to go, then it immediately reset to twenty minutes. "Guys, we just scrubbed!" I announced over the intercom.

We found out later that our right solid rocket booster indicated an overspeed in one of the hydraulic power units. With the Christmas holidays approaching, it was decided we would reschedule for January 6, 1986. It was a big disappointment for us and all our launch guests. We flew back to Houston to face our crew trainers again, and my launch guests returned home.

My crew and I went back into quarantine on New Year's Eve 1985, and Greg Jarvis brought us a bottle of champagne, God bless him! He was such a wonderful, charming personality, as demonstrated by this act. It was shaping up to be a boring ring-in when several of our crew trainers left another party to join us. I don't know how they had talked their way past the guards and into the space center, but they were dressed to the nines, having come from the other New Year's party. It greatly brightened up our quarantine.

We left Houston again on January 3 for our next launch attempt in three days. Only a few of our launch guests made the trip back to Florida. We walked out of the crew quarters to the Astro Van for our second trip to the launch pad and into *Columbia* for our second countdown. Everything went smoothly until we were inside with three minutes to go. Then, the anomalies started to pile on. At T-2:55, the external liquid oxygen tank started to be pressurized by helium to 21 PSI, but it was taking twice as long as normal. The team in the LCC was discussing the situation when another problem came up—helium bubbles in the liquid oxygen were causing the high-level sensors to read dry. Then came another problem. The shuttle main engines were too cold and were outside the start limits. We began procedures for how to mask the limits, and that was when the Director of Engineering at KSC, Horace Lamberth, came up on the launch network and said, "This countdown has been a disaster. Something is wrong. I don't know what it is, but engineering is 'No Go' for launch."

The only remaining hold point was at T-minus thirty-one seconds, so we counted down until that point and halted. Engineering did further analysis of the problem and determined Horace had saved the day for us. They discovered that when the liquid oxygen fill valve on the launch pad was commanded to close, it had not. The supply lines on the launch pad were then drained of LOX ahead of engine ignition, but since the LOX fill valve was still open, it drained 18,000 pounds of LOX out of our tank. This explained why the tank had taken so long to pressurize and why there had been helium bubbles in the tank at the high-level sensors. In fact, the high-level sensors had indicated dry because we had lost so much LOX. Had we launched, we would have had an early engine shutdown of all three main engines and wouldn't have reached orbit. This would have more than likely been followed by a high-speed abort and a landing somewhere in Africa. Horace Lamberth had the courage to speak up when the rest of the team were making excuses for the anomalies we were experiencing. The oxygen tank took twice as long to pressurize, our "helium bubbles" were actually dry sensors, the engines were too cold because we were chilling them down with extra-cold liquid oxygen from deeper in the tank than usual, and the engine person was going to mask the cold engines so the computer would ignore those readings. The "herd mentality" was that we were determined to launch, but the Director of Engineering had saved us from ourselves. My guardian angel was watching over me once again.

We recycled back to T-minus twenty minutes, started a new countdown, and were headed toward another try when the satellite customer, Satcom, was notified that the ARIA airplane flying over the Indian Ocean had heard we had scrubbed and had returned to Diego Garcia. The ARIA was on station to monitor the satellite perigee burn, and without that information, Satcom reported a 'No Go' for launch. We had scrubbed two countdowns in a single day, which had never happened before.

But it turned out to be a good decision because in reconfiguring the orbiter for a twenty-four-hour delay, it was found that a temperature probe had broken loose and had jammed the pre-valve in shuttle main engine two, which prevented it from closing. That situation would have been catastrophic if we had launched and suffered the early engine shutdown. With no way to close the pre-valves, the turbopump would have run dry of LOX and exploded.

We were starting to feel "snake-bit" with *Columbia*, but there was plenty more to come our way. We did a twenty-four-hour recycle and attempted to launch on January 7, 1986, but never got closer than T-minus nine minutes because of poor weather at KSC, in Dakar, Senegal, and in Moron, Spain, which were our Trans-Atlantic Landing abort sites. We couldn't try again until January 10, 1986, and on that day, we manned up *Columbia* and sat through a series of thunderstorms till we realized that the storms would persist. So we scrubbed again. It became known as "the S-word," equivalent to swearing if "scrub" was said out loud.

January 12, 1986, arrived and the weather was beautiful everywhere. We did the same departure from the crew quarters to the Astro Van, now for the fifth time. It was beyond frustrating and starting to get a bit depressing getting suited up for launch, going through all the issues of strapping in, counting down for over four hours, and then cancelling the launch so many times. I think I had two launch guests remaining from my initial fifty, my brother, Jon, and one of the pilots from Clover Field, Teresa Stokes (my time at Clover Field will come up later). Despite this, I was optimistic that day because it looked like all the stars were beginning to align for us. The weather was beautiful, and we were now very experienced in launch procedures.

But for this final attempt, we had decided that our astronomer, Steve Hawley, was a jinx because he had also suffered through the pad abort on *Discovery* STS 41-D, so we put him in a clever disguise and put duct tape over his name tag so that the Shuttle *Columbia* couldn't identify it was him. The disguise worked, and right on time,

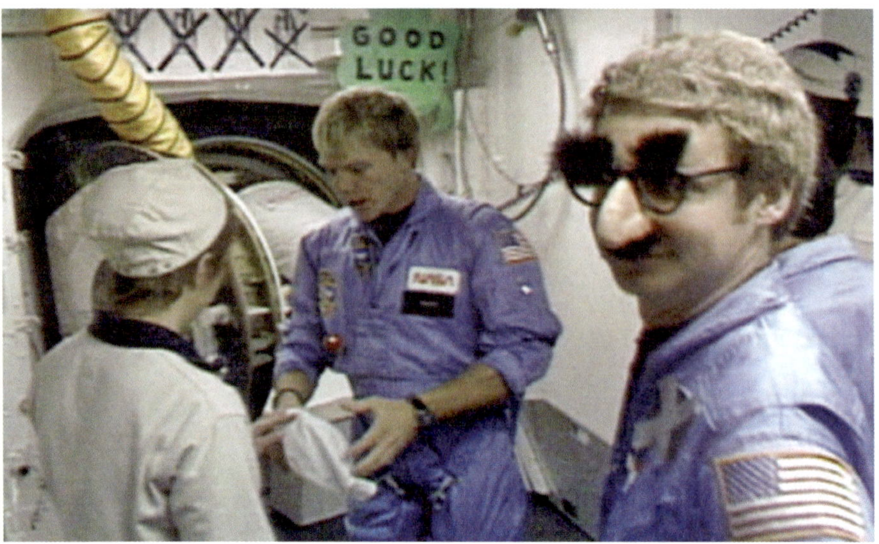

Steve Hawley's clever disguise. Credit: NASA

at 6:55:00 EST, we finally launched and were on our way to space.

Our families told us it was a beautiful launch. We started in the dark down on the pad, but as we climbed into the sunrise, our sunlit smoke trail reflected all the colors of a rainbow, some of which were captured on film.

Meanwhile we were busy immediately upon liftoff with malfunctions, none of which had happened to me during my first mission. Before we had cleared the launch tower gantry, we had a systems alert telling us of a change in one of our electrical buses, but the really exciting anomaly was in one of our shuttle main engines. An indicator alerted us to an apparently excessive helium usage in shuttle main engine one. If we used all the helium in that tank, the main engine would shut down because the helium purge was needed in the turbopumps to keep the high-temperature hydrogen fuel separate from the high-temperature oxygen. I was so impressed with our Pilot, Charlie Bolden, in working the procedure to try to isolate the helium leak. The system had dual regulators and pressure lines, an A and a B side, and Charlie had to cautiously close one side (A or B) and see if that slowed the helium consumption. When it didn't stop the leak, he needed to re-open that regulator and try the other side. If he had inadvertently shut off both regulators at the same time, the engine would have failed, and we would not have made it to orbit.

After watching the apparent leak continue, Charlie reversed the switches to see if the other leg might be where the problem was, but the helium loss persisted. I was uncomfortable with one regulator turned off because the pressure to the engine dropped from 750 PSI

Columbia launch on STS 61-C. Credit: NASA

on both regulators to only 650 on only one. Later, I just happened to be looking directly at the display when I saw the "change in pressure over time" indicator jump to a high positive.

"The Dp/Dt just went positive," I said to Charlie. "We can't be increasing in helium. We must have an erratic pressure sensor on the helium tank! Turn both regulators back on."

He did, and I updated Mission Control with our assessment of what we believed to be the actual problem. We flew the rest of the way to Main Engine Cut Off and on to the OMS-1 burn. Mission Control had been regularly updated on our issues and status throughout launch, but we hadn't received much more than "Roger" in response each time. Charlie Bolden was so impressive in the way he had handled a stressful malfunction on his first space flight while enduring all the G-loading and maneuvering.

(After the mission, in our Ascent and Entry team debriefing, Flight Director Gary Coen hung his head and said, "I wish we had been more help to you during the launch, but you guys had it all under control." It was a tribute to the excellent training we had received and our philosophy to be autonomous as a crew.)

We deployed the Satcom Ku-1 satellite at nine hours, thirty-two minutes Mission Elapsed Time. This was a satellite that was somewhat like the two I had deployed on my first flight in that it was a spinning deployment from the cargo bay, mounted on a Payload Assist Module. This contained the rocket booster motor that would perform the perigee-boosting burn forty-five minutes after we had released it from *Columbia*. Following deployment, we had plenty of other work

Satcom KU-1 Satellite deployment. Credit: NASA

and experiments to do, including work on the Get-Away-Special bridge and preparing the second version of the Materials Science Lab.

CAPCOM Fred Gregory then called us and said, "Don't shoot the messenger, but it has been decided that your flight will be shortened from five days to four days."

This reflected the schedule difficulties we were having early in 1986. My launch had been delayed by nearly a month, we still needed to get STS 51-L launched, and then Astro-1 would come soon after that. I was told that Astro-1, which was an astronomy mission, was failing science objectives every day it was delayed. One of those objectives was to observe Halley's Comet from space. It was present in 1986 but would not be back until 2061. All of this set the stage for the rush to launch *Challenger* on STS 51-L right after us. However, we were able to accomplish all the objectives of STS 61-C despite our mission being shortened by a day.

We prepared to do the deorbit burn on day four, but the weather in Florida was below our minimums, and Mission Control waved us off until the next morning, which was standard procedure to try for the landing at the Cape. It was highly desirable to bring the shuttle back to Florida to save the trip from California on the 747 shuttle-carrier aircraft. The next morning, we were waved off again due to weather. We assumed then we would make one more orbit and land in California at Edwards AFB, which was standard procedure after a one-day wave off. We were surprised when CAPCOM Fred Gregory called us with more than a little annoyance in his voice, and said we were to be delayed another twenty-four hours. Our four-day flight had been extended to five days, and had now become six. The KSC team had asked for the twenty-four-hour delay to put the recovery team and vehicles in place at Edwards for the next day, which would save about a week in the turnaround time for the orbiter, yet another indication of the intense scheduling pressure we were under in 1986.

It was getting to be as difficult to get home as it was to leave Earth. That night, I wrote a song to the tune of "Where or When," a 1958 song by Dion & the Belmonts. Bolden and I sang the lyrics in harmony to Mission Control as we were turning in for the night:

It seems that we have talked like this before,
the deorbit pad that we copied then,
but we can't remember where or when.

The clothes we're wearing are the clothes we've worn,
the food that we're eating's getting hard to find,
since we can't remember where or when.

Some things that happened for the first time
seem to be happening again,
and so it seems we will deorbit burn,
return to Earth, and land somewhere,
but who knows where or when?

We received an ovation from Mission Control, and I'm sure they enjoyed the brief break from the endless drudgery of the control center.

The next day, as we were getting ready for the deorbit burn to Florida, I called Gregory and warned him, "If you wave us off again, you're going to get another song!" but my threat made no difference. We suffered one last delay on day six because the KSC weather was still "No Go," and Gregory told us, "Make one more orbit and bring it back to Edwards."

I called him right back and said, "Fred, we are writing the words to the song now!"

He replied resolutely, "I will see you in Houston today!"

Down in Mission Control, they had made a poster reading "WANTED" in large lettering across the top, with images of our seven crew members and the words, “IF FOUND, RETURN TO EARTH.”

At least Mission Control was able to keep their sense of humor as the mission relentlessly dragged on.

We finally received the “Go” for the deorbit burn to Edwards, which meant I would be making a night landing about one hour before sunrise. It would only be the second night landing by a shuttle, the previous having taken place three years earlier. I had foreseen this possibility, because if we didn’t land at KSC at sunrise, any other landing opportunity would have to be a night landing by simple geometry of the orientation of the Earth to the sun, so Bolden and I had done most of our training for the mission at night.

While my previous reentry in *Challenger* had also happened at night, and had not experienced any anomalies, this time would be different. Just after the deorbit burn, we saw that we had an excessive usage rate of water cooling to Auxiliary Power Unit 1, which powered Hydraulic System 1. We could see that the water spray boiler was dumping too much water and was over-cooling that system. Once again, Bolden was instrumental in managing the system by turning off the water spray boiler, letting APU 1 heat back up, and turning the water flow back on. This was occurring while we were in “blackout,” a normal part of every reentry, so Mission Control could not see any data from the shuttle, and we couldn’t communicate with them.

It was critical we keep from losing APU 1 because it was the system that unlocked the landing gear, allowing it to deploy. Without Hydraulics 1, the gear would be lowered by a pyrotechnic system, causing damage to the orbiter. This was exactly why we had trained to be autonomous—with no connection with Houston, we were on our own. We came out of blackout at about Mach 12.8 about an altitude of 200,000 feet. I told Mission Control about our anomaly, and they concurred with our configuration and assessment of the problem. From that point on, the reentry and landing were nominal and went as expected. I landed *Columbia* on Runway 22 with main landing gear touchdown at 5:58:51 Pacific Standard Time and wheels

Artwork of *Columbia* Post Landing. Credit: Mark Pestana

stop at 5:59:50. I landed 1,530 feet down the runway, a little shy of our target 2,500 feet, and I was a little fast at 212 knots with a sink rate of -2 feet per second. But it is said that any landing you can walk away from is a good landing, and if the plane can be used again, it's a great landing! By this definition, I'd flown well, though the landing was less than perfect.

We worked the post-landing checklist, and I was about to power *Columbia* down when I decided to check in with Mission Control, and I'm glad I did. Immediately, and somewhat frantically, they said, "No, don't power down! We have the recovery convoy there to take over, so you are go for extended power up." They had never told us about deploying the convoy to Edwards, and we narrowly averted having shut *Columbia* down to cold metal. This is another lesson in proper communication, because in this instance, it had been poor. Another lesson was to be certain before taking any irreversible action, which powering down *Columbia* would have been.

Later, we were allowed to call our families over the phone. They were all waiting on the opposite coast, expecting us to land at KSC. Steve Hawley's father told him, "You're just like the airlines. You're in California, and all your luggage is in Florida!"

We did our post-flight medical testing at Edwards AFB, and then we flew back to Houston on the Shuttle Training Aircraft that had been positioned at Edwards to cover the landing. There was the usual large crowd to welcome us back home, and Rhea and our three-and-a-half-year-old son, Paul, came running out to hug me, even though Paul wanted to be somewhere else. He was having a great time sitting on one of the tractors, and Rhea had to drag him out to see me. During the hug, she was hanging onto him so he couldn't hurry back to the tractor, which to a young child was more important than Dad, even after his challenging mission!

Following the mandatory brief speeches, we were all celebrating, and suddenly, Teresa Stokes from the Clover Field gang called out, "Hoot. Look up!" I looked to the sky and was dumbfounded. There was a nine-plane formation approaching the airfield, all my Clover Field friends. I was speechless and gave them all a big thumbs-up as if they could see me while flying in close formation. The first three of the nine-plane formation were two Pitts Specials and a Great Lakes Biplane, the second three were Ray Lancaster in his Vari Eze, Don Davila in his Cassutt, and Stacy Williams in my Cassutt! The final three were a Bellanca Decathlon, a Bellanca Super Viking, and a Hughes 500 helicopter. I had been thoroughly welcomed home, and it was a thrilling flyby.

15

The face-to-face debriefings from a shuttle flight can take up to two or more weeks given all the participants that make the missions happen. On January 28, 1986, my crew and I were in the middle of one of these debriefs when another astronaut stepped into our large conference room in Building Four and announced, "*Challenger* is inside five minutes to go. Do you want to take a short break and watch the launch?" I said, "Yes," so we gathered into a smaller conference room with a video link and the voice loops so we could monitor crew discussions with Mission Control. There were several astronauts and support personnel in the room all watching as *Challenger* lifted off at 11:38 a.m. Eastern Standard Time. Everyone was jubilant because this mission, STS 51-L, had accepted the many delays my mission had caused as well as several postponements and two launch scrubs on January 25 and 27. And because of the delays, there had been significant schedule pressure to get the vehicle launched.

As I watched the screen, I felt something was off, and at first, I couldn't fathom what had just happened. Seventy-four seconds after launch, a large, extraneous puff in the smoke trail appeared, and then

Challenger Breakup. Credit: NASA

both solid rocket boosters (SRBs) took off in weird, wavy flight patterns. But despite that, I thought that the vehicle was still flying. It was only when one of the more senior astronauts present said, rather coldly, "That's it," that I realized we had just watched *Challenger* break up and our friends die.

Sylvia, one of the secretaries who was a close friend of Judy Resnik, ran crying from the room and the rest of us stood in shock. After several minutes of silence, we heard the call to Mission Control announce, "Range Safety said the vehicle exploded."

Our entire world had just turned upside down. Everyone left the conference room, and people were crying all over the space center. I went back to my office, and from there I saw my wife, Rhea, hurrying back to Building Four, coming in from a meeting. I hurried downstairs and met her outside the front door, and we both broke down crying together. I saw Bob Crippen walking to our building from Mission Control with tears streaming down his face. No one had any words to say to each other in the face of such a tragedy.

We knew right away that the crew had not survived because in those days, we didn't have so much as a lightweight parachute or a pressure suit. We launched in cotton flight suits with a helmet that provided us with ship's oxygen, but there was no crew escape system on the space shuttle. NASA's philosophy had always been, "It's the airliner to space." You don't wear parachutes on airliners, so we don't need them on the shuttle. It had been a large part of NASA's public relations efforts in those days to pretend that the shuttles were fully operational and completely safe to fly. Those of us from the tactical jet communities knew better, but we could not convince NASA otherwise.

It was a miserable day, and sleep was difficult that night as we lay thinking of our friends on *Challenger*. The next day, Rhea and I went to fly in a T-38 to try to bounce back a little and if nothing else, take our minds off our friends who had perished. It was just a quick out-and-back to El Paso, but the minute we landed, the duty officer told me I was to call Deputy Chief Astronaut Paul Weitz right away. Paul told me to pack my bags and go to Kennedy Space Center immediately to be part of the accident investigation. He said he didn't know how long I'd be there or what I'd be doing, but I was to report to Gene Thomas, Director of Vehicle Processing. I packed a bag, and that same day, January 29, 1986, Steve Hawley and I flew to X68, the space shuttle runway. We checked in with Thomas, who told us we would be part of the *Challenger* investigation at KSC in support of the Rogers Commission that had been appointed by President Ronald Reagan to report on the accident.

At that point, we had no idea why the shuttle had been destroyed. The launch films and videos had shown there was a glow near the right side of the vehicle, and then, suddenly, *Challenger* broke apart. It was several days after the accident when Astronaut Mike Coats pulled me aside and said the films from the northern theodolite showed a breach of flame from the right solid rocket booster. The flame impinged on the external tank and either caused the aft attach point to fail, or the tank was breached, causing the breakup. From that point, we knew why the accident had happened, but we on the KSC teams needed to answer the question of whether the breach had occurred because of incorrect SRB assembly or due to some other factor. Our portion of the overall investigation was to provide answers to the Rogers Commission on all elements of the space shuttle. The teams investigated the SRBs, the External Tank, the Orbiter, the launch pad, and every other element.

I was assigned to the SRB assembly and ET teams. There was a team to examine the Orbiter, the joint of the right SRB that had failed, the footage of the accident, or any possible indications whether this being the first launch from Pad 39B could be to blame. All prior shuttle flights had launched from 39A. All shuttles were grounded at this point, and we used the time to do a complete review of all the systems involved in flying the shuttles. I needed to pore over every page of the Orbiter Maintenance Instructions that governed how the work was accomplished and recorded. The stack of the OMI paperwork for just the SRBs was four feet tall, and every page had to be scrutinized for the accuracy of how the work had been performed and signed off and certified. I was also on the ET team, which was working through a stack of paperwork about three feet tall. We interviewed the technicians and engineers who had done all the work. I would spend all of February and March 1986 working this effort, and often I was only able to return home for a day or two on the weekends. I would fly a NASA T-38 to X68 at the beginning of the week, then fly back to Houston at the end of the week.

I had another tragedy in my life that March. I had decided to call my Dad from KSC the night of March 11, 1986, after the workday was over. I was surprised when Carol, my brother Don's wife, answered the phone. She asked me, "Did someone call you?"

I didn't understand why she had said that.

Then she said, "Your Dad just passed away."

My Dad was such an important part of my life, and I had worried for many years that he might die someday soon. It had finally happened, and during the *Challenger* fiasco.

Mom took the phone from Carol and said, "Oh, but he had a great day today! He talked about rebuilding aircraft engines and all about flying, all day." Then he quietly passed away while he was at home. The first responders were still there at the house.

I had to escape. I couldn't stop the tears, and I felt cooped up in the crew quarters and didn't want anyone to see me like that. I went outside and walked in the dark by myself for nearly two hours before returning to my room. The next morning, I attended our daily tagup with our lead astronaut, Bob Crippen, and the rest of the astronaut team. At the end of our meeting, I said, "Crip, I'm going to have to leave. My dad died last night." I managed to get the words out without losing my composure.

Crip was so compassionate, without hesitation, he said, "Oh! Go home."

I told him I had a meeting that morning that I needed to be in, and that I would fly back to Houston later that day.

But Crip said it again. "Hoot, go home."

When I landed at Ellington Field that afternoon, Kandy Hosea, our Ops lady, told me that Astronaut Steve Thorne was standing by to fly me to California the next day in a T-38. My Mom told me to bring my Navy uniform, and my brother Jon and I both attended Dad's funeral, Jon in his Air Force Dress Blues and me in my Navy Dress Blues. Losing my father is still one of the major tragedies of my life. I flew back to Houston on Saturday, March 15 and spent the rest of the weekend at home before flying back to X68.

Back to work.

We were getting close to the end of our investigation at KSC by April, but we had answered the basic question of whether the right SRB had been assembled correctly. The paperwork review did show that all the steps in the OMIs had been followed correctly and that there had been no anomalies with any of the hardware in the SRBs or any elements of space shuttle systems. A closer look at the film footage of the launch revealed a puff of black smoke flowing from the aft joint of the right SRB immediately after ignition. The smoke was evidence that the O-rings in that joint had been burned and were compromised. For some reason, the joint did not leak again until the shuttle entered jetstream winds at about 30,000 feet. *Challenger* encountered the strongest wind shear any shuttle launch had seen, and the turbulence had apparently caused the leak to start again and intensify until it had destroyed *Challenger*. Each SRB was made of four segments that were cast in Utah and shipped by railcar to Florida, where they were assembled and joined to the external tank to start the stack that the orbiter was attached to.

Each segment of the SRB weighed 300,000 pounds and was twelve feet in diameter, and they were the largest and heaviest items

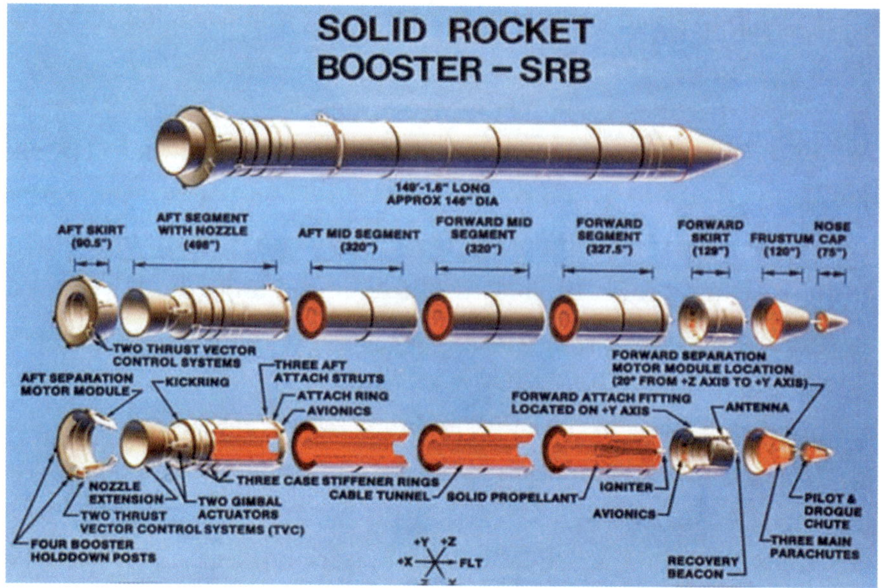

Solid rocket booster segments. Credit: NASA

that could be sent on a railcar. The segments were stacked at KSC with two O-rings in each joint, a primary and a secondary seal. At ignition, the SRB would pressurize to 1,000 PSI in 0.3 seconds, and the segment and the gap at each joint would grow larger. The O-rings needed to be able to expand to seal the joint, but the O-ring Viton material was too cold to expand enough in the freezing temperatures that morning and the right aft joint in the right SRB could not seal properly.

The investigation revealed the engineers at Morton Thiokol, the contractor who had built the SRBs, did not want to launch in the cold temperatures that morning and had made that statement in the management review the night before. But NASA SRB managers had put so much pressure on Thiokol with statements like, "I'm appalled by this recommendation!" and "When do you want me to launch? Next *May*?" Management had overruled the engineers. Thus, the stage was set for disaster.

We also found that the SRBs had routinely been burning and

eroding the O-rings in the segment joints as well as in the joint where the nozzles attached to the aft segments. I had burned O-rings on both of my first two missions. The problems with the O-ring erosion were not as evident as they should have been because NASA had opened only one anomaly report when it first happened on STS-2, and had then lumped all the rest of the incidents in that same report. As a result, management only saw one instance of the problem. Anomalies and close calls were talking to us, and we at NASA were ignoring them!

The right SRB had broken loose, rupturing the external tank, and *Challenger* had pitched nose-down, with 15 negative Gs, and had broken apart at 48,000 feet. The crew module broke away and coasted upward to 65,000 feet before it started back down to the ocean. The crew was cut off from onboard oxygen and only had a Personal Emergency Air Pack (PEAP) for emergency breathing. They could not have had more than a few seconds of consciousness after breakup, and the medical assessment was that they could not have regained consciousness before water impact. The 15 negative G's would have been extremely uncomfortable but should not have caused injuries to the crew. It was also discovered that several of the PEAPs had been turned on by the crew, so we knew they had survived the initial breakup. *Challenger* did not explode as it has been frequently reported, but was torn apart by aerodynamic and structural loads.

After April 14, 1986, my last day at KSC as part of the investigation, I was immediately assigned to another team, this one at the Marshall Space Flight Center in Huntsville, Alabama. Since I had learned a great deal about the SRBs during the investigation, I was assigned to serve as lead astronaut on the SRB redesign team. MSFC was the NASA lead center for propulsion and managed the shuttle main engines, the SRBs, and the external tank. I reported to the MSFC chief engineer in Huntsville on April 15. I would spend the next year and more working on the redesign of the booster rockets in Alabama and in Utah working with Morton Thiokol.

While I was in Brigham City, Utah, I worked closely with Thiokol engineer Alan McDonald, the man who had the courage to interrupt a meeting of the Rogers Commission to reveal to them that he and the rest of the Thiokol engineers had recommended against launching STS 51-L. He had endured a great degree of persecution by NASA but was eventually regarded as a hero for speaking out and was promoted for his bravery. He was an absolute pleasure to work with, highly competent, and instrumental in the successful redesign of the SRB system. He retired as Vice President and Technical Director for Advanced Technology Programs from ATK Thiokol Propulsion in 2001. He wrote a book titled, *Truth, Lies, and O-Rings* describing his travails after his courageous stand. I was honored to write an endorsement for him and the book that referenced me many times.

1986 had been a terrible and stressful year for NASA, particularly for the astronauts. We had been extremely busy working on the investigation, but we also had to say goodbye to our fellow astronauts who had died. We attend many memorial services. Dan Brandenstein from my 1978 class had taken over as the Chief Astronaut from John Young after the *Challenger* accident, and he decided we needed to throw a party that summer to give ourselves a break from all the misery we had been through. We decided we would hold a 1950s sock hop, and everyone was encouraged to come up with dances and lip sync acts and dress like people from the '50s, poodle skirts and the like.

Brewster Shaw and I had played our guitars and had sung at several of our astronaut parties. He walked into my office and said, "Hooter, you think we should get up a four-man rock band?"

I said, "Great idea," so Brewster, Pinky Nelson, and I got together at Brewster's house with our acoustic guitars to learn about nine songs.

Pinky and Brewster both had big excuses why they couldn't be the lead guitarist, and I only had a weak excuse, so they said, "Hoot, you're lead guitar."

We decided to name our band "Max Q" because the shuttle had flown through the Max Q (or maximum dynamic pressure) region after liftoff. We held practices two days in a row without our drummer, Jim Wetherbee, then I was out of town while he played with the two others. The first time all four of us played together was at the actual sock hop! I didn't have an electric guitar at the time, so I ran down to the pawn shop in Webster, Texas, and bought a cheap one and an amplifier.

It was a great party, and the entire astronaut corps and support group loved our performance. We were asked to be the dance band next for a huge party called the "Fajita Fiesta" that we held each year in the largest NASA hangar at Ellington Field, and at that event, they loved us all over again. We played at weddings, in the local and downtown Houston hotels, and even live on "Good Morning America!" The band went on for many years.

Back at work, we completed our redesign efforts and fired several static SRBs in Utah at the test site, some of them with intentional flaws built into the motor insulation to prove that the new design had an additional safety margin over the pre-*Challenger* boosters. NASA began to look ahead to returning to flight with the space shuttle and assigned an experienced crew to fly STS-26 aboard Space Shuttle *Discovery*. The crew of five astronauts included three members of my 1978 class—Rick Hauck, the commander, Dick Covey, the pilot, and "Pinky" Nelson, a mission specialist—and two mission specialists from the 1980 class, Mike Lounge and Dave Hilmers. It was the third flight for Rick Hauck and "Pinky" Nelson, and the second flight for the others.

I found out toward the end of 1987, while having a drink with

George Abbey, that I had been selected to command the second launch of STS-27, which didn't rest easy with me at first.

"George, it's not my turn," I said. There were ten pilots in my TFNG class who had not yet flown a mission as commander, and I was going to command a second mission before anyone else would get a chance at their first. I felt a little guilty about it.

But Abbey replied, "Turns don't have anything to do with it."

On September 14, 1987, I was asked to meet with Chief Astronaut Dan Brandenstein in his office at 8:15 a.m., along with Guy Gardner, Mike Mullane, Jerry Ross, and Bill Shepherd. I knew right away that this was my crew for STS-27 since the group consisted of two pilots and three mission specialists.

"George Abbey wants to see you guys," Brandenstein announced to the room. "I'll walk over with you."

Abbey engaged us first in a little small talk, and then made the offer official. "I was wondering if you guys would like to fly STS-27."

Immediately, there were big smiles, and all five of us were thrilled to be named to the flight. We were the last crew Abbey assigned. He was directed to transfer to NASA Headquarters in October to serve as Deputy Associate Administrator, a role he did not want. Since the first launch, he had been so instrumental in astronaut selection and flight assignment that a book would be written about him in 2018 titled, *The Astronaut Maker*, by Michael Cassutt. George considered his new role a demotion, but in the coming years, he would work his mysterious ways at NASA Headquarters and eventually make his way back into the senior leadership at Johnson Space Center.

16

STS-27 would be a mission unlike any other in my career. It was a top-secret, classified mission, and all five crew members were active-duty military officers. The crew members were USAF Col. Guy Gardner making his first flight as pilot, USAF Col. Mike Mullane on his second flight as Mission Specialist One, USAF Lt. Col. Jerry Ross as MS-2 on his second mission, and Navy Commander Bill Shepherd as MS-3 on his first mission.

It was interesting that as a Navy commander, I was outranked by the two Air Force colonels, but I was still the mission commander. It's been said that rank has no place in the cockpit, and we were evidence of that. STS-27 was an interesting and challenging mission. We were to place a highly classified satellite in a high-inclination orbit, which was different from my first two shuttle flights, which had been low-inclination orbits. "Inclination" refers to the latitude at which the shuttle would fly. My first and second flights had traveled as far as 28.5 degrees above and below the equator, but this mission would fly to 57 degrees north and south. We would see much more of Earth's surface. The flight would take us as far north as Sitka,

STS-27 all-military crew. Credit: NASA

Alaska, and south below Tierra del Fuego.

The top-secret classification of the mission made it more challenging for training and travel because simulations and documentation were limited only to people who needed to know the information. At the "secret" security level, we couldn't discuss the satellite with anyone. We felt a little like James Bond because we needed to cover our tracks when we traveled. We couldn't use credit cards to pay hotel bills, we would fly into a different city than where our meeting was being held and drive in rental cars. It seemed the security measures were somewhat ineffective, particularly in one case when we flew into "City A" in our NASA T-38s, and the ramp assistant said, "Oh, I remember you guys. You're the ones who fly in and then drive to 'City B.'" All five of us looked about the same, and one day, when we were checking out of a hotel, the person at the checkout counter said, "Let me guess, you want to pay with cash, too." We could only look at top-secret documents in specially cleared offices at Johnson Space Center, and we always had a security officer at meetings who would announce before the start of discussions, "This meeting is classified, security-level...," and then name the classification.

We developed a crew emblem that contained a great degree of symbolism. Bill Shepherd designed it depicting a rainbow symbolizing the passing storm of the *Challenger* tragedy and seven stars representing our seven friends who had perished.

We did the standard "training by fire hose" with the added complication of the high security level. My crew and I were at Kennedy Space Center for training on September 28, 1988, when STS-26, the first mission after *Challenger*, launched aboard *Discovery*. We were on the roof of the Launch Control Center, and I saw George Abbey. He was standing by himself at a distance, so I walked over to talk with him. He was no longer the director of flight operations, so he wasn't a member of the firing room team, hence his observation from the roof. With tears in his eyes, he said, "It never gets any easier, Hoot." I agreed, weeping too, as we comforted each other. I always got sweaty palms and a rapid heartbeat watching my friends fly to space, particularly while watching my wife on her missions. We flew shorter missions in the wake of the *Challenger* accident. We realized during the investigation that we didn't know as much as we thought, so *Discovery* landed after only five days. The philosophy was to launch, accomplish the major objectives, and return to land to do a thorough inspection of the shuttle after a minimum-duration flight.

My crew and I were next up, and it was interesting because throughout our year of training, I had heard, "Well, we've been this close to launch before," from Guy Gardner, Jerry Ross, and Mike Mullane alike. They had been assigned to fly the first polar launch of a shuttle, STS-62A, in July 1986 from Vandenburg Air Force Base in California. Launches from Vandenburg would not be able to use steel SRBs and planned to use carbon fiber filament-wound cases to reduce launch weight for additional performance. After NASA had learned the limitations of the steel SRBs, using "plastic" booster rockets was deemed too hazardous, and the mission was cancelled. I replaced Bob Crippen as commander, and Bill Shepherd replaced Dale Gardner as MS-3 for STS-27 aboard Space Shuttle *Atlantis*.

I stood up at our last all-astronaut meeting on November 21 and said, "We will be going into quarantine on Thursday, and I want to thank all of you for all your work on this flight. I know this has been a difficult mission to work on, but hopefully the crew has not been difficult."

We received a big round of applause from our fellow astronauts after my speech. We went into quarantine on Thanksgiving Day, 1988 and then flew to KSC on November 28 for a planned launch on December 1. We manned up and spent more than five hours strapped in only to scrub because of high jet stream winds at 30,000 feet. (As was the case with *Challenger*, a fast jet stream causes extreme wind shear that places dangerous structural loads on the shuttle at supersonic speeds.) We tried again on December 2, but the high winds were still with us. We had just about used up our entire launch window when last-minute balloon data showed we were within design recommendations for the shuttle's structural load, so we resumed the countdown.

We were at less than five minutes to launch when Houston Flight Director Gary Coen announced on the audio loop that he had to call for a hold because the weather in Spain had gone below minimums. The only hold point remaining was at T-minus thirty-one seconds, so we held there. That's when I looked at my Pilot, Guy Gardner, and chided him. "I'll bet you've never been this close to launch before."

I was sure we were out of the launch window and were about to scrub again when Gary Coen said, "We have a 'Go' to launch." The countdown clock resumed immediately, and we counted down to T-minus zero and were on our way to space. Our orbit parameters had

STS-27 launch on *Atlantis*. Credit: NASA

been highly secret, but as soon as we established a northeasterly heading after liftoff, it was apparent that we were going to a 57-degree orbit inclination. At 276 miles above the planet, this was the highest I'd ever flown, and we traveled over most of the populated Earth.

Our first-day activities included deployment of the satellite, but it almost didn't happen. There had been a flight rule in place that the crew could not exceed an eighteen-hour day, and because of our extended hold, we could not complete the deployment within that time frame. The satellite customer was the Department of Defense, and I knew they wanted the equipment to be deployed immediately, so I asked my four crew members how they felt about extending our day. They agreed enthusiastically. There's always plenty of adrenaline flowing on launch day, and it was easy for us to go longer than planned. I called Mission Control and said, "The boys are on a roll, and we want to complete day one." I know that the DOD and Air Force Satellite Control Facility must have been very pleased because we were able to deploy the satellite successfully. The control facility was named Onizuka Air Force Station in honor of my former officemate, Ellison Onizuka, a designation that made me proud to be working with them.

The very large payload filled the shuttle cargo bay, and the deployment was performed by grappling the satellite with the Remote Manipulator System and moving it out of the bay. We performed some reconfiguration of the satellite, which we had named "Dino," before releasing it from the RMS, and then I fired a separation burn to move eighty miles away from it. We went into a sleep period, and Mission Control allowed us to sleep in a little after the long first day. Then things got busy.

Jerry Ross had soaked up a little water from the floor of the middeck in one of his socks. He took a towel to the water, which completely soaked it. We had water under the deck that we needed to eliminate so we could perform some rendezvous burns to rejoin with Dino. We had to remove a large insert called Volume B to get access under the floor, and I saw that there was a sheet of water of about two gallons clinging to a bulkhead. We used a vacuum hose to dump the water overboard into space. We were able to determine that Humidity Separator B had malfunctioned and was dumping water into the cabin. We switched to Hum Sep A for the remainder of the mission and completed all this in time for the rendezvous burns to begin. There had been a problem with Dino, and we needed to do an unplanned re-rendezvous to help Onizuka AFS solve the problem with the satellite. We fixed the issue, and Dino went on to complete a successful mission in space.

We were then confronted with another malfunction, one that could have resulted in disaster. The CAPCOM called and told us that a review of the launch videos had shown something hitting our right wing and asked us to use the RMS camera to examine the underside. We maneuvered the camera into place, and I'll never forget what we saw under the wing. In fact, I even said to myself, "We are going to die!" There was extensive damage to the tiles that protected our aluminum vehicle from the 6,000-degree plasma of reentry. I called Mission Control and said very clearly, "Houston, we are seeing a lot of tile damage on the right wing."

The video showed what appeared to be a trail of debris coming from the right wing during launch. The DOD was against any video download, but they finally allowed us to send encrypted video back to Mission Control. The next day, they called us back and only said, "It's no issue. Just reenter as normal."

I couldn't believe what I just heard and immediately called back. "Dave, what are they basing this on?"

He needed to get the answer to that specific question and called later. "They say it's no worse than previous missions."

"I've been here since before STS-1," I said, "and I've never seen anything like this, but you're the experts."

I caved, but in retrospect, I should have been persistent. Mission Control had forgotten that I wasn't seeing encrypted video onboard. I was able to see the damage clear as day. Apparently, the resolution on their end was so poor that the ground team had concluded we weren't in fact seeing tile damage but merely poor lighting and shadowing, but they never told us their opinion. If they had said they didn't believe it was tile damage, I would have sent them a clearer video so we would be working from the same images. Not inquiring further to press the issue was my mistake.

The night before reentry, I was on the flight deck, and one of the crew told me how concerned he was about our right wing. I told him to relax and enjoy the remainder of our mission and added whimsically, "There's no reason to die all tensed up."

There weren't many photos taken in orbit that we could show, but we did manage to capture a picture of the world's largest freshwater lake by volume, Lake Baikal in Russian Siberia. Located at a latitude of 53 degrees north and more than a mile deep, it holds about 20 percent of all unfrozen fresh water on Earth.

We performed the deorbit burn on December 6 and headed back to the surface. I watched the position display for the shuttle's elevons (combined pitch and roll control surfaces at the back of the delta wing) indicate all the way down during reentry because I knew that if we burned through the right wing that the drag would increase, and the flight control would deflect the left elevon down to balance.

Every two minutes, I would announce to the crew, "The elevons look good." I figured that if I saw the elevons fighting the drag, I might have no more than thirty seconds to tell Mission Control what I thought of their analysis before we perished.

The entry and landing were completely normal with no anomalies, and I landed Shuttle *Atlantis* on Edwards AFB Lakebed Runway 17 Left. We were the first space flight ever to fly the reentry without a communications blackout because STS-26 had deployed a second relay satellite into orbit ahead of our mission. We were able to transmit voice and data upward, bouncing it off the satellite in spite of the plasma surrounding the bottom of the orbiter.

STS-27 *Atlantis* landing. Credit: NASA

The damage to the black thermal tiles was clearly visible on the front of *Atlantis*. When we exited the orbiter, there was a crowd gawking at our right wing, which looked like a shotgun had hit it, but that wasn't all. We had one entirely missing tile we hadn't been able to observe using the RMS camera in space. A burn-through had been prevented only because there was a thicker plate there serving as part of the antenna ground plane. This alone allowed us to survive.

I have told this story many times as a classic example of a failure to communicate on the part of Mission Control. An analysis of the tile damage was made many years later, after the *Columbia* accident. With more than 700 tiles damaged, *Atlantis* was the most beat-up shuttle in history to land safely.

Damage to *Atlantis* showing its missing thermal tile. Credit: NASA

The excitement of the mission was over, but there would be more to come after several weeks of debriefings. I went to Utah to Morton Thiokol to thank the employees I had worked with during the investigation for producing outstanding SRBs, and the entire crew was part of the half-time show at the Super Bowl in January. We traveled to Washington, D.C., in February 1989, and we were all awarded a medal at the headquarters of the Central Intelligence Agency. Though our flight had not been an agency mission, the award is only given by the CIA, so we, along with our NASA Flight Directors, were awarded the National Intelligence Medal of Achievement by CIA Director Judge William Webster.

The award ceremony at the CIA was held in a large conference room, and an amusing moment happened when we were leaving. A security guard at the door held out his hand. Confused, I asked, "What do you need?"

"I have to get that medal back, Sir," he said.

Mike Mullane, one of the funniest men I've ever known, was right behind me with a big smile on his face. "You mean to tell us you've given us a medal we can only wear in a safe?"

"Well, yes, sir," the guard replied. "That's true, and you also can't tell anyone you were here. But anytime you're back in D.C., we can let you in to look at your medal."

It would take about four years and the final declassification of the shuttle mission for us to take our medals and accompanying citations home.

The other event we attended was an extremely memorable one, but far smaller. We went to the Pentagon office of the Chairman of the Joint Chiefs of Staff to brief them on our mission. We had compiled a top-secret film of our satellite operations and the story of the deployment, which was flown to Washington, D.C., by a courier who had it in a locked briefcase handcuffed to his wrist—real James Bond stuff. I divided our story into portions and assigned parts to be narrated by each of the five of us because I wanted all of them to speak. The briefing was held in their small, highly classified conference room, and the Joint Chiefs were seated at the table. You had to be a four-star admiral or general to be seated at the table. The other attendees, three-star or less, were seated along the walls. We narrated the movie live and answered all their questions, and then Admiral Crowe, Chairman of the Joint Chiefs, stood up and said, "Gentlemen, I think we owe these young men a standing ovation."

They all stood and applauded. That moment was a major highlight of my career.

Another blessing came in 1989—our second son, Edward Dann Gibson, was born on March 27. He was named Edward for Rhea's father since we had named Paul after mine, but Rhea didn't particularly care for the name "Edward," so we resolved to call him Dann. Everything went fine during his delivery, a relief after we had suffered all kinds of stress during Paul's birth.

After STS-27, I was briefly assigned to command STS-46 but was later moved to the following mission, STS-47, a joint mission with Japan known as Spacelab-J. STS-47 was a very interesting flight, and I was joining a trio of American astronauts who had been training for two years together—Mark Lee, Jan Davis, and Dr. Mae Jemison—and Dr. Mamoru Mohri, the first professional Japanese astronaut. They had all worked together with investigators on more than forty life science and materials science projects that would all be in the Spacelab module in our cargo bay. Lee and Davis would be the first married couple to go to space together. I joined them as commander, along with Curt Brown as pilot on his first mission, and Jay Apt as flight engineer/MS-2 on his second flight. We started the training and made a journey to Tokyo and Tsukuba to meet all the participants. I had been to Japan on two of my Navy cruises, but this time, we were treated like VIPs during all our meetings and social events. I learned to love the extremely polite Japanese people. There was so much excitement in Japan over Mohri's upcoming flight, he was adored like a rock star everywhere he went. There were two additional Japanese backup astronauts assigned to train along with Mohri,

Dr. Takao Doi and Dr. Chiaki Mukai. Mukai would later go on to be the first woman astronaut from Japan. There was an additional American backup, Stan Koszelak, whom we really liked and wished could have flown with us.

The seven crew members entered into quarantine on September 5, 1992, and flew our four NASA T-38s to the Cape on September 9 for a launch on September 12. Luck was with us, and we launched right on time at exactly 10:23 a.m. Eastern for the first on-time launch in many years. Our orbit was set at 57 degrees so we would fly over all of Japan, and we had no anomalies during our launch aboard the Space Shuttle *Endeavour*, on its second mission to space. We were the fiftieth space shuttle flight. *Endeavour* was the orbiter built to replace *Challenger*. My former crewmate, Senator Bill Nelson, had played a significant role for NASA in acquiring it, so I felt extremely honored to command its second flight. We got right down

Shift handover in Spacelab. Credit: NASA

to work, activated the Spacelab, and about three hours after we arrived in orbit, the "blue crew" went into the sleep stations for an eight-hour sleep period while the "red crew" went to work.

We found that there was a coolant leak on one of our furnaces in the Spacelab, and Curt Brown and Mark Lee did an inflight maintenance procedure to repair it. The delay in starting the science investigations caused our mission to be extended from the original seven to eight days. The red crew and the blue crew worked alternating shifts. Every twelve hours, we would brief the incoming shift on what had been accomplished on the prior shift.

The coolant leak was the only significant anomaly that occurred over the eight-day flight. We prepared to deorbit on September 20, 1992, and delayed one orbit due to rain showers at KSC, then flew a normal reentry and touched down at 8:53:22 a.m. This flight was the third to carry a drag chute for landing. The first two had deployed it with the orbiter de-rotated, and the nose landing gear solidly on the runway. In simulations, some of the drag chute characteristics had caused the pilot to lose control, but the restriction to have the nose gear on the ground was lifted for my landing, so I was determined to have the drag chute fully inflated with the nose gear still in the air. The chute would initially deploy reefed—that is, restricted—to a diameter of twenty feet, or half its size, and then dis-reef to the full forty feet after a delay. I was required to de-rotate at a pitch rate between 1 and 3 degrees per second, so I used a rate of 1 degree per second to achieve the full dis-reef with the nose gear off the ground.

In performing this maneuver, I was able to expose a problem in the drag chute, which is why we do flight testing. The drag chute moved to the right 8 degrees or more, which then pulled the orbiter nose to the left, causing us to deviate twenty-seven feet left of the runway center line. I corrected and completed the landing without further issue. My landing revealed that the chute did not have sufficient

Endeavour drag chute deployment. Credit: NASA

porosity and was unstable in the wake of the shuttle. The problem was solved by removing some of the ribbons in the parachute, resulting in a stable deployment utilized in all future landings. Other than the drag chute issue, I had made a nearly picture-perfect landing. My targeted touchdown speed was expected to be 205 knots, and I touched down at 202 with an officially documented sink rate of 0.0 feet per second. Though a sink rate of zero is technically impossible, I had descended to the runway more slowly than one-tenth of a foot per second. At a total weight of 220,195 pounds, it was my heaviest landing, but I had really "greased it on."

17

Following STS-47, the new rumor on the street was that I was going to be named the next chief astronaut. However, after Dan Brandenstein had left the astronaut corps, anything could happen, and it was hard to get excited.

In November 1992, after our mission debriefings were finished, Dave Leestma, the director of the Flight Crew Operations Directorate, asked me to meet him in his office in Building One. He told me that as of that moment, I was the new chief astronaut, following in the footsteps of Deke Slayton, John Young, and Dan Brandenstein. I was awestruck by the news and knew it was an incredible honor. At that moment, I wished my dad were still alive so I could share the news with him. I did call Mom, though, and she was very proud, yet the excitement of my promotion dimmed a bit when I thought to myself, *Wait a minute! Am I smart enough to be chief astronaut?* I had 113 extremely talented astronauts; thirty-two test pilots who had served as mission commanders and pilots, about thirty-five PhDs, ten MDs, and many with master's degrees. I suddenly realized I didn't have all the answers, and I knew I needed to do something about that.

My solution was to get input from all those talented astronauts, hear as many opinions as I could, and then make decisions as the leader of the astronauts. I had several big projects I needed to finish, so I got right to work. We were behind on assigning flight crews and needed to rotate job assignments. The shuttle crew assignments were particularly challenging because I had to match astronauts best suited to a particular flight's payload based on their degrees and expertise, consider when it was time for a particular astronaut to be given another mission and review their prior flights, and take into account compatible personalities to assemble crews that would work best together. It required a lot of background work and was extremely time-consuming.

Meanwhile, I had a constant influx of my branch chiefs coming to me with issues to solve or questions to answer. As a result, I was getting little accomplished because the branch chiefs had not previously been given the authority to make decisions themselves. At my very next meeting with all my branch chiefs, I told them that going forward, they would make all the decisions that affected their particular branch. Only if an idea was controversial or expensive would we then convene a meeting to figure it out together. For the most part, they would be on their own.

The change in structure accomplished several good things. It gave me time to get my work done, but it also elevated the standing of my chiefs within their branch. By pushing decision-making to the lowest level possible, the members of each branch could now count on their chief to make a timely decision, and the chiefs got accustomed to making decisions. Even after having given away a large amount of authority, I never experienced any bad outcomes.

I also needed to select a new deputy chief astronaut since that position was also vacant. I selected Dr. Linda Godwin, who had flown one mission and held a PhD in physics. She was a fine choice for the position, even-tempered and capable, and because there had never been a woman in the position of chief or deputy chief, her appointment gave a significant morale boost to the other women in the astronaut corps.

Among all the astronauts, a frequent complaint had been that they never knew their professional standing, so I resolved to meet with each of them one-on-one in my office over the course of a year. On the schedule, these meetings appeared as, "One-On-One with Number One," which I found amusing (after all, number one was the informal designation for the ship's first officer in the *Star Trek* franchise), but one of my engineers joked that what it really meant was "One-On-One with No One."

From my time in the Navy, I knew the most meaningful performance debriefings emphasized what a pilot did well, and what could improve. I made it a point to do the same with my astronauts—tell them what they excelled at, and if it applied, what I wanted them to change. As a leader, you owe it to your personnel to share with them how to get better. Occasionally, this was difficult for my astronauts to hear, and it was hard on me, too.

I was interviewed by *Space News* shortly after being named chief astronaut, and I'll never forget one of the questions I was asked. "Hoot, in about two years, the first *Mir* docking mission will be needing a crew. Are you going to assign yourself to that flight?" It was going to be a joint American-Russian mission with the space shuttle rendezvousing and docking with the Russian space station whose name translated to "world" or "peace" in English. It would be the most exciting mission to come along in quite a few years and would be the first-ever docking mission for a space shuttle.

I launched right into a speech. "That is not the purpose of a leader, to skim off the best deals for yourself. I will *not* be assigning myself to the *Mir* docking mission!" In fact, my thinking at the time had been that I really didn't need to fly another mission. I had flown four very significant flights and planned to spend the rest of my time at NASA taking care of and supporting my astronauts.

One of my most enjoyable tasks as chief astronaut was supporting the launches and landings of the shuttle. I would fly the shuttle training aircraft (STA) before every launch and landing to record the wind profiles at altitude and to make sure the cloud cover was acceptable and met the flight rules. We had a flight rule that there couldn't be any rain showers within thirty miles of the shuttle runway in case a launch went wrong and had to abort and return. To see whether there was any rain falling before launches, I would fly a T-38 around midnight over the Atlantic thirty miles out, cruising below 1,000 feet under cumulus clouds. I was usually alone in the dark on these flights, so I took extra care to keep from descending into the ocean. I remember Rhea was never happy about these flights.

On launch days, I would ride with the shuttle crew in the crew van, and when the van made the turn at the vehicle assembly building, I would wish them a safe trip and go to the shuttle runway to climb into the STA. I learned from the previous chief astronaut how to do a little prayer with the crew as I was leaving them, so I kept up the tradition. I would ask them to bow their heads, then say with great gravitas, "May the Lord help you," pause for a second, then continue, "…if you mess this up!" It always got a little chuckle from the crew.

For shuttle landings, I would take off several hours before the planned landing time to fly approaches to the runway and check for crosswinds, turbulence, and adverse weather. We needed to evaluate conditions because we needed to give a "Go" to the shuttle crew for the deorbit burn about an hour and fifteen minutes before landing. I would then join up to chase the space shuttle in a loose formation for the final portion of their approach and landing so I could record the wind profile the orbiter had flown through.

Shuttle Training Aircraft following the shuttle landing. Credit: NASA

After the shuttle landed, the runway at Kennedy Space Center was closed while the orbiter was on the runway. We would then land the shuttle training aircraft on Cape Canaveral's Skid Strip, named in honor of the winged missiles that used to land there on skid plates in the 1950s. I would climb out of the STA and into the waiting NASA helicopter, which would fly me back to the shuttle runway. I would meet up with my returning astronauts to congratulate them on their mission and then ride with them in the crew van back to the crew quarters. Being with them in the crew van was always so heartwarming to me. I never really said much, but I enjoyed listening. They were always so excited after their mission. Hopped up on adrenaline after having flown through their sizzling reentry and landing, they were all talking a mile a minute. I mainly sat back, smiling to myself, remembering my own trips to space. From 1992 to 1994, I flew supporting the launches and landings for ten shuttle flights and enjoyed every minute.

My time as chief astronaut was about to end later in 1994. My boss, Dave Leestma, called me one day and said, "Hoot, headquarters really likes your *Mir* docking crew." It was an extremely important mission given its international significance. It was only the second American-Russian docking in history, and I had assembled a great crew for it.

"That's great!" I said.

Then Leestma added, "With one exception." I fell speechless and was a little annoyed. In my two years as chief astronaut, none of my crew selections had ever been altered. I felt that, since I was the one who knew them the best, I was in the best position to select them, and my process was meticulous. "They want you to command it," he finally finished.

I was dumbfounded, struck silent.

Finally, to break me out of it, he asked, "What's your reaction to that?"

"Dave," I said, "I don't want to do that. I've been telling the world for two years now that I'm not going to assign myself to that flight. Steve will do a fine job, and I want him to command it."

I had chosen one of my fellow classmates from the 1978 group, Steve Nagel, a veteran of four shuttle missions, to command the flight. I had previously shown who I wanted on that mission because

I had called Steve, Charlie Precourt, Greg Harbaugh, and Ellen Baker to come to my office to tell them as much as I could. I didn't have headquarters approval for that crew yet, and I told them that I didn't have much information, but the Russian crew members would be in Houston for training, and it would be beneficial for the four of them to attend some of their sessions to get to know them. Obviously, they were my choice for that crew.

Dave told me he would try again to get the brass to approve my original selection, but he called me back in a few days and said, "Hoot, they still want you."

"I still don't want it," I said.

He tried once more, then called me back. "Hoot, do me a favor!"

I said, "Sure, Dave. Anything."

"Shut up and go do the *Mir* docking!"

At that point, I gave up. "Okay, I'll do it, but only if you come over to Building Four and make the announcement to my astronauts as to why."

He agreed. I had to step down as chief astronaut and go right into training for a fifth mission. I found out much later that the Russians were very nervous about the space shuttle docking with their *Mir* station. In the Apollo-Soyuz mission in 1975, there had been two dockings, one flown by mission commander Tom Stafford, and one by Deke Slayton. Reportedly, one of the dockings hit the *Soyuz* so forcefully, it nearly broke the mechanisms. The Russians never forgot that event, and now, twenty years later, our quarter-million-pound shuttle was preparing to attack *Mir*, in a way. NASA headquarters had told the Russians the docking was so important that their chief astronaut would be commanding the mission. I had really enjoyed all the challenges of leading such a distinguished group of high achievers, and it was with a large amount of regret that I stepped down from being chief astronaut, the most prestigious position I had ever held.

18

The announcement of the crew for STS-71 was published with Charlie Precourt as Pilot, Ellen Baker as Mission Specialist One, Greg Harbaugh as MS-2, Bonnie Dunbar as MS-3, and me as the commander. Dunbar was in Russia training as the backup for American Astronaut Norm Thaggard, who would launch aboard a Russian *Soyuz* in March 1995 alongside Russian Cosmonauts Vladimir Dezurov and Gennady Strekalov to spend four months aboard the *Mir* space station. Dunbar would join us in Houston after the *Soyuz* launched. Joining us on the shuttle were two Russian Cosmonauts, Anatoly Soloviev and Nikolai Budarin, who would take over the *Mir* Space Station once we docked. Precourt, Baker, Harbaugh, and I traveled to Russia twice for a total of twenty days to train in the *Mir* space station mockup and the *Soyuz* simulator.

We visited the major space manufacturers in the Moscow area and met with Vladimir Syromiatnikov at Zvezda, who had designed the docking apparatus we would use to dock with *Mir*. We were very impressed with the intricacies of the docking mechanisms, which included active and passive damping capabilities, and we felt it was running like a Swiss watch, based on its construction and intricacies.

Baker, Harbaugh, and I squeezed into the snug fit of the *Soyuz* simulator and flew it for a launch to orbit. The *Soyuz* vehicle is fully automated, which meant that all attitude maneuvers and firings of the rocket engines were made without crew involvement. We were

Shuttle Russian docking mechanism. Credit: NASA

also surprised there were no audio or visual cues provided for the crew to alert us when these events were about to happen. The *Soyuz* would maneuver to a burn attitude when it was time and fire the engines on its own. We were simply along for the ride.

Our first training session had been in September 1994, and we stayed at the Pentahotel in Moscow and had a driver to take us to Zvyozdny Gorodok, or "Star City" in English, and the Yuri Gagarin Cosmonaut Training Center. The challenging roads in Russia required an hour to make the twenty-mile ride. In the evenings, after training was over, we walked to restaurants and department stores.

Star City Soyuz Simulator. Credit: NASA

We were unimpressed with the quality and minimal quantities of choices in Moscow. We stayed in Star City for the March 1995 training and lived and dined in the Prophylactorium, the visitors' quarters, which were also quite minimal.

Astronaut Bill Readdy was the NASA Director of Operations at Star City, and he was instrumental in our handling on both training sessions in Russia. He also arranged for us to have the tour of a lifetime to the Central Russian Air Force Museum at Monino, about four miles from Star City. I was fascinated by Monino because as a "cold warrior," I had studied and trained to fight against many of the aircraft that were on display there. I must have shot at least six rolls of film and acted like a kid in a candy store for hours. I nearly had to be pried away when our time was over.

I was able to see and study up close many Russian airplanes I had previously only seen in intelligence photos, many of which were grainy and taken from the woods surrounding the airfields. I saw fighters like the MiG-21 Fishbed, the MiG-23 and MiG-27 Flogger, the MiG-25 Foxbat, MiG-29 Fulcrum, and even the MiG-31 Foxhound. Russian bombers were all on display as well, dating from the reverse-engineered Russian copy of the American B-29 Superfortress, the Tupolev TU-4 Bull. I saw the TU-22 Blinder, TU-22M Backfire, and the TU-160M Blackjack, a swing-wing bomber similar to our B-1 Lancer. The prototype of the Russian supersonic transport, the Tupolev TU-144, was there along with the MiG-21I Analog, a MiG-21 flying testbed that was modified with the type of delta wing that would be used for the TU-144. One big bomber was the Myasishchev M-50 Bounder which was one of the larger aircraft on display. It had an interesting history behind it because it was a part of the Cold War-era "Bomber Gap" that was thought to exist in the late 1950s, the illusion that the United States lagged behind Russia in its number of bombers. It turned out that only one M-50 Bounder had ever flown, but the Russians had painted different numbers on it and claimed to have many of them. It was the perceived Bomber Gap that had resulted in U-2 spy plane flights over Russia.

Russian Myasishchev M-50 Bounder bomber. Credit: NASA

We enjoyed the company of our cosmonaut counterparts. Sergei had flown in space three times, his most recent on shuttle flight STS-60 in February 1994 as the first Russian to fly on an American shuttle, which had launched and landed exactly ten years after my first shuttle flight. Anatoly and Nikolai would launch with me aboard STS-71 and then stay onboard *Mir* for a total of seventy-five days. Sergei and Anatoly joined several of our training events and were a significant help. Sergei spoke English as well as I did while Anatoly was still learning in the same way I was learning Russian. I had about a year's worth of part-time lessons in the language, so I needed help when the discussions were only in Russian. We returned to training in Houston and then about one month before launch, our crewmates Anatoly and Nikolai, along with several backups, arrived for training at the Johnson Space Center in Houston. We grew to know Anatoly and Nikolai very well.

I took Anatoly for a familiarization flight in the back seat of a NASA T-38 out over the Gulf of Mexico. Our shuttle pilot, Charlie Precourt, flew with Nikolai. I had arranged with Anatoly that I would say to him, "Tolle, Te letayesh," which was his nickname, "Tolle," and, "You fly." He immediately took our throttles into full afterburner, accelerated to over 400 knots and performed high-G aerobatic maneuvers with loadings up to 6.5 Gs until our fuel was nearly spent. I smiled the entire time because that's exactly what I would have done if Tolle had taken me flying in a two-seater MiG-21. When it was time to return and land, I said, "Tolle, Ya letayu." I fly. We very much bonded with our Russian cosmonauts because they were just like us—they enjoyed flying in fighters as well as in space. However, we found their upper management to be not nearly as friendly or as easygoing. They were older, Soviet-era communists.

We needed a crew emblem, and I was able to prevail upon Bob McCall to make a design for us once again. He had designed the brilliant crew patch for the first crew on STS-1 and the crew emblem for the original Apollo-Soyuz docking mission in 1975, and he graciously agreed to design our patch for STS-71.

The crew patch depicted the approach to *Mir* as it was initially planned—fly to a position in front of and level with *Mir*, then slowly close in to dock, called an X Bar approach. It was later determined to be more fuel-efficient to fly from a position below *Mir* and approach vertically along a radius vector from the center of the Earth, an R Bar approach. The radius vector approach had the advantage of our ability to slow our closure rate in the approach to *Mir* using gravity. We needed to go into a braking mode of our upward-firing 900-pound thrusters, called "Low Z" mode, once we were within 1,000 feet of *Mir* to keep thruster firings from destroying their solar panels. The Low Z mode fired our forward thrusters at the same time as our rear thrusters which canceled each other along the X axis (fore and aft) but had a downward component that achieved some braking. Low Z used significantly more fuel for each braking pulse, and in an X Bar approach, would further raise fuel usage. From our combined simulator training, we were able to deduce a rule of thumb for our R Bar approaches to calculate what closure rate would allow us to coast to a stop at thirty feet without having to brake inside 250 feet. The formula was range-to-go, times two, divided by 1,000. If our range was 100 feet, times two equals 200, divided by 1,000 equals 0.2 feet per second. This is the highest closure rate that would coast to a stop at thirty feet without us firing braking pulses. The new training aspect of the mission was focused on the docking. Virtually every other evolution had been something the crew had previously performed. We did approximately a hundred dockings in the simulators, troubleshooting many anomalies and problems along the way, both in stand-alone sessions and integrated simulations with Mission Control Houston and Mission Control Moscow involved. The sessions with

Moscow occurred late in the evening in Houston because public transit in Russia shut down at night, and the controllers had no way to get to work.

I was awarded with another life blessing when my youngest daughter, Emilee, was born on June 9, 1995. My middle name is Lee, so Rhea decided we should spell her name with two E's at the end. Her birth meant a third C-section for Rhea, but the procedure happened without additional difficulty.

We went into quarantine June 17, 1995, and flew to Kennedy Space Center June 21, aiming for a launch on June 24. I flew the lead T-38 in our five-plane formation with Anatoly Soloviev in my back seat. Nikolai Budarin flew with Charlie Precourt.

The arrival of the crew was always a large press event, and we made brief remarks to the assembled reporters before heading for the crew quarters. We had three days to enjoy the beach house with our Russian friends and families, including Anatoly's wife and two sons. Emilee was only eighteen days old when I launched, but she was able to be with me at the beach house, as was my first daughter, Julie.

The management team made the decision the night of June 23 to proceed with tanking. The liquid hydrogen and oxygen were loaded into the external tank, and we were therefore committed to board *Atlantis* on June 24 for a launch attempt. As had been the case with STS 61-C, I was once again aboard a fueled orbiter in a thunderstorm with lightning in the area, and one fork of lightning actually hit the top of the launch pad, so the flight was rescheduled. Our second attempt on June 27 was successful, and we were on our way—America's 100th manned launch.

In the roll maneuver after liftoff, I made the radio call with a Russian word in tribute to Yuri Gagarin, the first human to go to space. I called, "Houston, Poyekhali, *Atlantis* is in the roll." The word means "let's go" in Russian, and Gagarin had broadcast that as he had lifted off. We flew a direct insertion launch to a 159.5 nautical mile high apogee into an orbit at 51.6 degrees inclination with the lowest perigee any shuttle had flown, eighty-five nautical miles. It was an on-time launch which maximized our ascent performance since we were able to launch the moment the window opened. That occurred when *Mir* passed over Cape Canaveral, and we were 2,000 miles behind them. By flying a lower apogee and perigee, we were traveling a shorter distance around the Earth than *Mir*, which was up at 212 nautical miles, so we were steadily closing the distance. We kept the low eighty-five-mile perigee for two orbits, and then did a burn called NC-1 that created a new apogee for us at 212 miles and made our perigee 159.5 miles. Over the next two days and twenty-one orbits of Earth, we made three more burns and drew closer to the *Mir* station by flying the lower orbit as we led up to the Terminal Intercept burn. That should have put us on a collision course with *Mir*, but the computed TI burn turned out to be inaccurate. We would have been 8,000 feet short. We performed four mid-course correction burns after TI which solved the problem.

After our fourth burn, I moved to the aft orbiter station to fly the manual phase of the rendezvous. We intercepted the earth radius vector (R Bar) at 2,647 feet below *Mir*, closing at 6.97 feet per second. I performed burns to diminish our closure rates to four FPS at 2,000 feet, three FPS at 1,500 feet, and 1.5 FPS at 1,000 feet, where I selected the Low Z braking mode. We continued closing to 270 feet, where we had planned to hold for fifty-six minutes in the event there were any problems or issues to be resolved.

After the hold, I fired our thrusters to move to the next planned hold at the range of thirty feet. I needed to maintain an approach corridor within eight degrees of the *Mir* docking port at a distance of 270 feet from *Mir*. At 150 feet, I slowed to a 0.1 FPS closure rate to the hold at thirty feet. In our simulator runs, we had determined that

Approaching MIR Station. Credit: NASA

a constant closure rate of 0.1 FPS was more practical than the original plan of a variable closure rate. The primary purpose of the hold at thirty feet was a chance to resolve any differences in the attitudes of *Atlantis* or *Mir*. I needed to line up the centers of the two docking ports within three inches of one other, and the relative pitch, roll, and yaw values had to be within two degrees. We would have needed to

MIR docking port from an approximate range of 30 feet. Credit: NASA

change the orbiter's attitude if it were outside the two-degree limit. The closure rate at contact was limited to 0.1 FPS, plus or minus 0.03 FPS. I was told that a contact speed of 0.2 FPS would damage the docking mechanism beyond repair. The day before we launched, the crew and I had a conference call with the NASA administrator, and at the very end of the call he said, "Hoot, I want you to know that when you dock with *Mir*, there will be eight million people watching you on television, so no pressure!"

We arrived at the thirty-foot hold point on time at eleven minutes before docking for a planned hold of about five minutes. From there, we had an extraordinarily clear view and could see that our relative attitudes were all less than one degree. We began the final approach at five minutes, fifty seconds to go, using a constant 0.1 FPS closure rate, and we achieved a very accurate docking.

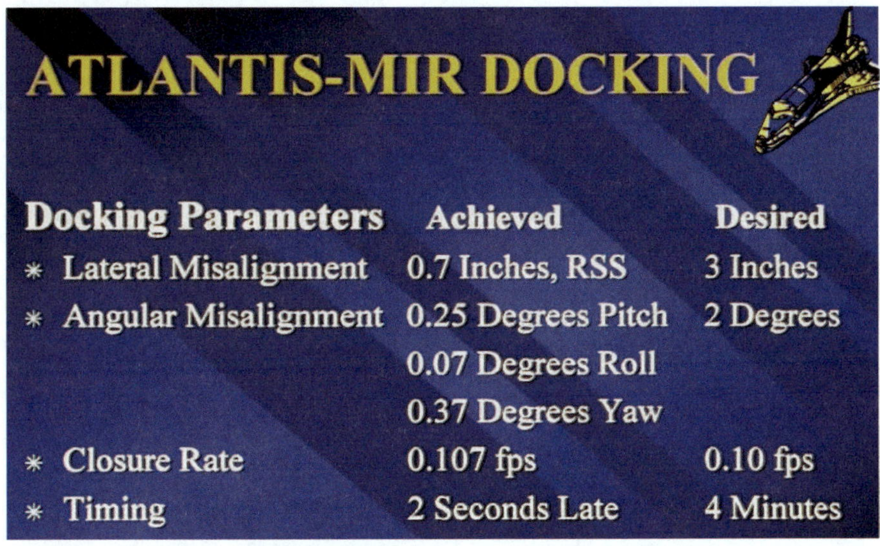

Atlantis docking parameters. Credit: NASA

I credit the excellent crew coordination we had with Pilot Precourt and MS-2 Harbaugh, both of whom who had plotted our progress every step of the way using handheld laser trackers to verify range and closure rates. We had been rigorous about checklist usage, working as a team, and flying every simulator session exactly the way we planned to fly the mission. We were given quite a compliment from the next two upcoming *Mir* docking commanders who had watched in Mission Control: "How are we going to beat that when we can't even match it?"

Harbaugh was our expert on the docking mechanisms, and he expeditiously performed the hard mate and latched the twelve structural hooks that securely attached us to the Russian station. We then transferred more than 135 pounds of air to *Mir* to equalize the cabin pressures before we could open the hatch. The protocol was that the two mission commanders would shake hands at the crew hatch, as it was done during the *Apollo-Soyuz* docking in 1975.

Atlantis - MIR commanders handshake. Credit: NASA

I shook the hand of Russian Air Force Colonel Vladimir Dezurov, a Russian MiG pilot trained for years to shoot me down just as I had been trained to shoot him down. President Bill Clinton observed our handshake and stated, "I guess this really means the Cold War is over." Since then, I've told everyone I ended the Cold

War. It always gets a laugh and usually a round of applause.

We spent the next five days docked with *Mir* and were extremely busy. We had over 400 items we needed to transfer to the station or from it to take back to Earth. We also gave *Mir* 1,067 pounds of water. We did the only Russian crew exchange in history using an American spacecraft, transferring the three cosmonauts from *Mir* to the shuttle, and Anatoly and Nikolai to *Mir* to take over. We also attended press conferences from orbit, sent to both the US and Russia.

At the end of our docking day, we said goodnight to mission control Houston and Moscow and were preparing to go to sleep, when Anatoly came back to *Atlantis* and asked us to join him for a celebration. We all went over to *Mir*, and the Russians opened some of their food containers and produced a white, plastic canteen with a dark liquid in it. NASA had worried that we would go to *Mir* and drink vodka with the cosmonauts. But after we landed, I told NASA in all honesty, "There is no vodka on *Mir*." The Russians weren't going to go to all that trouble for ordinary vodka; the dark liquid was cognac. They had many canteens filled with cognac and gave each of us a short straw to sip from the bottle. When the stopper was removed, the cognac would form a dome at the mouth of the canteen, which we would each dip our straws into and sip from. I had two or three swigs and felt a slight buzz floating through the tunnel back to *Atlantis*. I remember thinking a short prayer. *Please, Lord, no emergencies tonight*.

After five days of joint operations, it was time to leave *Mir* on the Fourth of July, 1995. Anatoly and Nikolai got into the *Soyuz* vehicle and undocked fifteen minutes before we left. They flew out to our left side 200 feet away and took the photo of the mated vehicles before I undocked, and then of *Atlantis* backing away.

After I undocked *Atlantis*, the situation deteriorated. Before the undocking, *Atlantis* and *Mir* both went into "free drift," meaning neither vehicle was attempting to control attitude. This was so there wouldn't be any inadvertent changes in the attitude of either vehicle that could cause a collision. At thirty feet of separation, I resumed thruster control of our attitude and mission control Moscow sent a command for *Mir* to resume control. Anatoly and Nikolai were both in *Soyuz*, and no one was aboard *Mir*. However, the command that was sent caused *Mir*'s computer to shut down, leaving the station dead in orbit and unable to resume attitude control.

Moscow frantically called for Anatoly to redock immediately, so we suddenly had three vehicles maneuvering that needed to stay clear of each other instead of only two. When Russia had proposed this idea of *Soyuz* flying free to get photos and video of undocking, I felt NASA would say no to the plan, but surprisingly, they had approved it. We were all approaching sunset, and there were no lights on *Soyuz* or on the *Mir* docking port, so Anatoly would have needed to hold for forty-five minutes until the next sunrise if he couldn't dock before dark. The *Soyuz* didn't have enough fuel to do that, so he would have had to do an emergency deorbit back to Earth in *Soyuz*, and the *Mir* station would have been lost. Luckily, Anatoly was able to redock, and *Mir* was preserved. The photo stunt was never repeated in any further Shuttle-*Mir* dockings.

We stayed in space for two more days. Then it was time for us to return to Earth. We performed the deorbit burn on July 7, 1995, from our orbit of 215-by-209 nautical miles and hit Earth's atmosphere traveling at 25,913 feet per second, Mach 25.9. We flew a normal reentry with no anomalies to the Kennedy Space Center Runway 15, touching down at 10:54:35 Eastern. This was my third landing at the shuttle runway in Florida. Our landing weight was 216,352 pounds and the speed was 201 knots at a sink rate of 1.8 feet per second. The flight duration was nine days, nineteen hours and twenty-two minutes.

After the usual post-landing reconfiguration and crew actions, we were able to disembark from *Atlantis* and walk around under our orbiter to marvel at its good condition. There were many high-ranking dignitaries waiting to welcome us back, including the NASA Administrator, the head of the Russian Space Agency, and my good friend and leader Dave Leestma, the Director of Flight Crew Operations and the one who had told me I needed to do this mission. All of them were extremely pleased with the outcome of our flight.

George Abbey was also there to welcome us back, and he said to me, "No one but you could have done that, Mr. Gibson." I disagreed but appreciated the kind words from him. He had apparently always been a fan of mine all those years, and I still appreciate him to this day.

After we finished walking around the shuttle and figuratively "kicking the tires," we were about to board the crew van. The NASA photographer asked if he could shoot a photo of us in front of *Atlantis*. He said, "Give me a big thumbs up!" which we did even though I was thinking to myself how hokey it was. But after seeing the photo, I liked it. There were only four of us in the picture because the three cosmonauts were in rehab, and MS-1 Dr. Ellen Baker was helping them.

When we arrived back at the crew quarters, we received one of our best welcomes. Our immediate families were there waiting for us, and it was always a joyous meeting when we walked off the elevator onto the third floor. I was always surprised by it, though this was my fifth trip to space and back. All four of my children were there with Rhea, and the photos we took with them are treasured memories in our family.

We completed our post-flight medical exams and changed into our blue flight suits. Charlie Precourt and I represented the crew at the press conference six hours after landing. My good friend Bill Harwood asked me, "Hoot, how does it feel after this flight?"

Shuttle crew after landing. Credit: NASA

I really appreciated the softball, and I answered, "Considering the degree of difficulty of this flight, and looking at how well it turned out, it feels really good."

I was smiling for weeks after. We had another "welcome home" waiting for us back in Houston at Ellington Field when we landed our NASA airplanes, and the crew exited. I was holding my new daughter Emilee as we arrived.

We all made brief speeches and thanked the several hundred Space Center employees and friends who had turned out to welcome us back. Then we went into the usual debriefings that occupied several more weeks to wrap up the mission. Because of the large amount of press coverage of this flight, people recognized me, and for several weeks, they would walk up and shake my hand. There had also been a newspaper article with the heading, "Do you think Hoot Gibson can parallel park?" in reference to the challenging docking maneuver I had flown. This mission attracted more attention than any other flight I made. Head of Mission Operations Tommy Holloway was quoted as saying, "This mission was our finest hour." My crew and I were highly honored to be a part of it.

Crew meeting with President Clinton. Credit: NASA

We made a trip to Washington, D.C., to meet with President Bill Clinton in the Oval Office. I had all of my crew there for the event, minus Anatoly Soloviev and Nikolai Budarin, who were still aboard *Mir*. We had a very special gift for the President—a model of the *Atlantis* and *Mir* docked as we had done in orbit. It was mounted onto a base on which was written a proclamation in English and in

Russian that all ten crew members had autographed while in space. We made only two of these, the other given to Russian President Boris Yeltsin. Our time in the Oval Office was very short, however, considering how far we had traveled for it. NASA didn't allow us to bring spouses to the event, though that had been the previous standard for presidential meetings, claiming it was an excessive travel expense. The NASA administrator at the time was particularly unsympathetic to his employees and had been previously quoted saying, "I don't give a goddamn about anybody's career." This was all occurring while he was giving the Russian space agency $400 million for the "privilege" of us docking with *Mir*.

This was my only White House visit that excluded the spouses from the event, both for my missions as well as my wife's. Vice President Al Gore was with us for the ceremony, and I believe he felt sorry that our time was cut so short, so he suggested we go to his office in the White House and talk for a while. We spent more than half an hour in his office and enjoyed our time with him.

Rhea had been ready to leave NASA after her third mission in 1993 but stayed on because I had been promoted to chief astronaut. Then I was assigned to the *Mir* docking, and we remained even longer, but she was eager to return to her hometown of Murfreesboro, Tennessee. Leestma asked me to be his deputy, a job I did for one year after STS-71, and he was a great leader. I really enjoyed working with him. After that, Abbey offered me the position of chief astronaut again, but Rhea and I both had already decided to retire from the astronaut corps.

I left NASA in November 1996 to fly as a pilot for Southwest Airlines. I thought I would only do that for a year or two, but there was not much need for an astronaut, a test pilot, or an aeronautical engineer in Murfreesboro, so it would end up being my career for the next ten years.

19

During my time in Houston, I was also involved in other aviation pursuits that had little to do with NASA. I had always been fascinated by racing airplanes because they were fast and sleek. I guess I've always been an adrenaline junkie. I admired the famous racing pilot Roscoe Turner and his quote, "There's no excuse for an airplane unless it's fast!" I can remember riding my bike in my youth to the library in Long Beach to read for the hundredth time, *Racing Planes That Made History* by David Cooke. Most racing planes were long and sleek and looked fast just sitting still. Growing up, I knew I wanted to be a race pilot as much as I wanted to be a fighter and test pilot. I couldn't afford a racing P-51 Mustang, but in 1983, I found a homebuilt racer called a Cassutt that I could afford. It was a type of airplane that was raced in the Reno Air Races in the Formula One Class—planes with a maximum engine size of 100 horsepower—but these were capable of more than 200 mph. I drove to Baton Rouge, Louisianna, in a rental truck and took the airplane apart to move it to my house in Houston and begin a restoration that took half a year. The airplane was thirteen years old when I bought it in the summer of 1983, and it needed to be rebuilt. I had the fuselage out in my driveway, and Rhea and I put our baby son, Paul, in the seat and he tried to chew on the control stick.

My experimental homebuilt airplane. Credit: Hoot Gibson

By the end of 1983, I had assembled the airplane. I had run the engine a number of times in my driveway and was getting close to being able to fly it for the first time. I put it all together in the driveway so I could get photos of it after I had completed the rework and painting. It looked good all put together.

I was having a drink with another astronaut and George Abbey one evening, and the astronaut asked me about my experimental plane. I tried to answer quietly, but Abbey's ears pricked up, and he asked, "And just when were you *planning* on flying this experimental airplane, Mr. Gibson?"

I knew what I needed to say, especially since I was about a month out from my first launch. So I answered, "Oh, probably not until after my space flight."

My racer completed. Credit: Hoot Gibson

Abbey said, “I think that would be a good idea.” It wasn’t a direct order, but it was obvious that I had just been grounded from test-flying my Cassutt.

A friend of mine kept a Great Lakes biplane at Clover Field in Friendswood, Texas, and invited me to store my plane in his hangar. He said that Clover was a fun airport full of experimental airplanes and aerobatic biplanes and that I should be there. After the debriefing for my space flight, and at the end of February, I was finally ready to move the Cassutt to Clover Field. I hauled the disassembled airplane in several trips using a borrowed trailer to get it to the airport. I finished assembling it on Leap Day, February 29, 1984, and then logged 0.3 hours of time doing taxi checks. My dear friend, John Kiker, was there the next day to witness my first flight.

That flight, March 1, 1984, was a very short one, only 0.1 hours. I lifted off from the runway and pulled the nose up slightly, and the airplane overshot the pitch angle I wanted. I eased the nose down, and then it overshot in that direction.

I said to myself, "I have an unstable airplane!" and decided to land immediately. I turned downwind and briefly tested slow flight to about 100 mph to make sure I wouldn't stall during landing. That was the whole flight.

I met a large group of pilots and made many friends during my time at Clover Field. It was easy to get a formation together and go fly. We did local air shows, and I was able to do some air racing at some of these, so I finally became an air race pilot. These races would factor into my racing at Reno many years later.

One of the first pilots I met at Clover was Ray Lancaster, who had a Rutan VariEze that he had built at home. Ray was a member of the Greatest Generation, having served as a fighter pilot in World War II flying P-47 Thunderbolts and P-51 Mustangs. He scored three kills against German fighter pilots, two Messerschmitt Bf-109s and one Focke-Wulf FW-190. He and I were both combat fighter pilots,

Ray Lancaster during World War II. Credit: Ray Lancaster Photo Collection, 1944

so we became good friends from the moment we met.

Ray was living proof of the adage, "fighter pilots never grow up." Several times, I remember sitting in my kitchen early on a Saturday morning drinking coffee, and the peace and quiet would suddenly be broken by the sound of Ray's VariEze buzzing me at 200 mph right over my rooftop, the smoke system he had rigged into the plane delivering a dense trail. Rhea would look at me and say, "Don't look now, Hoot, but you just got smoked!"

Another pilot I met right away at Clover Field was Bruce Bohannon. He was very much into competitive aerobatics competitions and owned a Pitts Special that he let me fly. Its registration number was N35PJ, and Bruce delighted in calling it "Piece o' Junk" based on the last two letters. I had not flown a Pitts Special before, and it was a hot rod! It wasn't nearly as fast as my Cassutt, but it was extremely maneuverable and aerobatic. It could be a handful on landing because it was quick to deviate from where it should be, and it could be a bit slow to correct. My Cassutt, on the other hand, was both quick to deviate and correct, so it was easier to fly.

Bruce became a very good friend over the years. I had converted him away from aerobatic competitions and into the air racing scene. He went on to be very successful in racing and set aviation world records.

Clover Field was a real "Boy's Ranch" for pilots. I met a circle of friends that lasted for decades, and I was able to fly a great many airplanes there. I was able to fly Lancaster's VeriEze, Bruce Bohannon's Pitts Special, a Great Lakes biplane, a Smith Miniplane, a Taylor Titch, and many more experimental planes, more than two dozen in all. We could be found at the airport nearly every weekend and during the week for special events and could put on an air show with very short notice. These were pilots who were there for the pleasure of aviation, whether that meant aerobatics, racing, or dogfighting. I flew in many dogfights from Clover Field, usually against Pitts Specials that could outturn my Cassutt, but I was able to use speed and the vertical dimension, so I rarely ever "shot them down," and rarely ever got "shot down."

Lancaster, because of his experience and age, was our de facto "commanding officer," and had the respect of all the aviators who flew out of our airfield. He was always there on weekends but ran his own insurance agency during the week. Years later, a P-51 Mustang was decorated in the markings of his "Galveston Gal" from World War II, and photos were taken with Ray and that airplane to imitate his photos from World War II.

Ray Lancaster and the Clover Airport women pilots. Credit: Hoot Gibson

There were also a number of women pilots who flew with us at Clover, and they were just like the boys. They were flying for the fun of flying and were fond of experimental and aerobatic airplanes. And they were good pilots. One of them, Teresa Stokes, was also a well-known wing-walker on Gene Soucey's biplane, the Show Cat.

She flew in countless air shows over the years. Kathy Galassini also flew with us, and I sent her out in my Cassutt several times. She really enjoyed flying a hot rod like that. She had flown hundreds of flight hours doing pipeline patrol missions in a Cessna, but the Cassutt gave her a much higher degree of excitement. She later became an airline pilot and captain. Another "Clover Girl" was Maggie Asher, who came to us a few years later but caught the bug and had her own American Champion Decathlon aerobatic airplane.

Constructing my new wing design. Credit: Rhea Seddon

I made many modifications to my Cassutt over the years to increase speed and performance. Since it's an experimental airplane, it's legal to make minor changes to it. I took advantage of that and added a new engine cowling, wing fairings, wheel pants, propellor, and spinners. Three years after the first flight, I started building a new wing for the plane. The original wing was a wooden, constant-chord, low-aspect-ratio wing using a 1930s airfoil. I knew I could design and build a more efficient wing with a low-drag laminar flow airfoil. I built the wing in my garage using a foam core and a carbon

My final airplane configuration. Credit: Hoot Gibson

fiber main spar with fiberglass for the rest of the structure. Over many years, I added an improved engine cowling and a new canopy. I've been fond of saying I've flown the airplane for more than forty years, and I still enjoy flying what I call my "Gibson Cassutt Racer."

I was able to do some actual sanctioned air racing when Bruce Bohannon asked if I would race his Cassutt racer at Reno, Nevada, and Casper, Wyoming. The Reno Air Races were the modern-day embodiment of the Thompson Trophy Races of earlier years, and I was thrilled to fly there in 1989 in the Formula One class. I raced against former astronaut Deke Slayton, one of the original Mercury Seven Astronauts, and I finished in third place in the Silver Category.

In July 1990, six of us were asked to fly a demonstration of a Formula One air race for the annual air show at the New Braunfels, Texas airport. It was not a sanctioned race, and all the pilots were friends I had known for years. Deke Slayton was one of the racers, along with Bruce Bohannon, Don Davila from my Clover Field gang, Rocky Jones, whom I raced against at Cleveland and Reno, and Jim

Miller. I had then been assigned as the commander of STS-46, which was scheduled more than two years later, and I didn't think there would be any problem with my participation since we normally assigned crews only a year prior to launch. The race was start-flagged on Saturday, July 7, 1990 by none other than Tom Cassutt, the designer of our air racers, and I was in the lead from the start. In the third lap, disaster struck when Rocky Jones crashed into my right wing as we were passing one of the race pylons. He had come from behind me, and I never saw him when he hit my wing. I thought I had blown my engine when I heard the noise of the impact, so I immediately pulled left inside the racecourse, shut off my magnetos to kill my engine, and began to maneuver for a dead stick landing. I went into a hard right turn, and that was when I noticed that my right wingtip was shredded. I immediately realized that this was the reason for the noise and not a blown engine, so I flipped the magnetos back on and recovered.

None of the racers had radios, so I had no idea that Rocky had hit me or that the race was cancelled. I landed and shut down my airplane, and Don Davila hurried over to talk to me.

I opened my canopy and said, "Don, what happened out there?"

He replied, "So you didn't know that Rocky hit you and he went in?"

I said I didn't know that and put my hands over my face for several moments. Rocky's left wing had disintegrated when he'd hit me, resulting in a fatal crash. He had been a new friend after the Cleveland and Reno races, and I was devastated. Our simple little demonstration race had turned tragic in an instant. The very strong wing I had built, and my guardian angel, had saved me.

The National Transportation Safety Board dispatched an investigator immediately, and I had to stay in New Braunfels to be interviewed. I wasn't able to go back to Houston until late Sunday. My airplane was not flyable, so it remained in a hangar in New Braunfels.

Wing damage after the midair collision. Credit: Teresa Stokes

When I arrived home Sunday evening, Rhea told me that I was to call Chief Astronaut Dan Brandenstein immediately. When I dialed Dan, he said, "Meet me in my office in 15 minutes." He told me he was going to fire me and that I should start looking for another job. I didn't argue with him and simply left for home. Once I was there, I got to thinking that the punishment was a bit excessive, so I called him. I told him I had been a loyal and hard-working astronaut for many years and felt I had contributed much to the space program. I asked him to reconsider his decision to fire me. I finished by saying, "I don't need an answer right now, but you could ground me indefinitely and make it permanent later on, if that's how you feel."

I asked our administrative leader to put me on leave for the next week because I was so devastated. I drove back over to New Braunfels on Monday to get my airplane and bring it back to Houston. I borrowed Don Davila's airplane trailer and Bruce Bohannon's Suburban, went back and disassembled my plane, and started driving back to Houston. On the car's radio heading home, I heard that another astronaut named Dave was being grounded for three months for safety violations, and that I was being grounded for a year and removed from command of STS-46. I was so pleased to hear that I wasn't being fired that the news was both good and bad at the same time.

It turned out that NASA had planned to publish a press release that Monday grounding Dave and decided I could be lumped in on the same announcement. This way, NASA would only look bad once instead of twice. NASA rushed my grounding and then needed to backtrack later after they decided my grounding was excessive. I was saved from being fired because Brandenstein had spoken with Mike Coats, another Navy mission commander, who had told Dan, "You can't keep Dave and fire Hoot! That makes no sense at all."

Dave had several years of safety exceedances, and I was only guilty of one apparent violation of our rule against high-risk activities while assigned to a shuttle crew. While air racing was listed as high-risk, my mid-air collision had happened two years before STS-46 was scheduled to launch. It wasn't the intention of the high-risk rule that astronauts couldn't water ski or participate in any activity for two years or more prior to their mission, and crew assignments were officially made one year prior to launch. I was grounded from T-38 flying, removed from command of STS-46, and fired as safety branch chief because I failed to act in a safe manner.

Honestly, I didn't mind losing the command of the tethered satellite mission because it had not been my favorite flight. I resolved to work diligently after I was grounded and went to work as the astronaut office representative to the Program Requirements Control Board and the Space Shuttle Program Office. Dan Germany was the head of the shuttle program office and had asked me several times to be his astronaut assistant. I very much enjoyed both of those assignments, and six months after my grounding, I received a letter from the chief astronaut saying that because of my excellent work, I was being quietly returned to flight status. At the same time, the high-risk rule was rewritten to say what it should have said in the first place: *When assigned to a shuttle crew, and within one year of launch, no high-risk recreational activities are allowed.* I was then assigned to command the very next flight, STS-47, a joint mission with the Japanese Space Agency called Spacelab-J. It became obvious that NASA had excessively rushed my year of grounding and should have thought it over more carefully. I felt partly vindicated, and after I finished flying STS-47 and was promoted to the position of chief astronaut, completely exonerated.

After I repaired my Cassutt, I did more flight testing and saw that the new wing I'd built had improved its speed and climb capabilities. I flew it to an altitude of 25,000 feet on one of the test flights and afterward saw that the world record for "Altitude in Horizontal Flight" was only 25,000 feet. I did more testing to altitude, and then on January 31, 1991, I flew to 27,040 feet, setting a new world record for piston engine aircraft in international category C-1A. I had to fly out over the Gulf of Mexico ten miles before I could go above 10,000 feet without certain avionics in my airplane, but I had a barograph and video recording to document the record. Some years later, after an engine rebuild adding some of Bruce Bohannon's racing cylinders, I broke the World 100-Kilometer Closed-Course Speed Record. I flew from the Murfreesboro, Tennessee, airport to the McMinnville airport and back in sixteen minutes, twenty-one seconds, coming in under my good friend Jim Miller's record that had stood for nearly twenty years. With a smile, I tell pilots to think of my Cassutt like the SR-71 Blackbird since both aircraft have set world altitude and speed records.

20

One of the pilots I met at Clover Field became a good friend of mine for many years and opened a door to another realm of aviation for me. Jim Robinson had a Pitts Special at Clover, but in 1987, he started collecting surplus jets. He first acquired a T-33 Shooting Star, and I enjoyed flying with him in it. I had flown a Calspan NT-33A during Test Pilot School, configured as a variable stability airplane, so Jim's T-33 was not totally new to me. Next, he bought an F-86 Sabre Jet, which was just cool, but then he bought a Russian MiG-15, an iconic jet fighter from the Korean War. I was fascinated with the idea of flying a MiG, so I asked him if I could fly it. After studying the minimal flight manual, I was checked out on it in 1988 while I flew the MiG with another pilot, Ed Schneider, flying chase in the F-86. The FAA had already signed me off for both the MiG-15 and the MiG-17 because they were so similar, though I never got the chance to fly a MiG-17.

This was the beginning of my new participation as an air show pilot in the MiG-15. I met a former Navy fighter pilot named Chuck Scott who had flown the F-8 Crusader in my squadron, VF-111,

The first MIG-15. Credit: Chris Henry

before they transitioned to the F-4B Phantom. He had made the final VF-111 cruise in the F-8 the year before I had gone to Vietnam with the squadron. Chuck and I became an air show team and flew a simulated Korean War dogfight, him in the F-86 and me in the MiG. I had a smoke system in the MiG, so of course I always got "shot down" in our dogfights, turned on the smoke, and landed.

We flew in air shows in Texas and at the huge Experimental Aircraft Association Fly-In at Oshkosh, Wisconsin. The theme at Oshkosh in 1989 was "Jennies to Jets," and we were invited to fly our dogfight routine in the show. An amusing story from that year was that there was a contingent of Russians invited to attend, and after I was "shot down" in our show, I asked one of them, "How did you like our dogfight?"

Not surprisingly, he showed me a brief frown, and then said, "Not so much."

He was an interesting-looking Russian, extremely muscled and fit, and he told me he wasn't a pilot but had a habit of "showing up unannounced" in places. I was convinced he was KGB through and through. He probably could have killed me with his bare hands.

It was fascinating to fly the MiG-15. It had a centrifugal flow turbojet engine that had evolved from the British Rolls Royce Nene engine. The British government sold fifty-five of the Nene engines to Russia in 1946 with the requirement they wouldn't be used for military purposes and trained seventeen Russian engineers on how to maintain and repair them. Joseph Stalin, the head of the Soviet Union at the time, was incredulous that the British would sell him the engines and was reported to have said, "What fool will sell us his secrets?" The Russians reneged on their promise and reverse-engineered the Nene engine to produce the Klimov RD-45 followed by the Klimov VK-1 for the MiG-15. The MiG-15 was an unpleasant surprise for the allies in the Korean War and had better performance in some areas than the F-86 Sabre Jet, notably at higher altitudes. The centrifugal flow engine was slow to spool up from idle rpm to 100 percent power, which had to be carefully managed. The steering on the ground for the MiG-15 was done using differential braking and was powered by an air bottle using a brake lever on the control stick. With the rudder pedals centered, activating the brake lever applied both the right and left brakes, while depressing one rudder pedal and the brake lever resulted in only the left or right brake for ground steering. The air bottle was filled before every flight since there wasn't an onboard air compressor, so once I started taxiing, I was gradually depleting the brake air supply. I needed to be judicious with the brakes because I needed them not only to take off, but also after landing.

The systems in the plane were not refined to the extent that I was accustomed to in Navy jets. For example, with a hydraulic failure in the F-4 Phantom, I could "blow down" the landing gear by putting the gear lever in the "down" position and pulling out on the gear handle to connect the air bottle to the gear down lines. In the MiG-15, I had to turn the valve manually to open the air bottle that connected to the landing gear. There were several air valves in the MiG cockpit for various functions whereas Navy airplanes were more user-friendly. The flight controls for the elevator, ailerons, and the rudder were simple and purely mechanical, so no hydraulics were involved. While the control forces could be fairly high at airspeeds over 350 knots, or 400 mph, the MiG-15 was a pleasure to fly, and I was impressed by its turn capability at 250 knots.

The only emergency takeoff I ever made was in the MiG-15. I taxied out on a very hot summer day in Houston, and when I arrived at the runway, my "Fire" indicator light came on. I didn't see any smoke or evidence of fire, so I taxied back to the hangar where crew chief Mike Peters told me it wasn't unusual to have a fire light after driving downwind all the way to the runway, and it would clear once I was airborne and had some airflow. I went back to Runway 22 and took off, and about the time I was airborne at 130 knots, the fire light went out.

Chuck Scott and I flew a great many dogfight routines in air shows for two years while Jim Robinson continued to buy more jet fighters. He acquired a second F-86 and an F-104B Starfighter, a Hawker Hunter, a Douglas A-4 Skyhawk, and a de Havilland Vampire. He named his collection the "Combat Jets Flying Museum" and kept them in a large hangar at Houston Hobby Airport.

I called Jim one day and said, "I really like the MiG-15, but you need to buy me a MiG-21."

He chuckled and said, "Yeah, right."

I didn't say anything else about it, but a month or two later, he called me and said, "I just bought you your MiG-21."

I was ecstatic! The MiG-21 was the fighter I'd trained to fly against in the Vietnam War, and it was an incredible jump in performance over the MiG-15 and 17, a Mach 2-capable air superiority fighter.

Our MiG-21 was a PF model, NATO designation "Fishbed D,"

and it looked like it was flying supersonic while sitting on the ground. It was the smallest 17,000-pound airframe that could be wrapped around a Tumansky R-11 afterburning turbojet engine with more than 13,600 pounds of thrust in afterburner, giving it a 0.8 thrust-to-weight ratio at takeoff. It was the first Soviet fighter capable of flying twice the speed of sound and was designed to be a rapidly climbing interceptor. It didn't carry a lot of fuel, so the flight time was relatively

Combat jet MIG-21. Credit: Hoot Gibson

short, but that was the nature of a point defense interceptor. The designers, Mikoyan and Gurevich, designed it with small, ultra-thin wings of 4.2 percent thickness at the wing's root and 5 percent at the tip, but it had a cool delta-wing planform.

With the relatively small and thin wings, the MiG-21 had a fast final approach speed of 175 knots with full flaps, and with inoperative flaps, the landing speed would be 190 knots, around 219 mph. It had a drag chute to counter this issue, but it was so challenging to repack it, I rarely ever used it. The MiG-21 did have an interesting brake arrangement, however. It used an air bottle the same way that the MiG-15 operated with a brake lever on the control stick, but with a brake on the nosewheel as well as on the two mains. The nosewheel brake could be selected on or off with a lever on the instrument panel. It was more difficult to steer the plane on landing rollout with the nosewheel brake selected, and the fast touchdown speed ate up a lot of runway on landing.

The MiG-21 was the world's original lightweight fighter, and it was a pleasure to fly, similar in several ways to the NASA T-38 that I'd flown for years. It needed to be at high cruise altitudes of more than 37,000 feet due to its limited fuel load—thinner air caused less drag, thus preserving fuel—and it cruised around Mach 0.85 like the T-38. Even its fast approach speed was similar. I only went supersonic in the MiG-21 once after I had gone way out over the Gulf of Mexico, where I accelerated to Mach 1.2, then headed back inland. I was impressed at how easily the MiG-21 passed through Mach 1 in full afterburner. The F-4 Phantom and F-14 Tomcat accelerated rapidly to about Mach 0.95, then the transonic drag rise took effect and the airspeed hung up briefly until the planes exceeded the sound barrier. But the sleek and streamlined MiG-21 sailed right through Mach 1 and beyond.

There was a maneuver that I enjoyed doing in the MiG-21—a 360-degree horizontal turn right in front of the grandstands. It was similar to what the Air Force F-16 would do in air shows, flying a 9-G turn. The F-16 was flying so fast, that to be able to pull that many Gs, the turn radius was huge. In the MiG, I flew my horizontal turns at only 300 knots in full afterburner and was at a high angle of attack with a lot of buffeting, but I was able to do the turn in half the radius that the F-16 could pull. The MiG would try to depart slightly in the turn, so I used the rudder to keep the nose going straight ahead.

The other maneuver that the MiG did impressively was a full-afterburner climb. I did a "drag race" at Oshkosh against the F-104B

Starfighter from 500 feet over the runway to 10,000 feet of altitude, and both airplanes were impressive. The F-104 series was so high-performance, the plane was called "the missile with a man in it," so I was genuinely uncertain who would win that race. We agreed to start at a speed of 350 knots. I called, "Afterburner now," over the radio, and we both went to full power. I accelerated to 400 knots and went vertical first, pulling ahead while the F-104 was still accelerating to the 500 knots it required to enter the climb. We did the race several days in a row at the air show, and the result was always the same—it was a dead heat, a tie every time we flew the vertical race as we both consistently passed the threshold at 10,000 feet at exactly the same time.

I was able to fly Jim Robinson's jets for four years, and then he decided to change direction. He wanted to marry and settle down and felt that the airplanes were getting in his way. He decided to donate all of them to the Experimental Aircraft Association in Oshkosh. Jim had accumulated nine jets by then. It was a sad day to be flying all of them up to Wisconsin in early 1992. I flew the two MiGs there and in July was able to demonstrate the MiG-21 at the huge fly-in.

I learned later that NASA administrator Dan Goldin was there for the air show, and when the announcer said, "Here goes Hoot Gibson flying the MiG-21," I heard that Goldin had said, "Hey, we have an astronaut named Hoot Gibson!"

Not wanting to blow my cover, Tom Poberezny, the EAA President, simply replied, "Yes, we've heard of him." I was just under two months from commanding my fourth space shuttle flight, and it might have been risky to be flying a Russian MiG that close to my launch date. Luckily, nothing ever came out of that conversation.

I didn't fly MiGs for a few years, but then I was asked to do the initial flight test of a two-seat MiG-21UM in 1996. I went to Quincy, Illinois, and met Don Kirlin to do the first checkout flight of his MiG.

That was where I first met Mike Keenum, and it was there that he asked me to race his Sea Fury, which would later become Riff Raff. This would lead to a friendship of more than twenty-six years.

I remember the test flight in Kirlin's MiG because of several malfunctions. The first challenge was the radio. Though the receiver was working fine, the push-to-talk button wasn't working, so I was unable to transmit. The Quincy Regional Airport was normally an uncontrolled field, meaning there was no control tower, but for the weekend fly-in, an Air Force mobile tower had been put into place along with Air Force controllers. I talked with them, and they were in favor of letting me fly without a radio transmitter because I could monitor their transmissions, and they could give me various light signals. I briefed them that I would be ready for takeoff when I got to the runway and would leave the airport vicinity to test the MiG, then return in an overhead break pattern and make a full-stop landing.

The other anomaly was the plane had no oxygen in the tank, so I said I would stay below 10,000 feet. I would simply leave my oxygen mask supply hose disconnected so I could still wear the mask but would only be breathing cabin air. I had set myself up for yet another emergency takeoff.

I left without incident and flew the MiG for about thirty minutes with everything working fine. I came back to the airfield and entered the overhead pattern and did about a 4-G break turn to a downwind leg abeam Runway 04. I extended the landing gear and wing flaps, and that's when I started smelling electrical smoke. A few seconds later, the smoke entered the cockpit, and it was thickening rapidly. Because of my poor judgment in deciding to fly a faulty airplane, I couldn't even share my misery with the control tower or anyone else. Additionally, since I had no oxygen, I was breathing ever-thickening smoke through my disconnected mask hose. I was expediting my landing by then.

On my short final approach, the smoke was thick enough that I was leaning forward to get closer to the windshield to see clearly. It was at that point I thought of my wife's pet sentiment, "Why do you keep risking your life doing dangerous things?"

Peering through all the smoke, I said to myself, "Maybe she's right this time."

I landed uneventfully, turned off the runway at the first available taxiway, stopped, and immediately opened the canopy to breathe some fresh air. I had the taste of electrical smoke the remainder of the day and found myself asking people, "Do I smell like smoke to you?"

The reason for the electrical fire was traced to the rear seat periscope that was supposed to extend above the instructor seat to provide a better forward field of view. It had jammed and stalled the electric motor that had then burned and produced the smoke. It was never repaired, only disconnected and unused after that.

I flew the MiG-21UM for about four years after the incident along with another pilot named Doug, and we were a hot item on the air show circuit. Doug was also a former Navy fighter pilot and a captain with a major airline. He and I flew the MiG at many air shows ranging from Virginia to Monterrey, California, and it was an impressive and fast airplane.

The 500-liter drop tank on the underside of the jet was a source of disagreement between Doug and me. It was cumbersome to remove and reattach, so it was left on the airplane for shows, but it limited the maximum airspeed to 540 knots. The MiG had so much power in afterburner, it could blow through 550 knots with ease, so I had to work to stay below the drop tank speed limit. Doug did not let that limitation bother him and routinely went well over 550 knots in air shows. I told the airplane's owner, Don Kirlin, that it probably wasn't my place to rein in Doug about the speed, but as the owner, he should talk with him about it. I don't believe that discussion ever happened.

At shows, Doug would also fly the blind-side pass, a maneuver often performed by the Navy's Blue Angels—fly low over the grandstands from behind and startle everyone. The Navy was allowed to do that, but we were not military and weren't authorized to overfly people on the ground. The FAA representative at the air show would pull Doug aside after he did that maneuver and explain this to him, so Doug would proclaim innocence and promise not to do it again, then he'd do it at a different show with a different FAA representative. They eventually figured out what he was doing, and I was shown an internal letter that stated they were keeping an eye on us because the issue kept happening when Doug was flying. I was a bit annoyed because I was being lumped into the FAA's scrutiny. Doug was known for pushing it in the MiG, and he had an incident where he narrowly avoided a tragic end. He was flying his MiG-17 in an air show and tied the world record for the lowest pass ever in recovering from a "split-S." It was only by the smallest margin that Doug survived that event.

In August 1999, Don Kirlin called me and asked, "Do you want to do some fun flying with the MiG-21UM?"

I asked him to share more, and he said, "Mach 1 at 1,000 feet making runs against a Canadian Navy guided missile frigate."

I immediately thought to myself, *Mach 1 at 1,000 feet? Will the plane even hold together at that speed?* But I kept that to myself and told Don instead that I just couldn't get away the day it was supposed to happen, so he said Doug would do the flights.

Later that month, Kirlin called me and said, "Hoot, we lost Doug."

I was in shock and asked Don, "What about Louie?" Our crew chief, Louis Ihnen, often flew with us in the MiG-21when we took it to air shows. Fortunately, he had not been riding along in the flight against the Canadian Navy ship. "What was Doug's configuration for the flight?"

Don said, "I knew you were going to ask me that. He had the drop tank on the airplane."

I spoke to Ihnen sometime later, and he told me that Doug was doing a practice run from Victoria, B.C., at 12,000 feet flying toward the Navy ship. At thirteen miles out, he was to do a 4-G turn so they could see different aspects of the MiG on their radar, but during the manuever, the MiG had disintegrated. It appeared that Doug had attempted to eject but didn't survive, and he was lost at sea. Louie told me the ship had tracked the MiG at a groundspeed of 680 knots at 12,000 feet, which meant Doug was probably flying the plane at just over 600 knots of airspeed. That was faster than the MiG-21UM airframe limit and well above the drop tank limit of 540 knots.

Doug's lack of respect for aircraft limits apparently cost him his life. We will never know what truly caused the airplane to break up in that final turn, but it may well have been due to the drop tank failing. I have used this tragic story many times when I talk about aviation safety. Airplanes have limitations, and it isn't just to spoil all your fun. It was a tragic case, and I've wished many times that we could have had that discussion with Doug to rein in his flying.

21

For more than five years, I raced my Cassutt. My time in the Reno Air Races in 1989 led to an invitation to race a Hawker Sea Fury in the Unlimited Class at Reno, a dream come true. I had been asked so many times during interviews, "You have done so many things in aviation as a fighter pilot, a test pilot, and an astronaut. Is there something you haven't done that you would like to do?"

I routinely answered, "I would love to race in the Unlimited Class at the Reno Air Races."

There was no way I could afford the type of racing plane needed for that class which included mostly surplus fighters from World War II like P-51 Mustangs, F-4U Corsairs, and Sea Furies. So, when I met Mike Keenum at an air show in the summer of 1996, and he asked if I would be interested in racing his Sea Fury, I jumped at the opportunity. I was required to get an FAA authorization from a long-time friend, Dennis Sanders, because the Sea Fury is faster than 250 knots and has more than 800 horsepower. After flying a checkout with me in the two-seat Sea Fury, I started flying Mike Keenum's single-seat model in August.

The Sea Fury is a large, powerful airplane with an empty weight of more than 9,200 pounds. The stock Bristol Centaurus engine of 2,450 horsepower had been replaced for racing with a Wright R-3350 with close to 3,000 horsepower. This was a supercharged, 18-cylinder twin-row radial engine which made the airplane significantly faster than stock. I was new to that type of plane, so Art Vance, the Unlimited Class president, said he wanted me to have at least eighty flight hours in Mike's Sea Fury before he would allow me to race at Reno. The plane was located at the Greater Kankakee Airport in Kankakee, Illinois, so I would fly into Rockford, Illinois, on weekends, fly the Sea Fury all weekend, then return to Houston to continue working for NASA all week. The flying had been progressing well, and I was returning to the Kankakee airport on August 24, 1996, at the end of a two-hour flight when I faced a serious problem.

I was flying downwind, paralleling the runway behind a slower Cessna, and I was catching up to him. I made a 360-degree turn to get some spacing. He was flying a long, straight-in approach to land, so I had to extend my downwind in addition. I was just reaching for the landing gear handle when the engine suddenly stopped. I immediately turned toward the airport, but because of the Cessna, I was too far out and had no chance of reaching the runway. I made a mistake and tried to lower the landing gear, but I was forced to the ground, specifically into a soybean field, so quickly that my landing gear couldn't extend, which was fortunate for me. If my gear had come down, the rough ground would have flipped the plane onto its back, and I likely would not have survived the crash. As it happened, the Sea Fury slid on its belly for about fifty yards and stopped, one of the shortest landings I've ever made. It was another brush with death, and I've been allergic to soybeans ever since.

I was thoroughly deflated. It was now impossible for us to participate in the Reno Air Races that year. Another pilot and I returned to the airplane the next morning. We removed the oil dipstick, which revealed there was no oil in the thirty-gallon oil tank. It turned out that a three-inch-wide oil line had detached, and with an oil pressure of 90 psi, it had rapidly emptied, seizing the engine. Mike Keenum, the owner of the airplane, was very understanding. "First of all," he said, "you're okay, and that's what matters."

We set our sights on the following year to race at Reno, and Mike contracted with a mechanic to rebuild the airplane. Everything was looking good until one week before the 1997 races, when Mike was flying. As he was shutting down the engine, the "chip light" flicked on, indicating there was metal in the oil. When we removed the oil screens, they were full of metal parts, so Reno 1997 was also out of the question. We were back to square one. After another engine rebuild, we would be ready for Reno 1998 with a new name and a flashy paint scheme. Mike's wife, Kay, came up with the name Riff Raff because it described who we were—the new guys, the rookies.

Hawker Sea Fury racer "Riff Raff". Credit: Hoot Gibson

In the summer of 1998, Mike and I went to Reno for a new training course, the Pylon Racing Seminar, which came to be known as "Rookie School." It was taught by experienced Unlimited Class racers and involved classroom fundamentals and representative air race scenarios flown on the racecourse. We practiced the race starts, which involved a line-abreast formation of nine airplanes, and how to properly pass on the course. We felt it was extremely beneficial for new air racers and recommended that it be made mandatory, which it was for 1999 and subsequent years. After all, Mike and I had graduated from the course, so it was like the old Navy expression, "I'm aboard, so pull up the ladder!" Every new race pilot after that was required to attend the course before racing.

After several years of disappointment, we finally made it to Reno for the races, and I was able to qualify for the first time and race in the Unlimited Class. We had many difficulties getting the engine to run at the very high power levels we needed for racing. The airplane had been set up, but some of the systems were inadequate since I was running full throttle and trying to get every possible amount of horsepower. I was running water-methanol injection and a water spray system for the oil cooler, and all of these needed to be refined. It was fortunate that Pete Law, a former Lockheed Aircraft employee and expert on these big radial engines, was on staff at the races. He managed to get us to an acceptable condition, and I finished in the middle of the pack, fifth in the Silver final race at an average speed of 376.1 mph. The eight fastest airplanes were in the Gold race, the second eight in the Silver, and the final eight in the Bronze. We were pleased with our finish given it was our first year—off to a good start!

We raced for nearly every year for ten years through 2009. Mike Keenum sponsored the venture himself, and he impressed me. He'd grown up a poor kid in Cicero, Illinois, graduated from high school, and enlisted in the Air Force. He served in Thailand as a crew chief working on F-105 Thunderchief fighter/bombers during the Vietnam war, graduated from college on the GI Bill, and then earned his Doctor of Physical Therapy degree. He founded his own company, Orthosport Physical Therapy, and grew the business into twelve clinics across Chicago and Indianapolis. He was a true self-made man and an excellent pilot. He had planned to race Riff Raff himself, but Kay had asked him to find someone else. That decision became my open door into Unlimited Air Racing. I joked that they needed someone expendable, someone they could never become attached to, and that was me.

The airplane became faster every year because Mike put an incredible amount of rework into improving the streamlining of the Sea Fury. He cleaned up the surfaces on the fuselage and modified a smaller canopy, and our speeds rose from 383.8 mph in 1998 to 447.2 mph in 2009.

I had always wanted to be in the Gold final race and often said I'd take last place in the Gold over first place in the Silver. I ran in

Mike Keenum wishing me luck. Credit: Lou Ann Baker

the Silver final our first two years and then made it into the Gold final in 2002 and five more times after. The Gold final was the culmination of a week of air racing and was the final event of race week. The Gold racers lined up across the grandstands, and the crews were all introduced to the crowd prior to the race.

The announcer would call out, "Gentlemen, start your engines!" All seven or nine racers would start and then taxi in order to the runway. The pace airplane was a T-33 Shooting Star. The pace airplane had to be fast enough to bring the racers onto the course since these were the world's fastest piston-engine airplanes, so they chose a jet. Steve Hinton, an air racer himself and former Unlimited Class champion, was the pace pilot.

Unlimited Championship race start. Credit: Lou Ann Baker

We fly in a line-abreast formation on the pace plane, who leads us to the starting line and when all is ready, calls, "Gentlemen, you look good! Gentlemen, you have a race!" Then he pitches up out of the formation, staying clear of the racecourse. The pace plane

Racing Riff Raff against Jimmy Leeward. Credit: Arnold Greenwell

remains overhead during the race and joins up on any "Mayday" aircraft, looks them over, and guides them during their emergency approach and landing. The racers head for the guide pylon, then onto the eight-mile unlimited course consisting of eight pylons.

Preliminary heat races were held on Thursday, Friday, and Saturday, and championship races on Sunday. Heat races were six or seven laps, and the finals were eight. The racing is very low-altitude at around fifty to seventy feet above the ground with speeds exceeding 450 mph.

Air racing has been described as "uncooperative formation flying." Two relatively even airplanes can be flying closely together, and neither of them want the other to be near them. All passing is required to be to the outside of the lead airplane, on his right, so it requires patience to pass another racer.

Flying the unlimited class racers was an intensive task, partly because of the care and feeding that the large piston engines required. The Sea Fury had a Wright R-3350 engine of 3,350 cubic inches of displacement and close to 3,000 horsepower. It uses a gear-driven supercharger to increase the volume of air fed to the cylinders by pressurizing the induction air to two atmospheres or more. In the absence of supercharging or turbocharging, a Cessna, for example, will see thirty inches of manifold pressure, the total pressure of the induction air. I would be running Riff Raff or Race 232, another Sea Fury I raced, at sixty inches of manifold pressure. Now, all that induction air under high pressure really heats up the air, which can quickly destroy the engine, so we used water-methanol injection, also known as anti-detonation injection, to cool it. This was a 50/50 mix

Instrument panel of Sea Fury Racer 232. Credit: Hoot Gibson

of water and methanol injected into the induction air after the supercharger to lower the temperature to a survivable level for the engine.

Induction temperature, oil temperature, and torque pressure were at the top of the panel—the three most important gauges—and they had to be constantly monitored during the race. Torque is a clear indicator of horsepower. Any reduction in torque was a loss of horsepower.

Oil temperatures were critical for power, and the standard oil coolers that used air flowing over heat exchangers weren't enough. The Riff Raff had a water spray bar to augment the air flowing through the cooler. The final championship race was an eight-lap event, and it was a struggle to keep my oil temperatures under control. We had to dump whole coolers of ice water into the plane's water tank to get me through that race.

I raced Riff Raff for ten years and after finishing fifth in the Silver race in 1998, I had three fourth-place finishes in the Gold Final in 2005, '06, and '07. Mike Keenum sold the airplane in 2010. I was then asked to race Sea Fury Race 232 in 2011 and flew it at Reno for four more years. Race 232 had a Wright R-3350 engine like Riff Raff, but it was the fastest Sea Fury ever to race at Reno—even faster than the R-4360 powered Sea Furys Dreadnought and Furias, both of which had more than 4,000 horsepower. The reason Race 232 was faster was because it had a boil-off system for the oil cooler and didn't suffer any of the air drag for the oil cooler that the rest of the Sea Furys had to live with. It was an oil cooler from a Douglas DC-6 airliner immersed in a "bath" in the aft fuselage filled with a 50/50 mix of water and methanol and a system to maintain a constant coolant level. The 50/50 mix would boil at 80 degrees Celsius, the perfect temperature for the oil.

My first year to fly Race 232 at Reno was in 2011, and things looked good for us up through my qualification run. I qualified fourth out of thirty Unlimited racers at 467.1 mph, but we received bad news after a check of the oil screens and cylinder compressions following the run. Cylinder 1 had no compression, I had burned a hole in the piston, and the piston rings were destroyed. I had not seen any loss of power in my qualification run because the engine had eighteen cylinders, and the reduction in cylinder 1 was unnoticeable. The big radial engines like the R-3350 could not be replaced quickly, so I was out of the races for 2011.

Since I couldn't race, my dear friend of more than twenty years, Jimmy Leeward, moved from fifth place into fourth. I had first known him from the Experimental Aircraft Association Fly-In at Oshkosh and then through air racing. Even though we were always in heated competition during the air races, the other race pilots were always good friends. The first day of the Gold Race qualifiers was September 16, 2011, and I attended the race briefing in the morning even though I wasn't flying. After the briefing, Jimmy came up to me.

"I'm disappointed you won't be in front of me at the start of the race," he said, "because what I was planning to do was stay behind you for a lap or two, and then I was gonna *smoke* your ass!"

He probably would have done it, too, because he was flying at more than 500 mph in a highly modified P-51 Mustang, The Galloping Ghost. The plane's wings had been clipped shorter than any other racer in history, and the large air scoop under the wing had been removed. Instead, it had a boil-off system for the engine coolant radiator and oil cooling. Jimmy had said he planned to win the Gold Championship using less horsepower than any other racer because he had reduced the drag so much, and he boasted he had flown the plane faster than 510 mph.

I was in the pit area, watching the race while standing on top of an F-7F Tigercat. Jimmy was steadily passing at least one of the other racers when tragedy struck. As he was passing the number eight pylon and entering the straightaway, the plane went out of control, pitching up and rolling to the right. A trim tab control surface had fluttered and broken loose from the airplane, causing it to pitch up at 17.3 Gs, rendering him unconscious immediately. The airplane rolled to the right and entered a steep dive, crashing into a spectator area in front of the grandstands. Jimmy and ten spectators were fatally injured, and dozens were injured in the greatest catastrophe that had ever occurred at the Reno Air Races.

The races were immediately canceled for 2011 as the National Transportation Safety Board took charge of the accident investigation. I was contacted by a lawyer I had worked with for twelve years and connected him to the Reno Air Race Association to help guide them through all they would have to do in the face of this disaster. I was appointed as the Party Representative for RARA to ensure that there was an experienced race pilot taking part in the investigation. This tragedy garnered so much media attention, it was decreed that the investigation needed to be completed before the Reno Air Races could resume. The final report was issued August 27, 2012. NTSB reports take longer than one or two years to be published, so it was an intense effort to complete the report in that time frame.

The accident hit me hard because Jimmy Leeward and I had been close friends for more than twenty years. Two years before the accident, Rhea and I had flown my Bonanza to Ocala, Florida, to help Jimmy and his wife, Betty, celebrate their fiftieth wedding anniversary. Two years later, we were flying to Ocala for his funeral. Jimmy

Sea Fury Race 232 taking off in 2012. Credit: Jarrod Ulrich

had been an institution at the Reno Air Races as well as at the Oshkosh fly-in. I was asked to be the master of ceremonies for a tribute we paid to Jimmy's legacy at Oshkosh in July 2012.

There was concern about whether the races would continue after the events of 2011, but the next year, they did. In 2012, I flew Race 232 and qualified eighth out of nineteen unlimited entries at 402 mph. I was running at greatly reduced power initially because Rod Lewis, the airplane's owner, would only let me use about fifty inches of manifold pressure after our experience with the burned piston in 2011. However, as we became more comfortable with the engine, he did allow me to increase the power to sixty-five inches. The airplane had a very small bubble canopy for reduced aerodynamic drag, and I needed to have it closed for takeoff at high power, but for landing, I would open it so I could get my head higher for a better field of view.

Unlimited Championship lineup in 2012. Credit: Jarrod Ulrich

Since I was initially running with reduced power, I was racing in the middle of the pack of the unlimited class and was stuck behind both Dreadnought and Rare Bear for the first two heat races. After I got past Dreadnought, I had a battle with Rare Bear and eventually passed him for second place in the final Gold championship race on Sunday.

I was passed by Rare Bear in the Gold final race, and it looked like I would finish in third, but Stewart Dawson in Rare Bear had an engine malfunction, and I passed him with one lap to go, finishing in second place, my best finish since joining the Unlimited Class. I raced 232 two more years in 2013 and 2014, but it didn't go well either year. I qualified second out of fourteen racers in 2013 at 480.249 mph, the fastest for any Sea Fury. Then, I was racing in second place in the Friday heat race when the intake air scoop for the engine disintegrated and was sucked into the engine. That caused a massive backfire that shredded the intake scoop, portions of the aluminum cowling, and the induction system. The pieces damaged my windscreen and the airplane's horizontal tail and sliced off the GPS antenna. The engine was still running, though damaged, so I made an emergency landing and was out of the races for 2013.

The airplane was trucked to Ione, California, to be rebuilt. A carbon fiber air scoop was fabricated to prepare for the races in 2014, but I never finished my qualification run that year. I was in my qualifier, running more than 460 mph, when the sound of the engine changed, and torque started to drop, losing horsepower. I pitched up off the racecourse and passed about 2,100 feet above ground level when the engine failed completely. The airplane shook violently, and I was getting smoke in the cockpit. The torque gauge went to zero, telling me I had lost engine power. I continued my climb to 4,000 feet to convert speed into altitude and to slow to the maximum landing gear extension speed. I immediately dropped the landing gear while I still had hydraulic power. I pointed toward Runway 14 and started down. The safety chase plane flown by Dan Vance joined up on me, and Vance said, "Hoot, you're trailing a lot of smoke."

I replied, "Yes, I've got smoke in the cockpit, too." We had practiced dead-stick landings, and this was the reason. After I hit peak altitude, the airplane was literally falling out of the sky like the space shuttle. I descended the first 1,000 feet at a rate of 6,000 feet per minute and the second 1,000 feet at 6,600 feet per minute. It happens quickly in total engine failure cases, and I touched down on Runway 14 a mere one minute and thirty-nine seconds after engine failure. I secured all the switches, and a crash truck was beside me before I had stopped on the runway.

Race 232 total engine failure. Credit: Jarrod Ulrich

It was the end of the 2014 races for me and the last time I flew Race 232. We reviewed all the onboard GoPro videos, then Rod Lewis, the owner of the airplane, told me, "Hoot, I have no complaints about the way you flew," which was a relief.

Race 232 never flew again because Rod was tired of fixing it. I had raced 232 for four years, and the one year that the engine didn't fail, I won second place in the Unlimited Class.

2014 was my last year to race the big Sea Furys, and it was rewarding to have taken Riff Raff from racing in the middle of the Silver Class racers into the Gold Finals and three fourth place finishes in the Gold. I did take a second-place Gold Class win flying Race 232 in 2012. I would have one more chance to succeed at Reno, but it would have to be in an entirely different type of unlimited air racer.

22

I would have one more year to race in the Unlimited Class at Reno. Bill "Tiger" Destefani had been after me for several years to race his airplane, a highly modified P-51 Mustang named "Strega"—or "witch" in Italian—that had won the unlimited championship eleven times. I was really tempted to fly it, but I had told Tiger I was tied to my 232 race team and I couldn't just bail on them. He called me right after I raced 232 for the last time and said, "You don't have a reason not to race Strega now, do you?" So I agreed to race her in 2015.

Tiger had stopped racing it himself because he told me, "Hell, the last time I raced it, I wasn't flying it; it was flying *me*!" That being the case, he hadn't done well his last time out and really needed to stop racing the plane. He had been disqualified for a racecourse altitude violation and had also blown the engine.

Strega was the height of refinement in an Unlimited Class racer. It had clipped wings which had been highly smoothed to reduce drag to the lowest amount possible. It was using the Rolls Royce Merlin engine and for racing produced far more horsepower than it ever generated in the Mustangs that flew in World War II. The air scoop under the wing, referred to as "the doghouse," had been greatly reduced in size, too, to further cut down on drag. The air intake area was so greatly reduced that the airplane needed a water spray bar in the doghouse for both the engine coolant radiator and the oil cooler, both of which were housed in the doghouse.

Race 7 P-51 Mustang "Strega". Credit: Hoot Gibson

I went to Bakersfield to fly Strega for the first time in early August 2015 and was very pleased with its flight characteristics. I was curious what the stall speed would be with the clipped wings and was surprised to see it was as slow as 90 mph with the flaps up. The plane also needed water-methanol injection because the boost level from the supercharger was over four atmospheres at racing power settings. Strega was a pleasure to fly and was far easier to manage than the big Sea Furys.

I flew Strega about six times over several days with a stock engine in the airplane—the racing Merlin was installed before it was time to leave for Reno. The airplane was easy to fly, but the engine required constant attention and had several unique controls particularly critical while racing with the Merlin engine. The three center gages on the top row, coolant temperature, induction temperature, and oil temperature, were critical to the life of the engine (and probably mine as well) and had to be actively controlled at race power settings. There was a rotary valve control to the right side of my seat that varied the water spray bar for the radiator and oil cooler necessary to keep the engine coolant between 90 and 115 degrees Celsius. The maximum allowable oil temperature was 125 degrees, and this was controlled via the water spray bar and opening or closing the coolant door at the aft end of the doghouse. The doors were controlled with a switch on the left canopy rail. The large aluminum knob on the left side of the instrument panel controlled the amount of water-methanol anti-detonation injection and was modulated to keep the induction temperature between 50 and 75 degrees to prevent the engine from exploding at the high manifold pressures experienced during a race.

The Rolls Royce Merlin engine required a lot of attention to survive at racing horsepower. The power settings in World War II were sixty-one inches of manifold pressure and 3,000 rpm for takeoff and military rating, and sixty-seven inches at 3,000 rpm for war emergency power, limited to five minutes. I would be using 128 inches of manifold pressure, nearly double the World War II war emergency rating. After the race engine had been installed, Steven Hinton took Strega on three short flights to break in the engine, then I flew it a couple of times before departing from Bakersfield for Reno. I flew to Reno and had several days to fly on the racecourse for practice followed by a qualifying run. I asked Tiger how much power he wanted me to use, and he said "WFO! We're here to win!" (In the parlance of air racing culture, "WFO" means "wide fucking open," if you'll excuse the language.) I qualified second of thirteen racers at 475 mph, just behind Stewart Dawson at 480.644 mph in Rare Bear. After the qualifying run, it was necessary to check all the rocker arms and lifters, similar to how the top National Hot Rod Association dragsters are managed.

I flew in the first heat race on Friday, September 18, 2015, and was unable to pass Stewart in Rare Bear. We had a lot of close-quarter racing, but no matter what I did, I couldn't pass him. He finished in first place at an average speed of 478.479 mph, and I was second at 472.871 mph.

The engine had to be reinspected after I had run it hard at full throttle during the heat race. The lineup for the Saturday heat race was Rare Bear "on the pole" in first place, me in second, and Steven Hinton third in Voodoo, also a reconfigured P-51 Mustang nearly identical to Strega that had qualified third at 464.246 mph. At the start of the race, Stewart in Rare Bear had flown slightly high and wide at the guide pylon, and I had to stay outside his turn on his wing. Steven in Voodoo, however, must have said to himself, "I'm not going high and wide." He cut to the inside and was instantly in the lead. It was a shrewd tactical move, and I was suddenly running in third. However, Strega's big breakthrough did finally happen. It turned out that the Merlin race engine was finally broken in enough, giving it much greater power than before. I was able to pass Rare Bear in one lap, then I made my way past Voodoo to finish in first place at an average speed of 484.793 mph. Hinton was second at 475.482 mph, and Dawson came in third with 474.760 mph.

The talented crew chief, L. D. Hughes, made calls on my second radio telling me when I was clear after the passes I made. It was a huge triumph after the disappointing first heat race, and the smile on my face walking back from the race debrief with all the race pilots told it all. This put me on the pole, starting in first place for the Sunday championship.

An anomaly had occurred in Strega, though, that I wasn't able to see during the heat race. I had burned through one of the exhaust stacks, and it was just barely noticeable, projecting from the right side of the forward fuselage. The second exhaust stack on the right side of the airplane had split open and had caused heat damage to the cowling. With years of air racing experience, the crew had spares of these parts, and the airplane was repaired in time.

Smiling after the Friday heat race. Credit: Marcia Lindstrom

The championship race started September 20. Hinton in Voodoo attempted to pass me and must have used an incredible amount of power because I was running full-throttle at 3,400 rpm and 128 inches of manifold pressure. He briefly gained on me, but then I was off and running and pulled away from the other racers. I ran full-throttle for about half of the eight laps during that race, and then Hughes called on the second radio, "Okay, first power reduction, come back to 125 inches," requiring me to limit my manifold pressure. This confirmed I was significantly ahead of the rest of the pack. Photographer Anthony Taylor captured an amazing photo at the end of the second lap of the race. I was timed at 503 mph in the first lap

Racers after the first lap. Credit: Anthony Taylor

and 498 mph in the second. Strega is in razor sharp focus while the top of the thirty-foot-high pylon is very blurred. Strega leaves a trail of water and steam from the water spray bar in the doghouse.

Several laps after the first power reduction, crew chief Hughes called, "Second power reduction, come back to 120 inches." Another lap later, he called, "Third power reduction, come back to 110 inches, open the coolant door some more, and you don't need to hug the pylons quite as tightly." I had been flying right next to the pylons in order to flying the shortest course possible, but I didn't dare "cut" a pylon. There was always an observer peering up through the 55-gallon barrel that formed the top of the pylon, and if any part of the airplane was seen through the barrel, it was considered a cut. A penalty

Strega at Pylon Eight. Credit: Anthony Taylor

of four seconds times the number of laps would be imposed. In the case of the eight-lap championship race, the result would have been a devastating thirty-two seconds lost. I had never cut a pylon in any of my unlimited class races.

I cruised to the finish line and took the checkered flag at 488.983 mph for the unlimited course, a record that has never been equaled. I had lapped the entire field of racers except for Dawson in Rare

Unlimited Championship trophy presentation. Credit: Marcia Lindstrom

Bear, who finished second at 471.957 mph. I had been fairly sure that going into the race, Hinton in Voodoo wouldn't finish the eight-lap final race. His airplane had been burning oil and had finished the prior six-lap heat race with an empty oil tank. He had to mayday out at the end of the fifth lap. Hinton is the most successful Unlimited Air Race champion with eight total unlimited class wins, and this was the first time in seven years he was not the champion.

Even though I had crossed the finish line first, I couldn't be certain I had won. There was still the possibility I had cut a pylon or committed a race violation. I had just climbed out of the cockpit when the race announcement was made. "The contest committee says we had a clean race, so we have a new National and World Unlimited Champion, Robert 'Hoot' Gibson!"

I was presented with the coveted gold jacket and posed for photos with the Perennial Trophy. It was a real thrill after eighteen years flying in the Reno Air Races to win the big prize, the Unlimited Championship.

I remember being asked in a television interview right after the race, "How does this compare with being a space shuttle commander?"

"This is such a thrill!" I answered. "It ranks right up there."

The awards banquet was held after all the races on Sunday evening and the entire team took the stage with me as we were given the championship trophy. I made some brief remarks, thanking about everyone I knew on Earth, especially my team. I hadn't won on my own. We had done it together.

23

I have lived a life that, as a child, I could never have dreamed. Thanks to my parents' inspiration, aviation had been my central theme and passion. I was able to exceed the goals I'd set for myself at ten years old of becoming both an aeronautical engineer and a test pilot like my father. I didn't grow up wanting to be an astronaut like most kids my age since rockets didn't have wings. At that time, life was all about the thrill of being an aviator and pilot and flying as many different aircraft as I could. It wouldn't be until the design of the space shuttle that I would choose to be an astronaut so I could fly that marvelous advancement in aviation into space. I was able to do everything I had ever dreamed and then some, both in flight and in orbit.

I enjoyed being part of some incredible teams, from my band of brothers flying in the Vietnam War to the astronaut corps at NASA, and was so very honored to have been named the chief astronaut and their leader. I had the pleasure of being part of a skilled team of mechanics and technicians on air racing teams over the course of more than eighteen years.

Mike Mullane, a dear friend and fellow astronaut whom I'd

flown with on my third space flight, wrote about me in his book, *Riding Rockets*. "If ever there has been a pilot who has worn out a squadron of guardian angels," he wrote, "that would be Hoot."

Over the years, having survived all the things I've been able to live through, that sentiment could not be truer. I've uttered the words, "Thank you, Lord," many times for seeing me through combat, aircraft emergencies, flight testing, more than 300 aircraft carrier landings, and during air races. I have joked about hearing a loud clank each time I walked away from a major emergency, some of my own creation—my guardian angel throwing his golden halo to the ground, saying, "I quit! Find another one. You're too difficult."

I'm reminded of the book by legendary aviator General James H. "Jimmy" Doolittle, titled, *I Could Never Be So Lucky Again*. I feel the same way. Even during my time at NASA, I remember thinking to myself on multiple occasions, *I can't believe they're letting me go to space*.

I grew up fascinated by racing airplanes and air race pilots and dared to dream that maybe I would be able to do that someday. I was able to break into the world of air racing with a very inexpensive home-built airplane to gain the experience necessary to earn my big break, the invitation to fly an unlimited-class racer in the Reno Air Races. That was what had made me part of the "Riff Raff" air racing team where I had made so many dear friends and had resulted in my being able to race for fifteen years in three different racers and even finish at the very top as the Unlimited Class Champion in my final year.

Over the span of more than sixty years, I've been honored to have enjoyed a flying career that covered three distinctly different phases: a wartime combat pilot, an astronaut, and an air racer. I was awarded many military medals while serving in the Navy as well as several from the Federation Aeronautique Internationale such as the Louis Bleriot Medal and the Yuri Gagarin Gold Medal. I've managed to establish six aviation World Records and three Space World Records. And I opened my eyes to my former enemies' perspective in becoming a "cold warrior," flying five different Russian MiGs. Looking back, I honestly believe the only thing I never flew was a blimp.

Perhaps most importantly of all, I've made so many friends along the way, lost some I will never forget, and stayed in contact with many. More than anything else, I will treasure all of *them* forever.

I returned to Vietnam forty years after my last combat missions there. I was happy to see that the country had totally recovered from the devastation of war. They know it as the "American War," but there wasn't any palpable resentment against the United States,

Military Headquarters in Da Nang. Credit: Hoot Gibson

The major channel in Ha Long Bay. Credit: Hoot Gibson

maybe because 80 percent of the population had been born after the end of the war. Saigon had been renamed to Ho Chi Minh City, and it was bustling with commerce and 8.5 million motorbikes. I visited several of the places I had attacked in 1972, like Hanoi and Hon Gai, and again saw Da Nang, the airfield where I landed many times. I marveled at the beauty of Ha Long Bay, a place I had flown over several times on combat missions inbound to Haiphong but had never really noticed. A UNESCO World Heritage Site, Ha Long Bay is quite a sight. Its name means, "Where the Dragon Descends into the Sea." The dragon's thrashing is said to have created the many limestone islands dotting its waters.

Today, I have four wonderful grown children, five precious

grandchildren, and five living brothers and sisters who have always been loving relatives as well as dear friends. Rhea, my wife of more than forty-four years, and I have enjoyed a wonderful life together and are now empty-nesters, but three of our kids live nearby in Tennessee, and we see them and our grandchildren often.

I was so fortunate to have been taught how to fly by my own father, Paul. I've always said, "If I have been successful as an aviator, it's because Dad taught me how to fly." But he didn't just teach me the how; he also taught me the why, the aerodynamics and structural considerations that made aircraft operate. I wanted to be my dad, and I believe I did achieve that to a large degree. He and Mom were always there for me and attended the big events in my life like college graduation, my commissioning as a naval officer, the pinning of my Navy wings, and my Test Pilot School graduation as the Outstanding Student of my class. Dad lived long enough to see me go to space twice and witness my second flight as mission commander. I believe I made Mom and Dad happy and proud, which has given me much satisfaction.

As I approach the "autumn of my years," I have no regrets and certainly don't believe I have missed out on much this world has to offer. I don't consider myself financially wealthy or overly encumbered with earthly possessions, but I am fabulously wealthy in experiences and memories, with good friends and family.

I've had the experience so many times of seeing Earth from the highest possible vantages in both air and space. I will never forget those moments, and I could never be this lucky again.

Hoot Gibson looking out the window from inside *Atlantis*. Credit: NASA

Acknowledgements

My first thanks go to my wife and partner of more than forty years, Astronaut Margaret Rhea Seddon, one of America's first six female astronauts. She published her excellent book, *Go For Orbit*, more than ten years ago, but she has been encouraging me to write my book for more than twenty years. It was her support that finally led me to write my story. To my four kids, Julie, Paul, Dann, and Emilee, I wrote this with all of you in mind. I never asked my dad and mom nearly enough questions about their lives, and I hope this tells you everything about mine. To Mom and Dad for pointing me in the direction of a career in aviation.

To my friend, Dr. Anthony Paustian, who provided the final nudge I needed to get me to start writing. He has been an extremely valuable guide, coach, and co-writer as I attempted to navigate through this process and turn the book into a relatable story. I never could have succeeded without his experience and wisdom as an author to lead me. And also to our editor, Jason Brandt Schaefer, whose efforts have been the key in helping shape the readability and overall quality of this book.

I had many mentors in the US Navy and at NASA that propelled my career, and I never could have climbed to the heights that I did without their support. To LCDR Jim Ruliffson, the operations officer of my F-4B Phantom squadron who selected me to go to TOPGUN and must have seen some ability in my flying. To my squadron "skippers" (commanding officers) CDR Bob Rice and CDR Tom Markley, who greatly furthered my navy career by selecting me to be their wingman and pilot. To the Director of Flight operations at NASA, George Abbey, who first of all, selected me to be in the 1978 astronaut class, and then put me into challenging technical assignments that resulted in my selection to fly as the fourth pilot from my class to go to space. To the twenty-nine astronauts and cosmonauts that I had the privilege of going into space with, thank you for being the vital team members that made us successful. There are too many of you to list here, but in particular, Vance Brand, Steve Hawley, Charlie Bolden, Mike Mullane, Charlie Precourt, and Greg Harbaugh. You are the reason we were so successful in our spaceflights.

Enjoy Hoot's Children's Book

First Flight

Illustrated by Michelle Rouch
with Czarina Salido

Readers and Reviewers Love It!

Get Your Copy Today!

First Flight is available from your local bookstore, Barnes & Noble, Amazon, other online sellers, or from the publisher directly at **HootSpeaks.com.**

Check the website for more information about books, public appearances, and much more!

Space Shuttle *Atlantis* separating from the Mir Space Station. Credit: NASA